TITUS OATES
AND THE
POPISH PLOT to KILL KING CHARLES II

TITUS OATES *AND THE* POPISH PLOT to KILL KING CHARLES II

JONATHAN OATES

AN IMPRINT OF PEN & SWORD BOOKS LTD.
YORKSHIRE – PHILADELPHIA

First published in Great Britain in 2025 by
Pen & Sword History
An imprint of
Pen & Sword Books Ltd
Yorkshire - Philadelphia

ISBN 978 1 03612 899 9

A CIP catalogue record for this book is available from the British Library.

Typeset in INDIA by IMPEC eSolutions
Printed and bound in England by CPI Group (UK) Ltd, Croydon, CRO 4YY

The Publisher's authorised representative in the EU for product safety is Authorised Rep Compliance Ltd., Ground Floor, 71 Lower Baggot Street, Dublin D02 P593, Ireland.
www.arccompliance.com

For a complete list of Pen & Sword titles please contact

PEN & SWORD BOOKS LIMITED
47 Church Street, Barnsley, South Yorkshire, S70 2AS, England
E-mail: enquiries@pen-and-sword.co.uk
Website: www.pen-and-sword.co.uk

or

PEN AND SWORD BOOKS
1950 Lawrence Rd, Havertown, PA 19083, USA
E-mail: uspen-and-sword@casematepublishers.com
Website: www.penandswordbooks.com

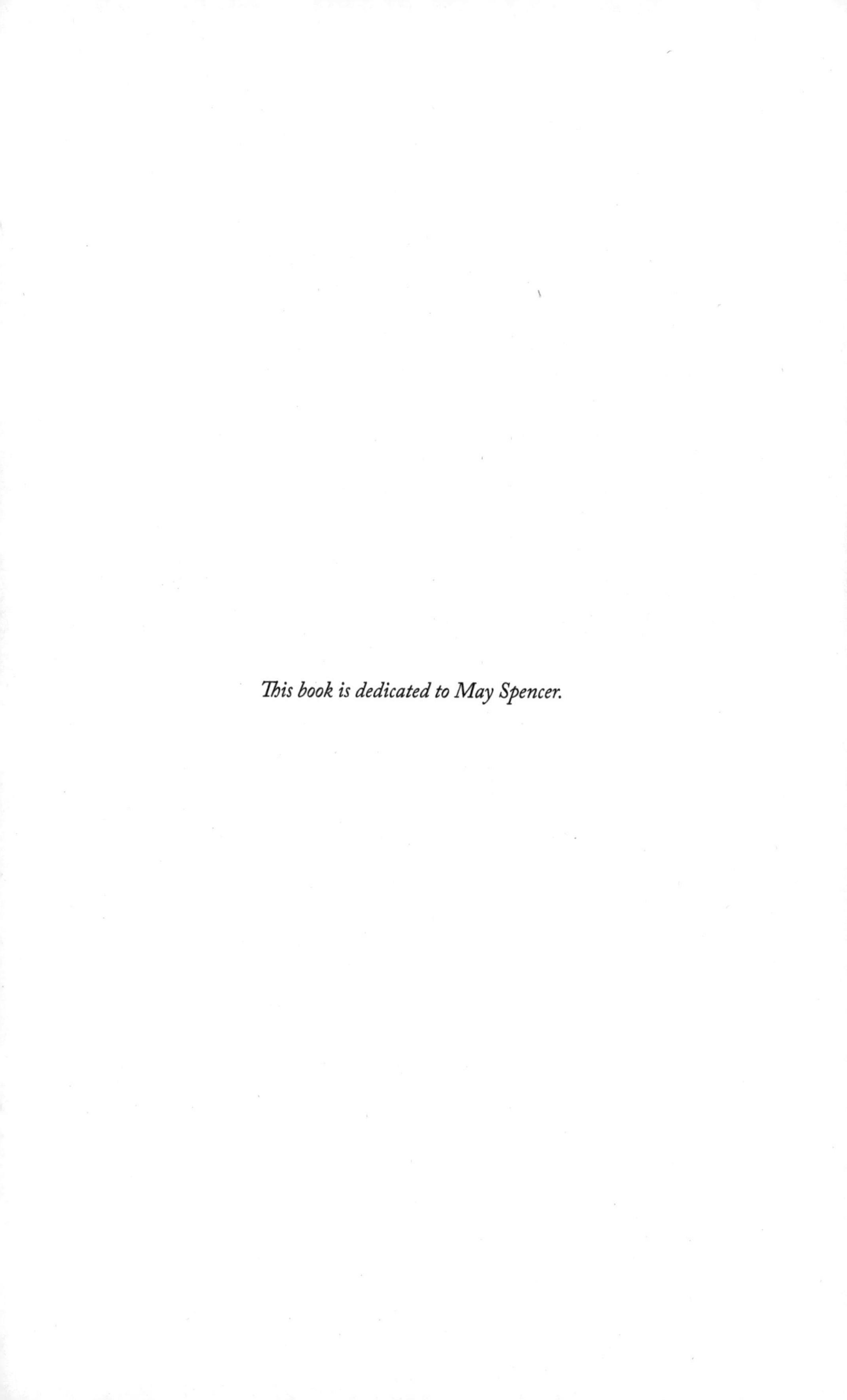

This book is dedicated to May Spencer.

Contents

Acknowledgements

Many people have assisted in the creation of this book. Several of the author's friends have read through some or all of the book and have made many helpful suggestions which have improved the content, though any remaining errors are the author's sole responsibility. I have also discussed aspects of the book with them. They are Lindsay Siviter (especially as regards the death of Godfrey) and John Coulter. Professor Victor Stater, Dr Anna-Lena Berg, May Spencer, Stephen Perrin, Sarah Taylor and Paul Lang have read and commented on the text which has led to its improvement. I have also benefitted from a discussion with my former doctoral supervisor, Professor Stephen Taylor. Dr Bill Shannon sent copies of documents from Lancashire Record Office. Judy Cubison showed Lindsay Siviter and I around All Saints' church in Hastings. Mike Webb at the Bodleian Library kindly sent a copy of a document to me. John Coulter kindly allowed me to use pictures from his collection. Staff at numerous institutions, namely the National Archives, the British Library, East Sussex Record Office, Surrey History Centre, the Bodleian Library and Lambeth Palace Library have helped in the provision of archives and books, without which this work could not have been written. My son, Benjamin, accompanied me on a research trip to East Sussex Record Office.

Chronology

1648?	Birth of Oates
1649	Execution of Charles I and beginning of the Commonwealth.
1652-1654	First Dutch War
1658	Death of Oliver Cromwell.
1660	Restoration of Charles II. Oates' father becomes rector of All Saints' Hastings.
1665-1667	Second Dutch War
1667-1669	Oates at Cambridge
1666	Fire of London
1669-1675	Oates serves as an Anglican clergyman in several parishes.
1672-1674	Third Dutch War
1675	Oates accuses Parkers of crimes.
1676	Oates briefly naval chaplain.
1677-1678	Oates at Catholic colleges in Spain and France.
1678	Treaty of Nijmegen ends war; discovery of 'Popish Plot'; Oates' revelations, discovery of Coleman correspondence, mysterious death of Godfrey, arrests of Catholics, first trials lead to execution of Coleman. Oates accuses Queen Catherine as accessory in conspiracy.
1679	Danby imprisoned; Parliament dissolved but Commons more hostile to court, more trials and executions of Catholics; but Wakeman and others acquitted.
1679-1680	Exclusion Bills against Duke of York fail.
1680	Further trials of Catholics, but few executed; Viscount Stafford. Deaths of Bedloe and Tonge.
1681	Archbishop Plunket is last man to be die due to the 'Popish Plot', Third Exclusion Bill fails and Parliament dissolved for remainder of the reign. Two Whig agitators executed. Oates loses apartment in Whitehall. Shaftesbury tried for treason but acquitted.
1683	Rye House Plot, execution of two Whig lords.
1684	Oates arrested and imprisoned.
1685	Death of Charles II; accession of James II, Monmouth rebellion fails. Oates on trial and imprisoned with flogging for the remainder of his life.

1688	Arrival of Dutch fleet under William of Orange in Torbay; flight of James II.
1688-1697	Nine Years War
1689	Accession of William and Mary. Release of Oates.
1693	Oates marries Rebecca Wild.
1697	Treaty of Ryswick
1701	Death of James II in exile; beginning of War of Spanish Succession.
1702	Death of William III, accession of Queen Anne.
1704	Battle of Blenheim
1705	Death of Oates

List of Characters

Thomas Ailesbury, (1656–1741), 2nd Earl of. Politician and memoirist.

Queen Anne (1665–1714), second daughter of James, Duke of York. As Queen reigned from 1702-1714.

Richard Baxter (1615–1691), nonconformist clergyman.

William Bedloe (1650–1680), rogue and informer against Catholics, notably alleged killers of Godfrey.

Duke of Buckingham, George Villiers (1628–1687), politician and womaniser.

Gilbert Burnet (1643–1715), Anglican clergyman, later bishop of Salisbury and historian.

Earl of Castlemaine, Roger Palmer (1634–1705), Husband of Barbara, royal mistress, diplomat and courtier.

Queen Catherine of Braganza (1638–1705), daughter of John IV of Portugal, wife of Charles II, 1662-1685.

Charles I (1600-1649), reigned as King, 1625–1649. Executed.

Charles II (1630–1685), son of Charles I, reigned as King, 1660–1685.

Edward Coleman (1636–1678), secretary to the Duke of York. Executed.

Stephen College (1637–1681), Protestant joiner, supportive of the Popish Plot. Executed.

Oliver Cromwell (1599–1658), politician and soldier. Lord Protector of the Commonwealth.

Earl of Danby, Sir Thomas Osborne (1631–1712), Lord Treasurer 1673–1679. Imprisoned in the Tower, 1679–1684.

Thomas Dangerfield (c.1650–1685), informer against Catholics.

John Dryden, (1631–1700), England's first Poet Laureate.

Stephen Dugdale (c.1640–1683), informer against Catholics.

Rev. Adam Elliott, (c.1649–?), Anglican clergyman accused by Oates.

John Evelyn (1620–1706), courtier and diarist.

John Fenwick (1628–1679), Jesuit. Executed.

Edmund Fitzharris (c.1648–1681), Irish soldier and anti-Catholic conspirator. Executed.

John Gavan (1640–1679), Jesuit. Executed.

Sir Edmund Berry Godfrey (1621–1678), Businessman and magistrate. Died mysteriously.

John Grove (?–1679), Jesuit lay brother. Executed 1679.

William Harcourt (1609–1679), Jesuit priest. Executed.

William Ireland (1636–1679), Jesuit priest. Executed.

James I, (1567–1625), King of Scotland 1568–1625; of England, 1603–1625.

James, Duke of York, later James II (1633–1701), King of Britain, 1685–1688.

Judge George Jeffreys (1645–1689), Lawyer, Lord Justice of the King's Bench from 1683.

Christopher Kirkby, amateur chemist who first approached Charles II about the Popish Plot.

Father Francoise de la Chaise (1624–1709), Jesuit confessor to Louis XIV from 1674.

Richard Langhorn (1624–1679), Catholic lawyer. Executed.

Louis XIV (1638–1715), King of France from 1643–1715.

Serjeant John Maynard (1604–1690), lawyer and politician.

Matthew Medbourne (?–1679), Catholic actor and playwright. Died in prison.

Duke of Monmouth, James Scott (1649–1685), Eldest illegitimate son of Charles II.

Duke of Norfolk, Henry Howard, (1628–1684), senior Catholic nobleman in Britain.

Francis Norwood. Churchwarden of All Saints' Hastings, 1670s.

Constant Oates. Sister of Titus Oates

Lucy Oates. Midwife and mother of Titus Oates

Rebecca Oates, nee Wild, (1670–1746), wife of Titus Oates

Samuel Oates (1614–1683), Father of Titus Oates. Anabaptist, later Anglican, clergyman.

Samuel Oates (brother) Naval officer.

John Okey, (1606–1662), Parliamentary soldier and regicide. Executed.

Duke of Ormonde, James Butler (1610–1688), Lord Lieutenant of Ireland until 1685.

William Parker (senior), Mayor of Hastings on three occasions.

William Parker (junior), son of William Parker.

Samuel Pepys (1633–1703), Civil servant, MP and diarist.

Thomas Pickering (c.1621–1679), Benedictine lay brother. Executed.

Archbishop Oliver Plunket (1625–1681), Catholic primate of Ireland. Executed.

Miles Prance. Catholic silversmith and informer against Catholics.

Sir John Reresby, (1634–1689), Tory MP for York and memoirist.

Earl of Rochester, John Wilmot (1647–1680), Poet and libertine.

Prince Rupert (1619–1682), Nephew of Charles I. Soldier, sailor, First Lord of the Admiralty, 1673–1679.

Judge William Scroggs. (c.1623–1683), Lord Chief Justice, 1678–1681; tried many during the Popish Plot.

Earl of Shaftesbury, Sir Anthony Ashley Cooper (1621–1683), Principal opposition politician, from 1678, died in exile.

William Smith, schoolmaster of Oates, later imprisoned.

Viscount Stafford (1614–1680), Catholic nobleman accused by Oates. Executed.

Dr Edward Stillingfleet (1635–1699), preacher and royal chaplain.

Earl of Sunderland, Robert Spencer (1640–1702), Secretary of State under Charles II and James II.

Dr Israel Tonge (1621–1680), Anglican clergyman, author and ally of Oates.

Simpson Tonge. Son of Israel Tonge.

Anthony Turner (1628–1679), Jesuit priest. Executed.

Sir George Wakeman (?–1688), Catholic and a Royalist, physician to Queen Catherine from 1670.

Sir William Waller (c.1639–1699), London magistrate, zealous against Catholics.

Edmund Warcup (1627–1712), London magistrate, active against Whigs from 1681.

Thomas Whitebread (1630–1678), Jesuit Provincial Executed.

Major John Wildman (c.1621–1693), radical soldier and politician.

William of Orange, later William III (1650–1702), Stadtholder of Holland, King of Britain, 1689–1702.

Sir Joseph Williamson (1633–1701), Secretary of State, 1674–1679.

Introduction

That Titus Oates has not enjoyed a wholesome reputation throughout history is an understatement. In 1955 Sir George Clark referred to him as being one 'of the vilest liars in the world' and a 'man of bad character and supreme effrontery'.[1] Sir Charles Petrie, a Catholic historian, wrote that 'there was hardly a vice to which he was not addicted, and he delighted in a variety of sins rarely combined in the same individual'.[2] In 1993 Geoffrey Holmes remarked that his 'chief gift was a breathtaking talent for mendacity' and that he 'was not the most prepossessing of students, for his Latin was primitive, his language foul and he was a homosexual'.[3] Six years later he was introduced thus, 'the even odder figure of the monstrous Titus Oates'.[4] Tim Harris has written that he was 'by all accounts a most unsavoury individual. His pastimes included lying, cheating, blasphemy and sodomizing young boys'.[5] More recently Don Jordan summarises Oates' many failings, describing him as 'a con artist' with 'foul mouthed conversation and disreputable habits' and 'by all accounts lazy and dim'.[6] In an article in the *BBC History* magazine in 2006, Oates, despite stiff competition, was declared by one historian (John Adamson of Peterhouse College, Cambridge) as the worst Briton of the seventeenth century, as being 'in a league of his own in the depths of his vileness'.[7] The author of a more recent book about the historical episode in which he is most associated writes of him as 'a shifty vagabond with a past so full of misdeeds and scandal that showing his remarkably ugly face in public was an act of courage' and of 'the squalid ambition of one very bad man' yet, quite uniquely, also credits the British party system to four men, one of whom is Oates.[8]

Oates' claim to historical infamy is his leading role in the invention and dissemination of the 'Popish Plot' in 1678-1681 which led to the executions of at least 27 innocent Catholics, mostly priests, in what was to be the last judicial murders of Catholics in England. This imaginary plot was the conspiracy to murder the apparently Protestant Charles II and replace him as King with his Catholic brother James. It seemed all the more plausible by the coincidence of the mysterious death (never solved) of Sir Edmund Berry Godfrey, the London magistrate to whom Oates first told his story. Oates alleged that a great many Catholics were involved in the conspiracy and provided their names. Briefly believed and feted in these years, Oates has been subsequently reviled by almost all those writing about this relatively popular period of British history. He was a faker and fraudster on a large scale.

Much of what has been written about him has appeared in books primarily about the 'Popish Plot', the mystery of Godfrey's death or about other prominent figures of the Restoration age, such as Charles II or the Earl of Rochester, or in general surveys of the era. A brief, derogatory character sketch is customarily given and an abbreviated account of his earlier and later career whilst the focus is his role in the Plot. These are, inevitably, incomplete accounts of his life, which sometimes repeat half-truths and myths, however this is how Oates has been portrayed to readers of history. The sole biography of Oates, published to coincide with the tercentenary of his birth, will be discussed in more detail later in this book. This is the work of an author once known primarily for her historical fiction and she certainly expresses strong views either for or against some of the principals. That said, it is well researched but limited in its treatment of some aspects of Oates' character.[9]

Despite having written a defence of another of the alleged 'Ten Worst Britons', (the eighteenth century soldier, the Duke of Cumberland) it is not this author's intention to act as Oates' defence counsel. Rather it is to investigate his life and public career in order to present a detailed account of a most unusual individual set against the background of some of the most turbulent events ever experienced in British history; civil wars, regicide, republican rule, the restoration of the monarchy, revolution, war and invasion. It was, unsurprisingly, a time of great political and religious instability and fears, when anything seemed possible. This work seeks to explore and understand, not to condemn. It will also consider his family and the society in which they moved in order to provide the necessary context to his existence.

There is a mass of contemporary writings about Oates, much of it very derogative. Likewise, many of the memoirs written years later are also highly critical of him. Retrospective accounts of his early life are coloured by such attacks. How much of this is true and how much the work of political muck racking is another question. One issue in particular is the question of Oates' sexuality. From the late twentieth century, it has been widely accepted and oft repeated that he was homosexual and sometimes even a paedophile. The only full length study of Oates' life was in 1949, not a period known for frank public discussion of this aspect of human behaviour, though in 1958 Petrie referred to Oates' homosexuality in passing.[10] This new study will investigate, as much as it is possible to do so after this length of time, this aspect of Oates' character and how it fitted into contemporary sexual morality at a time of both sexual puritanism, not just by adherents of the former Cromwellian regime but of respectable royalists such as John Evelyn, and licence as famously expounded by the likes of Sir Charles Sedley, the Earl of Rochester and of course, King Charles II.

It is both a blessing and a curse for the historian that the period of the later seventeenth century is not short of both manuscript and published contemporary material. Furthermore, as, albeit briefly, a figure of national significance, Oates was commented upon in public by many major historians, writers of private letters, diaries and memoirs. However, it is a great pity that Pepys' concerns about his eyesight resulted in him finishing his great diaries in 1669, a decade before Oates' prominence.

The mass of writings about Oates in published pamphlets has already been alluded to. As a clergyman in the Anglican Church and the Royal Navy, the son of a clergyman and as being frequently involved in trials as both witness and defendant and later as a recipient of public money, there is much official documentation about him. State Papers, Privy Council, Admiralty and Treasury papers at the National Archives, State Trials, quarter session records and Old Bailey proceedings all have much to relate about his public career. For the earlier decades there is relevant matter at East Sussex, Surrey and Essex record offices. Although Oates wrote some pamphlets and sermons it is regretted that there seem to be no personal writings by him, no correspondence, diaries or autobiography; perhaps not surprising for a man of his nature, though an apologia would have been of interest. As with the case of Dick Turpin (born in the same year as Oates' death) most of what is known about Oates has been written about him, sadly not by him, and this needs to be taken into account when assessing the available evidence. Yet perhaps we hear his voice through his actions?

I should add a personal note. I first became aware of Titus Oates in 1990 when in my second year at Reading University I chose to study the topic titled, 'Monarchy and Revolution, 1678-1690', supervised by the then Dr (now Professor) Stephen Taylor. I recall noting in an essay about the Popish Plot, somewhat irrelevantly, that Oates was no known relation of mine, and in later decades became convinced that this was the case. In part this was because Oates is only known to have sired daughters who would only have passed on their surname if they had given birth to illegitimate children.[11] Furthermore, my ancestors hailed from the north east of England not the south east as did Titus Oates' and also were of a rather lower social class than his. As a man of the late twentieth and early twenty-first centuries, though an Anglican, I do not share Oates' virulent (or indeed any) anti-Catholicism, though his beliefs were common enough in the seventeenth and eighteenth centuries for many Anglicans in England. This is not the case of a personal defence for surname sake. However, I do admit that one reason why I have decided to write about Oates is our shared surname. His shocking life and career are fascinating enough.

Chapter One

Early Years, 1648–1669

Evidence for the youth of most people is usually very limited unless they were of such importance, for example a royal prince, that contemporaries recorded their actions or that they were of an unusually precocious nature that they wrote diaries or letters as a child and youth. Oates was only thought to be of national importance from 1678 and versions of his life began to be published thereafter and in the following decades. Contemporary commentators made reference to his first three decades in their memoirs or public speeches. How accurate these are is another question. Almost all were derogatory. Although they cannot be ignored, they must be used with caution. This chapter will use additional sources as well as contemporary writings about those places that he was associated with.

Titus Oates was the son of Samuel Oates and Lucy, his wife. Samuel Oates was born in Norwich in about 1614. Samuel Oates had led a very colourful existence by the time his son Titus was born, and though less well known to history than his son he was far from being a nonentity throughout his life. His early career has been contested. Some have stated that he may have been the man who attended Corpus Christi College in Cambridge as a sizar in 1627, obtained a BA in 1630 and an MA in 1631, before being ordained and becoming rector of Marsham in Norfolk. However, this seems to have been a complete red herring, possibly the confusion lying in that there was another man of this name and Oates' father was an Anglican clergyman at one point in his life.[1]

Contemporary biographies of Titus Oates had varied comments about his father, possibly invented to denigrate his son by association. One published in 1685 noted that he was 'of mean parentage', that his father was born in Norwich and was 'brought up there in weaving Norwich stuff'.[2] Another contemporary source refers to his father as being a silk weaver from Norwich, married with several children and 'justly esteemed as a moste turbulent and factious fellow'.[3] These appear to be fairly accurate, judging from what information follows.

Samuel Oates married at St. John de Sepulchre, Norwich, on 3 October 1639 to Lucy Weld, who had been born on 3 January 1616 at Caistor St. Edmund, Norfolk. The biography of Oates of 1705 was less unsympathetic, though far from praiseworthy, referring to Oates' lowly social background, that he:

'came of a very renowned family, his father being an eminent Dipper in Spittle-Fields...a dextrous handler of the suttle, and sometimes a thumper of the cushin also; but he had always the character of an honest man'.[4]

It was during the British civil wars (1642–1651) that Samuel sprang to a modicum of significance. At the end of 1644 it was noted that he was in Norwich gaol, for an unspecified, but presumably petty offence, as he was allowed to be bailed.[5] As early as 19 February 1645 an Essex clergyman wrote of 'a base, but bold secratist named Oates a weaver in London came down, and vents and gaullimaufing (?) of strange opinions and draweing great flocks of people after him without all controul'.[6] The same noted 'Oates...hath been sowing his tares, booliminmg [sic] as wild oates in these parts these five weeks without any controul, hath seduced hundreds and dipped many in Bocking River, and when that he hath a Feast in the night, and at the end of that the Lords' Supper...no magistrate in the country have meddle with him'.[7] In more detail, 'Hee carryeth women about with him from place to place, being absent from yr families and husbands 2 or 3 weeks together, ployning from ym to maintain him. He dipps women naked & in ye night, fit for works of darkness'. Oates was deemed 'a man evill and scandalous in his life'. Because he was a weaver he had 'no lawfull calling to the ministry' yet he was preaching and administering the sacrament, sometimes even in churches. This was deemed scandalous and dangerous in the extreme. [8] It was also claimed that there was a sexual element to such dipping. A clergyman alleged that in Essex, 'where Oates hath beene dipping, that it was spoken of by many, that some young women, who having beene married divers yeeres, and never were with child, now since their dipping, are proved with child'.[9]

Adult baptism is a key tenet of the Anabaptist creed for they believe that an individual must make a conscious decision to come to Christ, when they are spiritually awakened (Jesus himself was baptised as an adult by John the Baptist, it should be recalled), which puts them at odds with the mainstream Christian practice of baptism of babies.[10]

The unsympathetic biographer of Samuel Oates wrote, 'he step'd from the Loom into the pulpit where he retailed sedition and Nonsense to the Baptists, being accounted among them a Famous preacher and a well Gifted Brother'.[11] A more sympathetic source notes that from 1645 he was based at a Baptist chapel at Bell Alley in London in association with a Mr Lamb, but that he was largely an itinerant and that he was an able preacher and disputant. He initially preached in Surrey and Sussex as well as Essex.[12]

Oates spent time in Yarmouth as an Anabaptist preacher having 'proceeded there with great applause of the factious rabble'. One of the women he baptised died thereafter, being heavily pregnant and was dipped in winter 'in water under his hands as he was performing his wickedly pretended function'. The jury at his trial who acquitted him of murder was 'consisting (as it was believed) of pickt rascalls of his owne gang'.[13]

However, an alternate version of these events was that Anne Martin, the woman in question, died several weeks after the baptism. Samuel Oates was committed to Colchester gaol where his followers flocked to see him. Even well wishers from London visited him until this was stopped. At the trial for murder at Chelmsford Assizes, the deceased's mother said that her daughter was well enough for some days after being dipped and so Oates was found not guilty. However, his enemies later threw him into a pond in Dunmow, a common enough practice used against nonconformist ministers unpopular locally.[14]

Oates was described as 'blaspheming, after the worst Usage of his Sect'.[15] On 16 March Oates, described as a 'woosted weaver from St. Thomas', London' and along with one John Hutchinson, a draper from Braintree, were forced to enter into recognisances from the Essex magistrates for their future good behaviour.[16] This was a result of Richard Wade of Bocking and others complaining of 'Oates as to his unlawful assembly of divers people together in Braintree and Bocking in disturbance of the peace and contempt of authority'.[17]

Women were especially drawn to independent preachers and congregations in the 1640s and 1650s. Here they were treated seriously, not as inferiors. Here too, they were taught the importance of an individual's personal relationship with God, without the need for a male family member or a clergyman. It was a liberation from restrictions and a form of sisterhood and shared community.[18]

It was enough for him to move to Rutland, however. Members of the county community complained to officialdom about his actions. Abel Parker of Hambleton wrote to Sir Thomas Hartopp of Burton Lazers, Leicestershire, on 19 March 1646, about Oates, describing him as a weaver 'who preacheth constantly in this county' and put it that it was 'for the consideration of the judges who may see fit to issue a warrant for his arrest and conveyance to the assizes of Oakenham'.[19] He moved on to Earles Colne in Essex, for on 29 June of that year the Rev. Ralph Josselin (1616–1683), vicar there, reported in his diary:

> 'This day I held against Oates, the Anabaptist, morning & afternoon, argum^t that they had no ministry, and yt particular Christians out of office had no power to send ministers out to preach, he confessed it and held only to doe what he did as a disciple; I shewed him it was contrary to scripture; our discourse was without passion; the man boldly continued in Towne till Wednesday, exercising all three days'.[20]

Oates was not only a religious radical but a political one as well. He was described as 'an Anabaptist & consequently an Enimy to Monarchy and Episcopacy'. [21] The 1640s produced Anabaptists, Quakers, Fifth Monarchy men and Ranters, but also Levellers and Diggers. The latter two groups preached a form of social and political equality, at least where Protestant men above the rank of servants and day labourers were concerned, and this went down badly with the elites on both sides of the civil war. A document known as *The Agreement of the People* was published in 1647 and Oates distributed copies at some of his meetings; to his many enemies it was deemed seditious. He was also critical of the monarchy, clergy and Parliament, with creating schism and mutiny among most.[22]

It would seem that Oates' activities were not curtailed because on 6 October 1647 Richard Horseman of Stretton, Lincolnshire, referred to the seditious activity of the preacher Oates; 'a dangerous schismatick'. On the same day he issued an order to the Stretton constables to arrest Oates for 'gathering together of unlawfull and disorderly assemblies'.[23] A further insight into Oates' activities is to be found in the reference to a petition of a number of presumably Anglican clergymen 'of the county of Rutland and the parts adjacent' on 11 December 1647, referring to Oates being involved in 'Arminianism, Anabaptism &c praying for his apprehension'.[24] There was a similar petition from Rutland clergy, stating that Oates was a weaver and as 'a known and professed anabaptist may be proceeded against for blasphemy'.[25] Oates was denounced in the House of Commons for heresy in this year, but there is no record of any formal action being taken against him.[26] However, by the end of 1647, he was brought to London. He escaped and an order was sent to the sheriffs of four Midlands counties to take him. On 22 January 1648 he was arrested but bailed for £200 to appear before the Rutland Assizes. The charge was presumably blasphemy as that is what the Rutland JPs proceeded against him for in May.[27] In 1649 Oates was in Barrow-upon-Soar, Leicestershire and there he met George Fox (1624-1691), who went on to found the Quakers, and who described him as 'one of their [the Baptists'] chief teachers'. A discussion about faith and sin, and the importance of water baptism ensued.[28] Oates' activities stirred up at least three authors to publish pamphlets between 1647-1653 condemning his practices as being antagonistic to the Bible's teachings.

Oates' opportunities came about because during the civil wars, lay and ecclesiastical order was weakened and so the opportunity for radicals, both secular and religious, grew stronger. Magistrates and clergy had other concerns to deal with and some were absent in the fighting. Furthermore, there was economic hardship caused by the disruption of war and so men and women were more likely to listen to unorthodox opinions. It was in these circumstances that Oates could flourish. In more settled times his actions would probably have been promptly curtailed.[29]

An early biographer sought to obscure the birthplace of Titus Oates, 'As for the place of his Birth, it is somewhat uncertain; some say he was Born at Coventry, others at London, others Southwark, others say in the place were he was got, viz., in a cow-house, but let the place where he was born be obscure as it will'.[30] Oates is generally assumed to have been born in Oakham, Rutland, on 15 September 1649 and though the former birthplace is mentioned by contemporaries the latter precise date is not. According to local historians, he was born in a small house in Mill Street or alternatively opposite the Crown in Oakham.[31] However, there is no contemporary record of this event (the first history of Rutland, published in Oates' life time, neglects to mention its most controversial son) and he was not baptised until 1660 in Hastings and then as a child not a baby. In 1678, Oates declared that he was 30 years old, which suggests a year of birth of 1648, if he was right in what he said, and others gave Oakham as his place of birth. In 1693 Oates claimed to have been 'about 45'. Some support for his birth being in 1648 is also supplied by the fact that as noted above his father was in Rutland in January and May 1648, and presumably his wife was, too, so Oates could well have been born in Oakham in that year, perhaps in a house they were renting or an inn there. His mother later said that when she was pregnant with him, 'she was with child of the Devil; if the Author did not mistake Of for By' and 'the pangs she had to bring him forth'.[32] In more detail, she apparently later told a schoolmaster of his, one William Smith, in 1678:

> You know, Mr Smith, I have had a great many children, and by my profession [as midwife], I have skill in women's concerns. But I believe never woman went such a time with a child and did with him. I could seldom or never sleep, when I was with him, and when I did sleep I always dreamt I was with child of the devil. But when I came to my Travail, I had such hard labour that I believe no woman ever had, it was but it had killed me.[33]

The name Titus was probably chosen because it is the name of one of the smallest Books of the Bible, to be found towards the end of the New Testament. His elder brother's name, Samuel, could be because of his father having the same name but also because that name is from one of the more significant Books of the Old Testament. Maybe Titus was chosen as a reference to the boy's size or as an uncomplimentary term. It is presumed that it was a name chosen at birth but possibly came about only at his eventual baptism in 1660.

As to Oakham itself, just a few years later John Evelyn (1620–1706), a royalist gentleman, was journeying northwards and he later wrote:

> riding through Ockham [sic], a pretty Towne in Rutlandshire, famous for the Tenure of Barons Harrington, who hold it by taking off a shoe, from every noble-mans horse that passes with his Lord thro' the streete: unless redeem'd at a certaine piece of mony: a toaken of this, are severall gilded shoes, nailed-up on the Castle Gate, which seemes to have ben large and faire.[34]

This was a most turbulent time in Britain's history. Between 1642–1648 two civil wars had been fought throughout England and Scotland. By the end of 1648 the forces of Parliament had triumphed over those of Charles I (1600–1649) and the monarch was a prisoner of his enemies. Such had not occurred in Britain since the civil wars of the fifteenth century. Worse was to occur. After a trial where the King, God's anointed, was accused of levying war against his people, and found guilty, he was executed in public at Whitehall on 30 January 1649. The shock of this unprecedented event is hard to imagine, both in Britain and on the Continent. As a contemporary royalist song has it, it was a case of 'the World turned upside down'.

Such a revolutionary act was only the start. Monarchy and episcopacy were abolished. The reins of government were taken over by Oliver Cromwell (1599–1658) as Lord Protector. Protestant nonconformist sects were able to flourish and Anglican clergy loyal to the monarchy often were replaced in their benefices by men supportive of the new order. For a time the army had an unprecedented role in society and politics. The late King's son and successor, the young Charles II (1630–1685), had escaped overseas, but despite his return with a Scottish army, he was crushed at the battle of Worcester in 1651 by the professionals of the New Model Army under Cromwell. Charles was able to escape alive to France but his cause seemed to be in ruins and any chance of a royal restoration seemed bleak at best.

The future is always, by its very nature, uncertain, but now it was even more so. All the older certainties of life had been done away with. It was unknown how long the new political and religious world would endure and whether the King and Church would return. So, lacking any real certainty, anything was possible.

Little is known for sure about Titus Oates' childhood. One biographer, after listing his father's many failings (rebellion, unorthodoxy, lack of principles, a suspected perjurer and adulterer) adds that this was to show 'Titus Oates was the bad egg of an old crow, and that he was fitted by his depraved education for the villainies he has since committed'.[35] This same biographer claimed that 'till he was five years of age, was much troubled with convulsion and fits and small hopes of life' were entertained. When he was stronger he was brought from Oakham to live in London, 'where in that time he was so famous for lying among his companions, that several did presage his future villainies'.[36] It is not uncommon for biographies of criminals to trace the seeds of their ill deeds back to their childhoods. Another contemporary biographer alludes to 'Passing by his many little Roguish Tricks and unhappy Pranks that he play'd, while under the Government of his Parents'.[37]

His mother later claimed:

> When he was growing up, I thought he would have been a natural, for his Nose would always run, and he slabber'd at the mouth, and his Father could not endure him; and when he came home at night, the Boy would use to be in the chimney corner, and my husband would cry take away this snotty Fool, and jumble about, which made me weep, because you know he was my child.[38]

Titus Oates was not an only child. He had at least two brothers, Samuel, probably the eldest, and later an officer in the Royal Navy, and Constant. There was also two sisters.

The law finally caught up with Oates (the father) on 30 October 1649 for on that day he was sentenced at Leicester by two justices of the peace for stating that infant baptism was unlawful and that Anglican clergy were not true ministers of God. He was ordered to renounce these statements in public at Leicester castle on the next day. As he refused to do so, he was gaoled until he did or could raise the necessary bail.[39]

Oates' father was not there for long. He became the chaplain to Colonel Thomas Pride's regiment in the victorious New Model Army, presumably after 1649. Pride was a lowly born officer who was also a political radical and Pride's Purge of 1648 resulted in the imprisonment or dismissal of those MPs hostile to the New Model Army. Possibly the radical Oates put himself forward for this regiment because of the colonel's politics and because it offered him a safe haven against conservative clerics and magistrates. The regiment was part of the Parliamentary army which fought and beat the Scots at the battles of Dunbar in 1650 and Worcester in 1651; perhaps Oates was present at both.[40]

Yet trouble and Oates were never far away. Several officers from this regiment, including Oates, a major, captains and lieutenants had been involved in a plot in 1654 to replace General George Monck (1608–1670) who was commander in chief in Scotland with his second in command, Major General James Overton (c.1609–1668), and then to march that army into England. Oates also wrote a circular letter which was distributed around the regiments in Scotland, which contained seditious suggestions, and desired that a meeting be held. After his arrest, Oates wrote a letter to a sympathiser to state that the earlier letter was not seditious, but merely a plea to send a petition to Cromwell and Parliament, for they believed that what they had fought for had been betrayed and if this wish was denied, they would resign their commissions and go home.[41]

The plot was discovered and the officers implicated in it were tried at court martial; it would have been deemed mutiny. On 27 February 1654, Monck, writing from Dalkeith, told Cromwell, 'having found him [Oates] to bee a very greate contriver and formentour of the late designe here, they adjudged him to be casheared from the army and to be imprisoned until such time as hee give in sufficient security for his future peaceable demeanour to your Highnesse and the government'.[42] Oates and Cromwell came face to face on 31 March 1655, but the latter 'gave him onely a sharpe reproofe for his folie, upon promise of his faithfull deportment for the future'.[43] It is not known where and for how long that Oates was imprisoned, but clearly his career in the army was at an end.

The Oates family may have lived for a time in London as it was later noted that as a young man Titus was a member of a Baptist church at Virginia Street, in Ratcliff (East London).[44] It is possible that Oates senior may have influenced his son's political beliefs as the older man was noted as being 'inferior to few in his hot blind zeal for the Good Old cause'.[45]

An early biographer wrote that as a child Titus was 'mark'd as a scholar…that he might become teacher forsooth, in one of their own congregations'. Apparently he was 'a pretty forward child, he had even in his cradle a very politick shrewd Aspect'.

His initial schooling was 'to a decrepit old woman, to be taught his prayers and his congees'. He was not a good influence on his fellow pupils 'he cou'd lie before he cou'd speak plain; he begun as he held on and was ever telling Tales, and making mischief among the children'.[46]

He then went to another master, a clerk of the parish, 'a precise formal Rascal and a great Scholard'. This 'Rural Preceptor' taught him to read and write and how to cast accounts. His parents were generous though Oates was accounted 'a Blockhead'. When a Baptist elder examined Oates at home, he perceived that 'his time had been all misspent; and that he was as great a stranger then to Latin as he ever was with morality'.[47]

By 1660 the Oates family were resident in Hastings on the Sussex coast, about 65 miles to the south east of London and then known as a small fishing town of perhaps 1,500 people, a far cry from its importance in the Middle Ages as one of the Cinque Ports and a major supplier of ships for the Navy. Daniel Defoe wrote of its insignificance, 'The towns of Rye, Winchelsea and Hastings have little in them to deserve more than a bare mention' and John Macky noted it was 'a very poor and indifferent place'.[48] It was divided into two parishes: All Saints and the older St. Clement's. All Saints' church is at the north end of a long lane leading from the seafront and is set on a little hillock.

This was when Samuel became rector of All Saints parish, despite his earlier radicalism. 'When the King came in, he wheeled about with the times', and was to be resident incumbent for another fifteen years (and at least nominally so until his death). The family resided in the rectory just to the north of the said church on Hastings' northern outskirts. Or as another wrote 'by his cunning suttle tricks and behaviour he became incumbent of a church in Hastings'. Of course, it was commonplace for servants of the Republic to transfer their allegiance to the new order; Anthony Cooper, Earl of Shaftesbury, who appears later in this book, was one such. Having been a member of the Council of State in the 1650s and backed Cromwell as Lord Protector, he served as a member of Charles II's first governments.

By now (1660) Charles II had returned in peace as King to much initial popular rejoicings and was determined not to go on his travels again. For the Church of England this was good news, with the restoration of not only monarch and lords, but also bishops. Royalist clergymen who had been displaced by their enemies in the 1640s and 1650s were returned to their parishes. A career in the Anglican Church was certainly inviting once more and with the loss of about 2,000 clergymen who were unable to swear allegiance to the monarch, there was scope for men like Oates' father who lacked the usual qualification of a university degree to become a clergyman – as well as being able to downplay his earlier principles, at least outwardly. John Injanes was the man who owned the advowson of All Saints' church and so made this appointment. The previous known incumbent was Christoher Dowe, from 1636 and so presumably by 1660 he was dead. Injanes appointed Samuel Oates.

Titus was here baptised at All Saints' church, Hastings, aged about 12, on 20 November 1660, as was his brother Constant. The parish register read 'the 20th of this month titus otes, an constant otes, sons of samll an Lucy otes were baptised'.[49] This is the first time that Oates is known to have been mentioned in writing anywhere. Regrettably no note as to their birthdates is given; it was not required at the time but some clergymen did record them.

Titus had a number of the town's principal inhabitants as his godparents. Sibling Euneke was baptised on 2 February 1661 and sister Ann and brother Samuel on 3 June 1661. As with Titus and Constant, these may have been child as opposed to baby baptisms.[50] Little is known about his early childhood in Hastings, but in 1679 Sir Denny Ashburnham (c.1628–1697), an MP for Hastings from 1660–1679 and JP from 1660, recalled, 'I do know Mr Oates and have known him a great while; I have known him from his cradle, and I do know that when he was a child, he was not a person of that credit that we could depend upon what he said'.[51]

Perhaps because of the need to emphasise his apparent change of political and religious allegiance, and to impress this on his children, Samuel took Titus and possibly other family members, on the comparatively lengthy trip to London in April 1662. This was to witness the hanging of John Okey (as with the elder Oates, an Anabaptist) and two other men, who had been among the regicides who had signed the death warrant of Charles I in 1649. The three were hanged, drawn and quartered on Tower Hill on 19 April 1662. Oates later recalled attendance there.[52] Children often attended public hangings, it being thought good for their moral education. The impression this made on the young Oates cannot be known, but presumably, given his later career, it did not lead him to be antipathetic to such spectacles. Possibly Samuel went there to pay respects to a former comrade or possibly to impress on his son the importance of allegiance to the new monarch as Okey confessed that he had been in the wrong.

After his initial schooling, Titus went to a more respectable establishment, at Sedlescombe, a few miles to the north of Hastings, where the master 'beat something into his indocile Noddle'. There was another experience he had there. A biographer wrote, 'The Doctor, man and Boy, was ever addicted to that shameful lewd Act of Sodomy' and he was 'catch'd with another of the scholars in that beastly Trick'. Hauled before the master, with his partner in crime and the two witnesses, Oates 'fell upon his knees, and wish'd he might never rise again (or some such wish) if ever he did any such thing'. The master thought that Oates was impudent and vehement in his expressions. Apparently Oates asked his fellow sodomite to deny everything to the last, but the boy confessed 'that Oates had importuned him to it and then made him swear not to discover it'. For his parents' sake, the crime was covered up.[53]

That was not all. Oates was determined to be revenged on his master. Seeing another boy enter the master's room with a tobacco box and then staying there some time, he decided to publicly accuse the master of sodomy with the boy. He swore an oath on this. Fortunately for the master, he had an impeccable reputation and Oates was known as a profligate youth and his evidence seemed incredible. The case was thrown out.[54] We shall see similar alleged patterns in Oates' behaviour in later years, especially in his desire for revenge and for accusing others of abominable, but only imagined, crimes. As a clergyman's son, Oates must have known of the commandment 'Thou shalt not bear false witness against thy neighbour' but he had no wish to keep it.

Meanwhile, Titus Oates was entered into the Merchant Taylors' School on 11 June 1665 and remained there for a year.[55] The school was founded in 1561 and was then located in the City of London; John Goad was then headmaster. Nicholas Delves took him to the school.[56] He was a 'free scholar', meaning that after an entrance fee had been paid, no further costs were payable. Apparently Oates cheated William Smith, his master, of the entrance fees, by keeping the money that should have been paid to him.[57] Smith recalled, 'he cheated me out of our Entrance Money, which his father sent me'. He added of Oates 'his perverse and wicked pranks, when he was a school boy'.[58] It would also seem that Oates bore a grudge against Smith; possibly the latter may have reproved or punished him at school and as we shall see, this Oates did not forget or forgive.

One account states that he was 'instructed in literature by Master Mackmillan, in London for one year, and under other preceptors for two years, more or less'.[59] A contemporary biography alleged that he briefly attended Westminster School (there is no record that he did so) 'but profited little in learning his Genius being wholly bent to baseness and Villainy'.[60]

Another biographer claimed that there, 'where, without mending his manners, he made some slow progress in his learning till with a kind of solid dullness he had perpetrated thro' the Classicks and could make a tolerable shift with a Latin author'.[61]

Formal education was not compulsory in Britain until the nineteenth century and many did without it, being put out to work as soon as they were capable of augmenting the family income. This was not Oates' lot. In order to become an Anglican clergyman it was conventionally necessary to obtain a BA degree as a minimum prior to ordination. As with his father before him, this was envisaged as Oates' career. There were then only two universities in England and being an Anglican was a prerequisite for entry.

It may well be a pointer to the elder Oates' political preferences that Cambridge was chosen. Oxford was well known as a centre of Stuart support in the seventeenth and eighteenth centuries. Charles I had established his court at Oxford during the civil war in 1642 and his son retreated there during the plague of 1665, and it is significant that in 1681 Charles II would hold his final Parliament there. Cambridge had been where Cromwell had been an undergraduate and traces of Puritan sympathies remained there after his death.

On 29 June 1667, Oates was entered as a sizar at Caius College, founded as Gonville in 1348, refounded as Gonville and Caius in 1557. He was under the tutorship of one Master John Ellys and George Thorpe. A sizar was the lowest of the low at the universities in this period, a poor student who had to undertake menial duties for wealthier students to earn his keep. One account states that he was the servant to a young gentleman there.[62] It is possible that this increased Oates' sense of injustice and envy that he felt against the world. Entering the college at about eighteen was relatively old to do so in the seventeenth century; Oates' near contemporary, John Wilmot, Earl of Rochester, matriculated at Oxford in 1660 aged a mere thirteen years old. Evelyn dismissed the college in his description of his visit to Cambridge in 1654 thus, after describing St. John's and Trinity colleges, 'Then we went to Caius, then to Kings Coll' and rhapsodising about the latter at length.[63]

In 1682 Adam Elliott, a fellow student, recalled Oates' time at the little college:

> I remember Titus Oates was entered into our Colledge; by the same token that the plague and he both visited the University in the same year. He was very remarkable for a canting Fanatical way conveyed to him with his Anabaptistical Education, and in our Academical exercises, when others declaim'd, Oates always preach'd...I moreover remember, that he staied not above a year in our Colledge, but removed to Saint Johns; what the occasions was, I cannot call to mind.[64]

The relationship between Oates and Elliott is never made clear, but it seems evident that as with Smith at school, Oates bore a grudge against him. In both cases, when he was able to take his revenge on them, he did so. Oates and Elliott certainly knew each other; in such a small college it would be hard not to. Whether they were on apparent good terms or not at college it is impossible to know.

According to Elliott 'he was so inconsiderable both as to his person and his parts'.[65] His first biographer retells the following story about Oates' time at university thus:

> he giving there a most remarkable instance of his roguery. He bought a Gown of a poor taylor and when he was Dun'd for the money, he swore before his tutor that he would take the sacrament upon it, that he had pay'd him; being asked by his tutor how he came by so much money, since all the money past through his hands, he said it was privately sent him by his mother, by a carrier, and Named him, the carrier afterwards being called, he neither knew Oates nor any thing of the matter.[66]

Apparently Oates sold the gown for twopence to a second hand clothes dealer. One account suggests that this theft and attempted perjury led to his expulsion from college in disgrace.[67] Dr Thomas Watson, his tutor, later recalled, that he did 'not charge him with much immorality, but says he was a great dunce, ran into debt, and being sent away for want of money, never took a degree'.[68] An early biographer states 'he was spewed out, for his litigious uneasy Temper'.[69]

On 22 February 1669, he entered St. John's College, founded as recently as 1511, and just a little north on the same road as his previous college. Apparently his father urged the authorities there to instruct him in Arminiamism, a Protestant nonconformist sect allied to Anabaptism, though it is unknown if the Anglicans there would have done so.[70] In 1654 this more prominent college made a rather greater impression on Evelyn than had Caius, with the diarist recording:

> Cambridg, & went first to see St Johns Colledge & Librarie, which I think is the fairest of that Universitie: one Mr Benlous has given it all the ornaments of Pietra Commessa, whereof a table, and one piece of Perspective is very fine, other trifles there also be of no great value, besides a vast old song book or Service, & some faire Manuscripts: This Coll: is well built of brick: There hangs in the Library the Picture of Williams ABishop of York, & sometimes Ld: Keeper, my Kindsman, and their great benefactor.[71]

Pepys was equally impressed with the college library, taking his wife and two others there on their visit in 1667. Later in the century, Celia Fiennes, who omitted any reference to Caius, wrote of it:

> 'St Johns College Garden is very pleasant for the fine walks, both close shady walks and open rows of trees and quickset hedges, there is a pretty bowling green with cut arbours in the hedges'.[72]

Apart from the escapade already noted, there were more general references made to his time at Cambridge, by the same source. Apparently, Oates was 'equally remarkable for his dullness and debauchery'. 'Oates was now but a fresh [young] man, but a Master of Arts in lying and swearing…he had stayed some small time in the university, being notorious for all sorts of Debaucheries he was called home by his father to be his vicar at Hastings, his father being by this means preventing his being expelled the university, he having neither wit nor learning'.[73] Another account states he 'obtain'd some little learning in Cambridge'.[74] A hostile critic later wrote about the results of Oates' education, that he was 'being no manner of a scholar, but as ignorant as any other poor curate may be imagined (for I will be a bond slave for ever), if he can translate six lines into Latin without a solecisim'.[75]

The debaucheries referred to could tie in with an early biographer, writing a quarter of a century later, he wrote 'he grew up to those Nauscious attempts of Sodomy or Buggery too often laid to his charge'. Homosexuality in the all male conclaves of university life was far from uncommon at this time, some of the unmarried male tutors taking a fancy to handsome young students.[76] An enemy later wrote 'The Doctor has an affection, I suppose to the masculine, because it is more worthy than the feminine'.[77]

Another enemy of Oates wrote in 1682 about his university experiences, that 'Dr Otes fall'n foul in language upon a senior in Cambridge, and was condemn'd to ask his pardon in a copy of verses as a composition'. The commentator added, 'And a copy of verse, let me tell ye, in those days went as hard with the Doctor, as fifteen or twenty thousand pounds did afterwards'.[78]

There was apparently another regrettable incident in his experiences at the college and this contrasts with his apparent predilection to date for the same sex. Although here 'his malignant Spirit of Railing and Scandal was no less obnoxious to the whole society', he did make, temporarily at least, one friend in college. Apparently 'he grew into familiarity with a pretty young Gentleman of the same college'; he may even have been physically attracted to him. On one occasion, the other student's relatives came to Cambridge to visit him. Among them was his sister, 'a very beautiful young Lady'. These relatives were entertained in part by Oates and 'this brutal Dunce of a Knight Errant constru'd quite contrary to proceed from the Result of a too free and compliable Disposition, and presently set his Impudence at work to commence an early suit of love to the Lady'. She was 'unwilling to take notice of' it but this did not deter him.[79] She was too polite and modest to give him a forthright negative.

Oates wrote her a love letter on the following day:

> 'If I may presume on the small Encouragement you were pleas'd to give me last Night, I have I hope, no reason to despair of your Favour, to the satisfaction of which nothing can add more than another opportunity of declaring how much I am, dear lady'.

The young lady was still indifferent on its receipt, but Oates, once again, took her silence to mean approval. After dinner, his college friend showed his relatives over the college, leaving Oates and his sister alone in his rooms. There was some conversation about her brother and then Oates 'with a brutal lust, seiz'd her in his Arms, and in a rude manner, fell a kissing her, which confounded her with surprize'. She then tried to let him down gently but without success, for he renewed 'his brutal attempt, offering to throw her onto the bed with no check to his lascivious passion'. Fortunately her cries brought her brother running back. The friendship between the two young men came to a sudden end and Oates was turned out of his rooms.[80]

His time at the college was mediocre, 'he was very inconsiderable both in his parts and person'. Yet, though he plodded for his years at Cambridge it was not wholly wasted, for it had given him a 'blind notion of Divinity, sufficient with a grave hypocritical Air, and outward Grace to qualify him for a country Pulpit'.[81]

Oates was probably the type of unfortunate student who has few, if any, real friends. He was probably one who gets talked about a lot by his fellows when he was not there, as an oddity and a freak. If he knew of this it might well have served to increase his sense of injustice with the world and his fellow men, and as will be seen he did, when he could, try and take revenge on those whom he had met and maybe crossed, earlier in his life.

As we shall see, Oates did not go straight from Cambridge to Hastings as a clergyman. Leaving either university at this time and for long after, without a degree was commonplace (Anthony Ashley Cooper, later Earl of Shaftesbury and a future patron of Oates, was one such). Many went to university for a year or two or even less, not for any pretence of study, but for the social life and the need to network. However, serious gentlemen scholars and those who needed a degree to pursue their chosen profession, whether it be the Church, Law or Medicine, had to continue and obtain, at least, their BA. Oates fell into this latter group but he dropped out. It was now time to make his own way in the world and for this he was lacking the conventional formal qualifications, but this was compensated for by his wily nature as we shall see and a career of public mischief beckoned.

Chapter Two

Titus Oates' Early Career, 1670–1678

Oates had left university without any qualifications and this would usually be an insurmountable handicap for a young man wishing to enter the Anglican Church. Yet for Oates it was not to prove so. His difficulty, rather, was to be holding on to any official post once he had obtained it. To become a clergyman, a testament that the candidate had led a moral life was needed from both his local Anglican clergyman and his university tutor. From what is known about Oates' university career it would seem that the latter would be unlikely to have been forthcoming. However, it is quite possible that his father as rector of All Saints', Hastings, would have given him more than adequate testimony. Furthermore, clearly no thorough check was made at his university.

Clerical career

It is recorded that Oates was ordained as a curate for the rural parish (with a population of but 334 in the first official census of 1801) of St. Mary's, Theydon Bois in Essex on 25 November 1669 by Benjamin Laney, bishop of Ely. Oates claimed he had an MA and either he was taken at his word or had forged the necessary documentation.[1] Nothing is known about his time there and it may have been extremely brief. The parish is two miles to the south of Epping and fifteen from London. However, the curacy was vacant in the 1650s and no surprise as the annual income was a beggarly £20, as a contemporary noted, 'no godly minister will accept of it'. This may of course be why Oates was offered it; the lowest of the low but perhaps better than nothing and all that his previous achievements would merit. Duties were probably slight, for by the early eighteenth century there was typically only one baptism, marriage or burial per year. However, there must be some doubt whether Oates was curate as the minister there, as in 1669–1670 John Strype was listed, followed by John Ailmer and finally William Davis from 1670–1706.[2] Possibly Oates' stay was very brief or he never took up the post to which he was appointed.

However, Oates himself said that he was curate to the Rev. Walter Drury, the rector of St. Nicholas' church, Sandhurst, on the border of Kent and Sussex. The parish, with a population of 887 in 1801, was 50 miles to the south of London, on the road to Rye. Its chief crop was hops and the church was half a mile from the village. Oates later claimed that at this time (1670) one Mr Cotton was attempting to persuade him to go over to the Catholic Church. Drury told him that Cotton had also attempted to convert him as well. Two years later one Keimash apparently tried likewise. Cotton and Keimash were presumably Catholic priests (assuming they ever existed in reality). Oates left the parish in early 1673 at the latest.[3] None of Oates' biographers or enemies seem to comment on this part of his clerical career; possibly because there was nothing scandalous known about it. Yet he left after a short period, but this may have been to better himself elsewhere, rather than being obliged to leave.

More is known for certain about his next parish. Oates then managed to secure the vicarage of St. Bartholomew's church in another little village, that of Bobbing, also in Kent, being presented to the benefice as 'Clerk and Bachelor of Arts' on 5 March 1673 by Gilbert Sheldon, Archbishop of Canterbury, and Sir George Moore of Bobbing Court, the benefice's patron. This was a step up from being a mere curate and financially more remunerative. It was 39 miles from London, ten from Rochester and one from Sittingbourne and a historian writing in the next century wrote of the place in slighting terms, 'It is not an unpleasant situation, though at the same time it has not the character of being very healthy'. It was 780 acres, with some very poor clay soil but some fertile land as well. The church had two small aisles, a tall spire and steeple at the west end and five bells. In 1640 the incumbency was worth £60 per annum and there were 88 communicants. The population in 1801 stood at 231 and so was probably even less in 1673.[4]

He did not stay long here, either. Formal authorisation of Oates' dispensation for his absence from the incumbency occurred on 14 September 1674. Not much of a contemporary nature is known of his time there, but he and the Rev. Thomas Turner, Vicar of Milton, signed documentation to show that certain individuals had taken holy communion according to the rites of the Anglican Church and thus were now eligible to hold civic offices, as per the Test Act of 1673. One such was one John Tweedy or Treedy of Bobbing.[5] The motive given in 1674 for this departure was 'by reason of the unwholesomnesse of the ayre'.[6] Six years later he said that he left the parish in the hands of Turner and the reason he gave was as before. 'The air was not a good air in that part of Kent, and I had my health, and that was one reason, and for other reasons best known to myself'.[7] However, several hostile sources claimed otherwise. One was that it was because Oates stole pigs and preached Catholic doctrines and so the bishop ended his tenure there.[8] Similarly Smith later claimed that at Bobbing, Oates was known for 'where amongst many other notorious exclamations against him, he was remarkable for Petty Thefts, his Neighbours pigs and Hens never escaping his Rapacious Clutches'.[9] Finally, Elliott claimed that Oates' patron, Sir George Moore, had Oates turned out of Bobbing.[10] This was in part due to 'several other irregularities in his conversation'. Among the parish Oates had allegedly caused 'continual strife and contention among the people, than ever he saved by his preaching, being always observed where ever he fortun'd to make his abode, to sow Dissension among the Neighbours'.[11] It seems odd that Oates, reared by an Anabaptist and then schooled in Anglican institutions should espouse Catholicism, and also curious that he should feel the need to steal pigs and hens, though earlier biographers and commentators have felt no need to question such allegations. Presumably these thefts, if such occurred, were caused by spite against their owners, rather than the need to eat. It was generally difficult to expel a beneficed clergyman and usually legal proof was needed of a heinous crime. The parish had not forgotten him for they later noted 'Our minister is gone to sea', by which they may have meant that he had gone to the coast.[12]

Having no other obvious place to go to, it was unsurprising that Oates went back home to Hastings. However, he did not go back there immediately, or so he said in 1679, 'I did go near about Chichester, and served a sequestration there'.[13] This is confirmed by his being a surety at the marriage of Robert Hitchcock, of St. Pancras, Chichester, needle maker, described as a kinsman, to one Alice Wattes at St. Peters' church, near to the Guildhall.[14]

Once in Hastings, 'he frequently assisted his father in his church duties of preaching etc.'. However, both father and son were problematic, 'both of them by their vile practices and behaviours became cumbersome and indeed odious to all or most of their parish…which together with many of their intollerable unjust dealings, moved and stir'd up the parishioners to exhibit articles to the ordinary to evict old Oates, of which, after a while, he grew to be in great apprehension and therefore essayed the solicitation of divers of his ffriends upon the parishioners, but without ffruit, for they persisted effectually'.[15]

They were not entirely destitute of supporters:

> Whereupon a certaine person who had been very instrumentall in endeavouring a reconcilliation amongst them, by accident meeting Tytus Oates, in conference (amongst other things) demaunded of him how now at last matters were like to goe between his ffather and his parishioners, who presently answered 'it was no matter, for there were now irons in the fire which if they tooke a right heat would doe the worke.[16]

An early biographer was scathing about his time there. Apparently his preaching was of such a quality that 'fisherwomen pulled him out of his pulpit' on one occasion. He was no more welcome to their social superiors for 'he was always quarrelling, and by his lies and false suggestions, setting neighbours by the ears'.[17] Oates was later accused of other behaviour, 'His debaucheries are notoriously known in and about Hastings'.[18] Quite what these were is not stated.

Given the small number of baptisms, marriages and burials in the parish, the work of the clergyman in officiating at such events was modest. In 1674 there were but 24 such services; in 1675 there were a dozen and of these all but ten were prior to May, but by then the Oateses were involved in other activities as shall be seen.[19]

Apart from ecclesiastical duties, the role of the early modern clergyman was to play an important part in what would now be called local government. Parish administration in both civil and church matters were then treated as one. The day to day work was given to a number of parish officers, appointed annually; churchwardens (then as now to care for the fabric of the church and its property), overseers of the poor, to distribute poor relief to the deserving poor of the parish and possibly the itinerant poor passing through the parish and the surveyors of the highway who were to see to the upkeep of local roads.

The appointment, and meetings of these officials was overseen by the incumbent. So in the book created to record such, we often see 'Samuell Otes, Rector' there. But his son also shouldered some of the work, as is noted on 4 January 1675, when John Faulby and Richard Sealtt presented their accounts as surveyors of the highways, for £1 3s 4d. This was witnessed by 'Titus Otes, Curate', Thomas Nicholas and John Wringfield.[20] This is the only explicit reference to Titus Oates in the parish records, but those for the seventeenth century, other than this book and the parish registers are scanty indeed, so he may well have attended other parochial meetings. There seems no official appointment of Oates as curate and so this post was probably given to him by his father unofficially, without any sanction from the diocese.

Father and son did not always attend to their parochial duties as the parish noted in 1675:

> Wee present Samuell Otes for his cattell annoying the churchyard and breaking downe the fence; secondly for leaving his cure and being absente from his benefice 32 weekes. Titus Ote for presuming to preach, having not orders. Wee present the chancell and churchyard fence is out of order, the parson to repair both; Titus Ots, curate as pretended, for serving a subpoena in the church upon Francis Norwood, one of the churchwardens; the said Titus for being a malicious, disorderly, scandalous person, also for not reading his certificate of the renunciation of the Covenant. Samuel Ots, clerke, for neglecting his cure ever since the last visitation and also for not observing holy days and for not catechising of children.[21]

Oates was also accused of thefts, 'a scarcity of poultry was in the parish' and this was resented by the housewives there.[22]

Norwood was a miller and was often churchwarden or overseer of the parish in the 1670s and he had a particular animus towards the Oateses and Titus especially. On 8 February 1676 it was stated that 'he the said Francis Norwood [said he] would beate him or strike him the said Titus in the hearing of the said George Jackson'. Apparently Norwood accused Oates of telling lies and we shall hear of Norwood again. Yet the Hastings court found in favour of Norwood on 27 May, not Oates and so Oates' allegation of being threatened by Norwood was dismissed, and they deemed 'he said Titus had voluntarily and corruptly committed perjury', binding him over for £40 to appear at the next Sessions.[23]

In particular both father and son were antagonistic towards the Parker family of Hastings, who were very prominent locally, with William Parker senior being mayor of the town on three prior occasions. In 1675, Oates senior swore that Parker senior was guilty of treason with the result that the latter was sent to London, but was soon released, but only after 'a great deal of trouble and charge'.[24]

In detail, Oates senior complained to the Privy Council that the elder Parker attend the Privy Council in London because of 'certaine irreverent, scandalous and opprobius words alleged to be by him spoken'. The Privy Council was made up of a number of senior politicians and often the monarch themselves, who met regularly. On 7 April 1675 Parker came before the council but they thought that Oates senior and junior should also be there and so ordered that they do so in three weeks' time.[25] Given that the regime was very sensitive to allegations of sedition and potential treason from real and imagined plots, all such possibilities had to be investigated.

On 17 April 1675 it was noted that next week Titus Oates was expected to attend in London to make good his information against the elder Parker before the Privy Council. He told them that he could not do so because he was giving evidence against the younger Parker at Hastings in a case where the younger man was accused of 'an unnatural offence' and so another day had to be allocated to Oates to provide evidence against the father.[26]

On 28 April 1675, Oates father and son, and the younger Parker, came at last before the Privy Council. Charles II was present and the conclusion of the hearing was recorded thus:

> 'His majesty, upon hearing the whole matter, and being satisfied by a certificate under the hands of divers gentlemen of the said county of the loyalty and good affection of the said Parker to His Majesty's service, was graciously pleased to order that the said parker be dismissed'.[27]

This was not to be the last time that Oates and the King would meet, but it is probable on this occasion the former made a relatively minimal impression on the latter.

That Easter, Titus 'swore a detestable crime against young Parker, said to be committed in the church porch'. This had allegedly occurred two months previously. Oates himself claimed that he had found the younger Parker, 'in the abominable and most unnaturall act of generacion with a young and tender man-childe'. Oates senior also swore that this was true.[28] Another writer put it thus, that Oates 'swore downright Sodomy against the honest schoolmaster…with one of his school boys in the church porch'. Apparently the quarrel was over Oates wanting the schoolmaster's post which was for 'a Religious and godly scholemaster'.[29] This is very similar to the allegation that Oates made against one of his schoolmasters in the previous decade; a scandalous offence for which physical proof can rarely be found to prove or disprove such. It would seem that Oates was motivated by money and wanted the master's salary. He may have been influenced by his father who was having to pay for his son's upkeep out of his existing stipend.

Yet at trial of the young Parker for sexual offences on 27 May 1675, masons and others at work in and around the church on that day could swear that Parker could not have been guilty without their observing it. Furthermore, on the day of the alleged assault, 'he was treating the parents of his scholars with a select Gaudy-day Dinner at his own House, and never stirred from the Company till night'. Parker lived a half mile from where the assault allegedly occurred. Another point in Parker's favour was that 'the child abused [was] neither produced nor heard of'. He was acquitted but Oates was sent to Dover Castle 'for speaking scandalous things of Mr Parker'.[30]

A later account of the case in court was as follows, that Oates:

> attested it at the Bar with all the Oaths and impudence imaginable: but the Jury nevertheless brought in the prisoner not Guilty, as remembering what an Accuser he had, and understanding by their Neighbours, that he was making merry with some of them at that very time of the Pretended Fact. This so enraged the very women of Hastings…That they stood at the Hall with rods to whip him, and Tubs of Water to wash him when bloody, so they might whip him again.[31]

Apparently 'infinite are the prancks of this nature [committed by Oates and his father] in that very one place'.[32] Despite Oates senior looking unfavourably on his son when the latter was an infant, they now seemed to be working together in disreputable partnership. How much each influenced the other is unknown. It is also worth noting that Oates decided to foist alleged (and untrue) sexual misbehaviour on the younger Parker and it is possible that this is a crime that Oates had spent time thinking about and so may be a clue to his innermost thoughts and fantasies. That these deceits ended in failure may also have taught him something about how to better indulge in such behaviour. That he was motivated by money is worth noting but also he may have been influenced by spite and envy of those he knew and were better socially placed than he.

The family, or at least the rector, seem to have left the parish shortly after this debacle. Anthony Wood recalled, 'Old Oats was outed of his benefice and lives sculking in London about Bloomsbury upon the friendly allowance of his holy sisters [presumably female sympathisers not nuns] till now'.[33] Whether others of the family moved with him is not known.

Naval Career

Although this aspect of his career is ignored by contemporary biographers, and Wood reported that it (impossibly) occurred in 1666 (when Oates was still undergoing his education), it is now necessary to state that most observers note that Oates then served as a naval chaplain upon HMS *Adventure* in 1675-1676. Oates' elder brother was a naval lieutenant and this, coupled to his recent residence in a coastal town, may have suggested this career avenue for him, as well as seeing it as an escape from his experiences on land. England had been at war with the Dutch Republic in the third Dutch War from 1672-1674. This had been in alliance with France but whereas France fought on land, England's contribution was primarily maritime. However, by 1674 hostilities (between England and Holland) had ceased and so the Navy was no longer on a war footing. This did not mean that it was inactive and with England's recently acquired colony of Tangiers in danger, the latter needed constant supply by sea. Naval chaplains were officers, but their status was seen as relatively lowly compared to their counterparts on land, though Oates' clerical options were now very limited, after his recent escapades in Bobbing and Hastings, so he could hardly hope for anything better. Naval chaplains had to say prayers once or twice a day and might occasionally preach but rarely gave holy communion.

HMS *Adventure* was a 34 gun ship launched from Woolwich in 1646. By 1666 she had 38 guns and had taken part in the Battle of Solebay in 1672. In 1675 Sir Richard Ruth became her captain. On 22 June the ship reached Tangiers. The Earl of Inchiquin, governor of Tangier, and his garrison were there disembarked.[34]

Yet did Oates serve on this ship? As noted early biographers do not mention it, but Dr Gilbert Burnet (1643–1715), a Scottish clergyman (and later renowned as one of the premier historians of the era and bishop of Salisbury), much later wrote of the ignominious end of Oates' naval career thus 'from which he was dismissed upon a complaint of some unnaturall practices not to be named'.[35] A letter of 1679 stated he was on a ship to Tangiers.[36] A listing of chaplains aboard Royal Navy ships lists him as being one in 1675 but does not name the vessel that he served on.[37]

His naval service, though, seems undoubted. Furthermore, Oates himself later recalled serving afloat, under the aforesaid Sir Richard.[38] However, the ship's crew roll does not only not list Oates among the 234 men serving onboard, but notes that one William Morgan was the minister (assuming that Oates was not using an alias). Furthermore, Sir Richard noted in the ship's log book that they departed from Spithead on 12 April 1675 and this is 16 days before Oates attended the meeting of the Privy Council concerning the charges against Parker and 45 days before the hearing against young Parker in Hastings.[39] It seems safe to note that Oates was not on HMS *Adventure* but as to which ship he served is unknown, barring a search of all surviving muster rolls of the Royal Navy in 1675.

Oates later wrote that whilst at sea, 'I found many Difficulties by Sickness of Body, I refreshed myself at Tangire'. Apparently he talked to one Gerard, an Irish Dominican, who asked him whether Catholicism was dominant in England and Oates said not, and the man said that in that case the war with the Dutch was pointless.[40]

Another account details the ignominious end his naval career and corroborates that given by Burnet:

> 'he fell into his old Tricks of Sodomy in the ship and was taken in flagranti, to escape hanging, according to his demerit, he adventured drowning, and stole away narrowly to shore in the cockboat'.[41]

Elliott wrote similarly:

> his monstrous lusts, which would make a satyr blush…I have heard those who were aboard with him report, that he has committed such crimes a-ship-board, as have obliged the captain, a gentleman of very fair conditions, to waive all civility usually bestow'd upon his Quality, and to order him to be drubb'd and ty'd neck and heels, and afterwards be set ashore.[42]

Unfortunately there is no contemporary record of this, no court martial records exist and failing the discovery of which ship he was on, no known reference in the captain's logbook where such remarkable events should have been recorded. Sodomy was rare in the Navy; it was unpopular among the men and such was the lack of privacy on board, detection was highly probable.[43]

At a loose end whenever it was that his naval career ended, after a matter of mere months (perhaps in the time it took to sail to Tangiers, spend some time there and then return), it seems that Oates gravitated towards London. In 1681 it was recalled by one Archibald Gledstanes that at the beginning of 1676 Oates was in Coleman Street, on the north edge of the City of London, on a Sunday. Although he was wearing the robes of an Anglican clergyman, he professed an interest in Socinian principles. Socinians were a small nonconformist Protestant sect, not unrelated to Anabaptism. Therefore, in accordance to Socinian beliefs, he denied the orthodox Christian tenet of the Trinity. On the other hand he alleged he was an Anglican, claiming to be a prebendary of Gloucester Cathedral and had subscribed to the 39 articles of the Church of England. Gledstanes accused him of perjury and asked Oates to explain the obvious dichotomy. Gledstanes thought Oates was blasphemous in denying the principal tenets of the Christian faith, the Trinity and Divinity. The Socinians were equally unimpressed by Oates. Furthermore, at Mr Ward's alehouse on Coleman Street Oates repeated what he had already professed to the shock of all concerned.[44] This episode points to Oates' essentially openly irreligious nature, whilst wanting to project the image of an Anglican clergyman. For contemporaries, raised in orthodox Christian faith, this would have been seen as a great outrage.

By the autumn of that year Oates was back in his Sussex haunts. In September 1676 William Parker, senior, as (yet again, for the fourth and final time) mayor of Hastings, had Oates put in custody. This was 'in default of security on his bail, was placed in the custody of the prison' in Hastings. This was presumably because he was being accused of perjury following his lies against the younger Parker in the previous year. John Strode (1627–1686), lieutenant governor of Dover Castle told Parker, 'I command you that the body of Titus Oates, debtor of our said Lord the King, by whatever other name or additional name the said Titus is known, to be taken and detained in the prison' and was to be taken to the Westminster Quarter Sessions on St. Michael's day (1 October), which was three weeks hence.[45]

These letters of Parker and Strode cast several interesting reflections on Oates. They suggest that contrary to what is known from other sources, that Oates was masquerading under pseudonyms, commonly used by anyone involved in crime or underhand dealings, and that perhaps after his naval career ended so ignominiously, he returned to haunts known to him, albeit under another name. It is also interesting that his case was to be held in London rather than locally, as such crimes would normally be dealt with there. However, either the case collapsed or he escaped because there is no record of any conviction in London.

Catholic career

With yet another career option closed off to Oates, it would seem that his flirtation with Anglicanism was coming to an end. A pariah in Hastings, it was back to London for him, by the end of 1676. Most of the remainder of Oates' life was spent in London, with the exception of brief sojourns in Spain and France and so it is worth briefly examining the London of the late seventeenth century.

London was by far the most populous city in Britain – and indeed Europe – with almost half a million inhabitants. After the Great Fire of 1666 it was in the process of being rebuilt. It was the centre of government and commerce. Many people visited the capital on business or pleasure. There were many villages just outside the capital, such as Hammersmith to the west, Islington to the north and Mile End to the east. Oates had probably lived in the capital as a small child and had visited it in 1662 and 1675. Now his residence would be more or less permanent. His former sins were as yet unknown here and so he could begin with a fresh slate. The contrast to the villages and small towns he had hitherto resided in must have been a shock but he adapted quickly and was not slow in grasping the opportunities offered before him.

There he took employment as a Protestant chaplain with Henry Howard (1628-1684), Earl of Norwich (and later sixth Duke of Norfolk), a Catholic. Despite the Earl's Catholicism, he had to cater for the beliefs of his Protestant servants, so needed a Protestant clergyman in his household. Yet he lost the post as 'he began to rail against the Church of England…intending to wind himself into the good opinion of the Roman Catholics'. This was so he could make his conversion acceptable to one Matthew Medbourne (c.1637–1680), 'a zealous Romanist', an actor and playwright.[46]

As an early biographer stated 'he found himself at a great loss, and so betook himself to his old Trade of lying and swearing'. Becoming acquainted with Norfolk, he was promised a benefice but in the meantime became one of the Earl's honorary chaplains. Oates became apparently increasingly critical of the Anglican Church and when speaking to some of London's many Catholics, 'pretended all on Fire to be joined to it and resolved to become a new man and so at last he was admitted' and 'prevailed by his seeming zeal'.[47]

He was not popular in the household:

> he was only a hanger on for maintenance, he was an Eye Sore among the servants, and grew into disesteem of the whole house; nay, such was his inordinate and gormandising way of living, that the chaplain in the Devil of a wife [possibly a reference to the play of this name], came short of the Devil of a Doctor.

Apparently Oates had eyes for the butler and the cook, and the housekeeper stopped his supply of sweetmeats and cordial drams because he slandered her concerning her romantic interest in the valet, the woman being seen by Oates as his rival 'in the lovely aspect of that charming young man, on whom he had cast many a Amorous Wanton Eye'.

It was also at this time that Oates began to make acquaintances with Catholics and to learn something of their habits.[48]

William Smith, the master who had last crossed Oates' path in the previous decade as his schoolmaster at the Merchant Taylors' School, met him again in 1676, having been introduced to him by Matthew Medbourne, a comedian. Oates was now wearing clerical attire again. The three men met at a club at The Pheasant in Fuller's Rents, Islington. The company there was both Catholic and Protestant, though apparently politics and religion were never discussed. Oates told Medbourne that he was a convert to Rome. Smith knew nothing of Oates' recent escapades but recalled his rascally nature as a schoolboy.[49]

Smith saw more of Oates in Islington, where he now taught. Dr William Sclater (c.1622–1691), Vicar of St. James' church, Clerkenwell, asked Oates whether he would preach in his church on Sunday and Oates agreed. Smith advised the vicar against it. However, his advice was ignored and Oates preached, 'speaking all along very bitterly against Calvin, he call'd him always Jack' (John Calvin, 1509-1564, a radical French Protestant reformer of international repute). The sermon gave offence to two (Protestant) magistrates in the congregation. Soon afterwards Oates cast off his clerical habit and began to be seen wearing a champagne coat and bearing a sword.[50]

Oates also met another man who was to be crucial in his career at this time. In 1681, Simpson Tonge, the son of the Rev. Israel Tonge, told Sir Roger L'Estrange (1616-1704), a courtier and pamphleteer and avowed enemy of Oates, that:

> When I came from the university, in the year 77, I found Oates with my Father, in a very poor condition, who complained he knew not what to do to get Bread; who went under the name Ambrose. My father took him home, and gave him Cloaths, Lodgings and Dyet, saying he would put him into a way. 'And then

he persuaded him to get acquainted among the Papists; and when he had done so, when my father told him, there had been many plots in England, to bring in Popery, and if he would go over among the Jesuits, & observe their ways, it was possible it might be Oates now, and if he could make it out, it would be his preferment for ever. But, however, if he could get their Names, and a little Acquaintance from the papists, it would be an easy matter to stir up the people to fear Popery. And again, my father and he (Dr Oates) went and lodg'd at Fox-Hall, at one Lambert's, a bell founder…and there Oates' narrative was written'.[51]

In other words, Oates should enter the Catholic Church in order to learn their secret plans and then to reveal these to the Protestants whom they were directed against, in order for the latter to preserve themselves. Oates was to be a spy.

The young Tonge also recalled that his father and Oates (known as Ambrose) also met at the Golden Horse Shoe on the Strand, at The Bush in Great Queen Street and also in York Buildings.[52] However, the two had originally become acquainted because Tonge lived at Sir Richard Barker's house in London and Barker had previously helped Samuel Oates and so knew the son as well.[53]

Dr Israel Tonge (1619–1680) had attended University College, Oxford, graduating there with a BA in 1643 and becoming a doctor of divinity in 1656. After a varied clerical career in Tangier (in the decade before Oates was there) and in London, at this time he was rector of Ashtead in Herefordshire and of St. Michael's church in the City of London. Tonge was an author of anti-Catholic tracts; later he published one titled *Jesuit assassins: or the Popish plot* and also *The Popish damnable Plot against our religion and liberties*. He had a strong animus against Catholics.[54] Gilbert Burnet described him thus, 'a very mean Divine, and seemed credulous and simple. But I had always look'd on him as a sincere man'.[55]

In February or March 1677, Tonge himself wrote that he showed Oates 'several treatises he had prepared for the presse' and that 'he had, by his owne intelligence & by discourse with very knowinge persons observe the Popish Plot to advance very strongly'. They decided that Oates should make further investigations.[56]

In London William Berry, a former Anglican vicar now Catholic, suggested that Oates join the Catholic Church and took him to a Jesuit priest. Oates later said that he was introduced to the Catholic Church in London by Basil Langworth, chaplain to Lord Petre, and was received in the faith on Ash Wednesday (28 February) in 1677.[57] Burnet wrote that the man who instructed Oates was one Hutchinson, also known as Berry, a Jesuit who had flipped between Catholicism and Anglicanism, not a man to be trusted but one who worked with would-be converts, 'He told me that Oates and they were always in ill terms'.[58] Apparently when Oates was confirmed, the priest later wrote 'he doubted whither Oates' heart was prepared to receive the Holy Ghost, the spirit of love in whose face he perceived signes of greate malice'.[59] John Fenwick, a Jesuit priest, recalled in 1679 that Oates came to the Catholics in a distressed state, 'He once came to me in a miserable poor condition, and said I must turn again, and betake myself to the ministry, to get bread, for I have eaten nothing myself these two days'. He was given 5s.[60] Thomas Whitebread, another Jesuit priest, spoke similarly of Oates' financial straits, 'a man that depended wholly on us to live and had no livelihood but what he had from us'.[61]

Oates later claimed he entered the Catholic Church as part of a plan to learn about any possible Catholic conspiracies and so act as informer and this is backed up by Tonge's son's later testimony. Yet it would seem that he had other motivations. These were the result of economic desperation. Needing money he sought refuge in one place which had not rejected him so far. Yet his character and learning made him inherently unsuitable for the role he sought out of necessity.

He was also apparently unsuitable as Whitebread was to continue:

> 'I found him a man not fit for that purpose and design which he pretended to…it was doubtful whether he was a good Catholic: For he had oftentimes maintained several propositions that were not soundly Catholic: and secondly, he led a very idle life, and was not found a man we were obliged to accept of, and therefore we desired him to retire, and for that purpose we furnished him, and gave him a good suit of clothes, and a periwig and £4 in his purse and he promised to pay me again when he had sold his library, which he said he had a very good one in London, but he never did'.[62]

Later that year, Oates, with the recommendation of his new friends, went overseas, first to the English College at Valladolid in Spain, where he was known as Titus Ambrosius. Founded by Robert Persons, an English Catholic priest in 1589, it aimed to instruct men to become priests for the English and Welsh mission. It was run by Jesuits. Catholic educational establishments were illegal in Britain since the reformation and it was an offence for nobility and gentry to send their sons there; but many did.[63]

Oates set sail at the end of April 1677, on the ship *The Merchant of Biscay*, whose master was Lucas Roach. He arrived in Bilboa, on the north coast of Spain, on 16 May and met Michael Hore and John Grace, Bilboa merchants. He was guided to the college by Martin Lornitz Espinosa, taking 10 days.[64]

His early biographer paints a dreary picture of Oates' time there:

> 'he had not been there long, but he gave many evident proofs of his incorrigible Nature and Blockishness so being a constant Quareller and Combatant with the servants and found altogether unfit to proceed'.

In 1679 William Frankland, a young Protestant merchant claimed that he had been to Valladolid at this time and saw two fellow Englishmen, William Bedloe and his brother James, there for several days and that they were in Oates' company; Oates later denied this and said 'My eyes are down; I will not swear I know you or any man, that I have been but once or twice in company'.[65] Apparently, one Clavering recalled in 1685 that 'he [Oates] told me he had been cheated by such a one of some pieces of eight in Spain'.[66] Bedloe's role in Oates' life was to assume a greater importance at the end of the next year as shall be seen. However, another account links Oates' meeting Bedloe at St. Omers, not Valladolid, so whether one account or two is true is unknown.

The Spanish there had a low opinion of him, 'an Ignorant Dolt that could not speak six words nor write three' in Latin. Furthermore, 'We have a mean opinion of the English hereticks since so ignorant and ridiculous an animal could gain entry amongst them'. He left the college on 30 October 1677 and travelled with a Spanish companion on a mule back to Torquemode. Oates did not hear mass there, but at the next town on their route, Burgos, both men did so. On 3 November they were at Bilboa and heard mass after breakfast. Oates' companion asked how he could do so, Oates replying 'That's no matter, I have several times said three or four masses after breakfast'. Oates was thus proclaiming his enthusiasm for Catholicism. After spending a few days in the city in the company of some Englishmen there, he took a ship, *The Bilboa Merchant*, whose master was Richard Thomas, and there sailed to Exeter. They were there on 26 November, and Oates took a coach to London.[67] In London he 'began to be very troublesome to his Romish acquaintances', whilst pretending zeal, and explaining the debacle at Valladolid 'only because he did not understand the Humour of the Spaniards'.[68]

Meeting members of London's Catholic community, he then received a second chance, 'hoping he should give them better satisfaction in a seminary of all English'. He left London for Dover on 10 December.[69] Apparently Father Richard Strange was persuaded to send Oates to the college.[70]

Oates then went to St. Omers College, which was in northern France and about 24 miles from Calais, so convenient for the English Catholic youths who were the constituency aimed at. It had been established in 1593. Apparently he said 'I shall either be a Jesuit or a Judas…If I do not become a Jesuit I will be damned'.[71]

Much of what is known of Oates' career at St. Omers is from his fellows there who recounted it at his trial for perjury in 1685, thus seven years after his stay there. It should also be recalled that the majority of those giving this evidence were themselves English Catholics and, given Oates' public career of anti-Catholicism in 1678-1681, they would be hardly sympathetic towards him, so how much this coloured their predominantly negative evidence is a matter of opinion. Oates arrived at St. Omers in December 1677.[72] At the college he went by the name of Sampson Lucy. He certainly stood out as a memorable character and one who was far older, aged nearly 30, than the teenage boys who made up the pupils there. It was known to some that he had been a minister of the Church of England. Apparently he did not think he would gain entry for his 'irregular and childish behaviour'.[73]

His early biographer gives a predictably downbeat account of his time there:

> 'he had not been long there, but he began to be so remarkable as he had been at Valladolid. The Boyes for his folly and stupidness flocking about him as small birds do about an owl, so that he was judged by all very unfit to go on to higher studies, not being able to speak two words of true Latin…besides he was very proud and disobedient, slighting the discipline of the House and perpetually murmuring and speaking ill of the Royal Family'.[74]

Another biographer claimed that his fellows called him Sampson because he was always 'being a very notorious profound blockhead'. Furthermore, he was 'very mutinous, troublesome and indeed inconsiderable'.[75]

As a student he was in the syntax class and in the rhetoric class. Mr Thornton, a fellow of his 'gives no great commendation of your scholarship'.[76] Elliott wrote that at the college he was 'an indocile Blockhead, that could never be brought to turn three lines of English into tolerable Latin'.[77]

Each Sunday or holy day from March 1678 he would be the reader of a book or piece of divinity.[78] On 5 May he 'preach[ed] a pleasant sermon…he said in it that the late King Charles the second halted betwixt two opinions, and a stream of Popery went between his legs'.[79]

Oates was a very memorable individual for other reasons. Statements made later by his fellow students were uncomplimentary. One Mr Price said 'he was so noted a man' and another that he was 'very remarkable both for Age, and that he had a particular table to eat at'.[80] Several of his fellows remarked upon his individual arrangement at dinner and supper and one Mr Conway gave the fullest description thus:

> He sate at a little Table in the Hall by himself, for he pretended, being a man in years, he could not Diet as the rest of the young students, did, and he obtained leave to sit above it at a little table by himself, and he sate next to the table of the Fathers, to which all the students were to make their reverence before they sate down.[81]

He was not much liked, with Price remembering 'he was very absurd, and always quarrelling with the students there'. As Doddingstone recalled, 'In general his conversation and canting stories after Dinner and Supper, and times of recreation, made him so remarkable that no one could miss him', adding, 'He was so remarkable by his stories and ridiculous Actions and falling out with every one of his college'. Lord Gerrard recalled similarly, 'he had a particular cant in his Tone which all men may know'.[82] He was annoying for other reasons, as Mr A. Turberville recounted, 'his conversation being so remarkable for a great many ridiculous actions, and a great many petty jests, that he us'd, so that he was like a silly person, as I may call him, that us'd to make sport and nobody could be missed'.[83] Mr Beeston was insulted by Oates after he had been congratulated on his singing and Oates said 'if I had paid for learning to sing, I had been badly cheated'.[84]

Things could turn physical. Turberville remembered 'I saw a little boy in Colledge beat him up and down with a Foxes Taile'. Quite possibly Oates provoked such. Turberville recalled that 'I see him very much abusive to persons that liv'd with him in the Colledge'. He added 'I was a person then the youngest in the whole Colledge, and Mr Oates being very abusive to me, I did what became me to right my self up on him'.[85] Mr Conway and others at one time broke a pan about his head.[86]

Yet he was not entirely obnoxious. Mr Smith (not his former schoolmaster) was in the infirmary from 21 April to 1 May and recalled that Oates visited him either every day or every other day. From 26 April Oates himself was ill.[87]

There is a possibility that Oates acted improperly towards one of the other pupils. In 1679 Thomas Billing recalled, that on 2 May 1678, 'I saw Mr Blunt walking in the garden, and Mr Oates with him; and observing him to be very intimately familiar with him'. Oates was then almost 30 and his fellow pupils were schoolboys. What exactly was going on is unknown but there is at least the possibility that Oates was indulging in an illicit same sex attraction.[88]

On a different instance, on 29 April 1678, an Englishman came to the college from Spain, begging alms. Mr Clavering organised a collection for him from among the scholars. He was asked if there was one amongst them who had been to Spain and when Oates was identified as being such, Oates refused to see the man. Apparently, Oates, recalled being conned out of money at Valladolid.[89] It has been stated that this man was, once again, William Bedloe, who came seeking alms and whilst Oates went to find him some food, he robbed his would-be benefactor.[90] It has also been suggested that he and Bedloe began to discuss their anti-Catholic schemes at this time.[91] We shall hear of Bedloe again. There has also been the suggestion that the two already knew each other before this French meeting, having met in London due to a common acquaintance, Sir Richard Barker.[92]

In January, Oates stayed away from the college for at least one night in Watton.[93] On 26 May, St. Augustine's day, Oates was confirmed as a Catholic.[94] He was still there in June 1678 at least by midsummer or St. John the Baptist's eve (23 June).[95] His absence was noted, as Doddingstone noted, 'We miss'd him in his place then, and 'twas discoursed of all over the town'.[96]

Although none of these students mention the story concerning his dismissal, and it is not known why this was, an early biographer spends a little time on the subject. On the night before he was turned out of the college, Oates was in the private oratory, set aside for private prayer and featuring an altar and a crucifix. A superior entered and:

> Sampson [Oates] was got upon the altar, and his hand upon the hand of the crucifix, he asked him what he was doing, he replied he was taking leave of Jesus Christ at his dismission he said to several of the students, he would be revenged upon the Jesuits to the full, for denying him entrance into their order, and for turning him out of the Colledge.[97]

Returning to London again, in June 1678, Oates once more spent time with those Catholics that he was acquainted with. Apparently he was 'very troublesome, being perpetually begging something for a poor student and a converted minister, who had voluntarily left a good Benefice to embrace the Catholic faith, which moved the charity of several'. Oates showed his vengeful side as well, telling some of the Jesuits 'that if they would not by such a time furnish him with such a sum of money they should all repent it'. They saw him as a 'mere vagabond and scoundrel and so paid no heed to him.[98] Oates later said 'I have not had two-pence in my pocket, and sometimes I have not had 6 pence'.[99] Apparently one way of earning money was to accompany fiddlers into 'places of publick resort' and after they had finished playing, for him to ridicule preaching by his 'presbyterian cant'. His vicious streak came when after befriending a young gentleman, he went into the country to the house of the young man's beloved. He wormed his way into becoming friendly with the family and they invited him to dine with them. Ingratiating himself with the householder, he told him that the young man was wholly unsuitable as a match for his daughter. The romance was thus over. Oates gained nothing from this but the knowledge he had created misery.[100] Possibly he wanted to break up the romance because he had eyes for the young man; if so it does not seem to have come to anything. Oates was now near rock bottom, living in a room in a house owned by a Mr Lowd, in Cockpit Alley, Drury Lane, near to the Red Lion.[101]

Oates, now wearing secular clothing, sought out his former associates, Smith and Medbourne, for further help. Apparently the latter weas 'instrumental in obtaining him some assistance for his relief from persons of quality of the Romish religion'. Oates was in extremis, 'complaining of his extreme necessity, he told them, he had not eaten a bit of bread in three days'. Medbourne and one Thomas Hughes fed him in an inn in the Haymarket and gave him some money.[102]

There is another reference to his poverty, written five years later. He was being charged eight or nine shillings for his board and lodgings, presumably on a weekly basis. He had to borrow 20s from one Mr Wilson, a neighbour. Apparently, 'He shew'd her [the landlady] 3s more and Bemoan'd himself that that was his whole Estate, clutching his Fist and swearing, without Book, that he would not be kept at that Rate'.[103]

Oates' politics came to the fore in a conversation in the Catherine Wheel pub in Islington. He argued with his benefactor, Medbourne, claiming that the monarch was answerable to others in the body politic. Medbourne and Smith opposed such radical views, arguing as he was speaking against the King's prerogative. By September, Oates' finances were improving as he was able to offer Smith between 30 and 40 shillings, perhaps in repayment of a loan or gift, but Smith refused.[104]

Oates also returned to seek out his old acquaintance, Dr Tonge and the differing experiences of both, combined with their prejudices, encouraged them to become inventive. Tonge thought that this was in late July 1678. Oates was probably also spurred on by monetary motives as he had needed an income, as well as a hatred of

Catholics. One author has suggested that Oates 'furnished with materials picked up at St. Omers'.[105]

Oates' first modern biographer has alleged that his inspiration for the plot came from reports of a French convert to Protestantism, one Luzancy. Apparently in 1675, after having worked in various menial roles in the Catholic Church, he renounced his faith and spoke in public against it. This was briefly financially remunerative, but then donations dried up. He then told a story about having seen Father St. Germain, the English Queen's confessor, as wielding a dagger and threatening him with death unless he returned to the Catholic fold. MPs and lords took it seriously as it ran well with their anti-Catholic agenda and so the priest was ordered to be arrested as well as other priests and Luzancy was recommended to be rewarded. However, on examination by the Privy Council, the young man talked at length of planned Catholic massacres of Protestants in London but also that the King was a Catholic sympathiser. The latter went down less well and lacking any details the former was not believed.[106] It is not known if Oates knew of this, or if he did, he made use of it as an inspiration, and certainly no contemporary links it to him. Other suggestions have been made that he took his inspiration from, and revamped and embellished earlier stories of the Habernfield Plot and the Prynne interpretation of the Civil War and transposed these to the present.[107] It was unoriginal and much conspiracy material both past and present was being recycled.[108]

L'Estrange, one of Oates' doughtiest foes, played down Oates' role in the creation of the 'plot':

> Now upon the whole Matter, Oates neither saw with his own eyes; nor heard with his own Ears; He stirr'd neither Head nor Foot; his tongue hardly wagg'd in his Mouth but by Tonge's Direction. His way was still chalk'd out before him; and all that he had to do, was to swear to Tonge's words and matter.

To put it succinctly, 'It was Tonge's invention' and 'the founder of the imposture was the chief manager too'. 'The invention, the contrivance and the conduct was altogether Tonge's'. L'Estrange wrote:

> He began with Habernfield's plot; he fancy'd Another of the same under the colour of that plot's going on still. He took a copy of it in his Royal Martyr, for a precedent; he shew'd it to Iates to consider of it…He design'd a plot.

Oates 'only drew the bellows' because 'Oates wanted bread'. Tonge told him 'Do but discover the plot says Tonge, and y'are a made man forever'. Oates joining the Catholic church and going to Spain and France was all apparently managed by Tonge.[109] Oates added to what Tonge had already written, based on 'the observacions he had made in his travels amongst the Jesuits'. However, it was Oates who wrote up the initial version of 43 articles. He read it to Tonge but kept the writings himself.[110]

Tonge had been writing anti-Catholic tracts for a long time, so it is not surprising that he should have written much of the plot. In Oates he had found his man, for Tonge's attempts at winning a receptive audience had been of little success to date. The two needed one another and as shall be seen their output was to prove deadly. Unlike Tonge, Oates had a smattering of knowledge of the Catholic Church and was acquainted with many Catholic priests and others, some of whom had helped him in the previous two years, though such help was now deemed by Oates as nothing, as we shall see. His knowledge helped to give a minimum of credibility to the fiction in giving names of real people. Another source of information, it was alleged, was from Thomas Lloyd, an employee of Lord Danby.[111]

It was later wondered about the true originator of the 'plot'. North wrote 'that Dr Tonge was Oates' pilot is certain', but who was behind Oates? He pondered that it might be one (Thomas?) Smith, a barrister whom Oates later employed. Or could it be the Earl of Shaftesbury, Anthony Ashley Cooper (1619-1683), a leading opposition politician? North certainly thought so, 'it is more than probable, he was behind the Curtain, and in the Depths of the Contrivance'.[112] The evidence does not support North's allegations, however. Burnet related a conversation he had with the King on this subject:

> We agreed in one thing, that the greatest part of the evidence was a contrivance. But he suspected, some had set on Oates and instructed him. And he named the Earl of Shaftesbury. I was of another mind. I thought the many gross things in his narrative shewed, there was no abler head than Oates, or Tonge, in the framing of it. And Oates in his first story had covered the Duke and the ministers so much that from thence it seemed clear that lord Shaftesbury had no hand in it, who hated them much more than he did Popery.[113]

However, as we shall see in due course, it was Oates who has been seen as the sole progenitor of the plot, as Tonge and Kirkby were to slowly fade out from both public gaze and historical record.

At this time Oates was living partly with Christopher Kirkby at William Lambert's in Vauxhall and also at Barker's house in the Barbican. In the first or second week of August Oates told Tonge that the account of the plot must be delivered to the King. On 11 August the papers were hidden under the wainscot of Barker's gallery, near Tonge's door, on the latter's suggestion. The doctor then copied them out.[114]

Chapter Three

Oates' Revelations, 1678

Oates did not appear in public about the 'plot' as it initially began to be disseminated. At noon on Monday 12 August 1678 it was Tonge who told Christopher Kirkby about the Catholic plot and showed him the 43 paragraphs that he and Oates had written about it. They agreed that the King must be told, but no one else was to hear about it. Kirkby went to the Palace of Whitehall that afternoon to try and find the King, whom he had an acquaintanceship with through their mutual interest in scientific dabbling. He was unable to locate him so returned to Tonge and they resolved he should try again on the next day.[1]

That day Kirkby planned to meet the King on his regular morning walk in St. James' Park, and to give him a note requesting fifteen minutes of his time to discuss a matter of great importance. It was well known that the King liked to walk in the park, which was just to the west of the palace of Whitehall. Kirkby met the King in the palace's outer gallery. Kirkby told him that his information concerned an assassination attempt on the King's life. Despite this, the King went for his walk and on his return met Kirkby again and they talked in the royal bedchamber. He told him Tonge's tale, namely, 'He had a great plot to discover, which concerned His Ma[ty's] life, the Protestant Religion, and present Government, but desired to come privately in the night, for should he be knowne, the Papists, he say'd, who were the contrivers of it, would knock him in the head'. Charles was given a bundle of papers which he passed to his Lord Treasurer to peruse.[2] In detail, Kirkby explained that the King was to be shot and failing that, poisoned. They met again that evening; this time Tonge went along too. They gave the King a copy of the papers listing the 43 articles. Oates retained a copy himself, but his identity was not disclosed.[3]

On the next day Charles showed his lack of deep concern about what he had been told, and went to Windsor, as planned, but had told Tonge and Kirkby that Sir Thomas Osborne (1632-1712), Earl of Danby, Lord Treasurer since 1673 and who headed the government, would investigate the allegations. Because the latter's son was very ill, Danby did not see the two until late afternoon of the 14th. They discussed the contents of the papers. Danby told Tonge that he needed more evidence than mere words, 'desiring to see some other proof by letters or papers from the conspirators themselves wch might convince the truth of the information…with what was fetched from one Mr Oats'.[4] Tonge claimed that the papers concerning the plot had been delivered to his house by an unknown person and that he had copied them, for safety.[5]

Tonge gave him additional information two or three days later and on 20 August announced that the two would be assassins could be arrested in the park as they lay in wait for Charles. There was discussion about the interception of the post to one John Grove, one of the alleged assassins.[6] Oates later claimed that on 22 August he met Tonge at the King's Head on Grey's Lane.[7]

Oates' rise to fame initially began on 2 September 1678 when he visited Kirkby at his lodgings in Vauxhall and the latter gave him money and a new suit and gown, for the two men were now allies, presumably at Tonge's behest. In the next few days, Kirkby went to Windsor to speak to the King and Danby, without much success, returning on 9 September when the three conspirators met at The Flying Horse on King Street, Westminster. Thereafter, Oates stayed with Kirkby in Vauxhall, allegedly for his own safety, travelling there by separate boats. Oates wrote copies of the allegations, adding to them, whilst Tonge sought out Danby, now at his Wimbledon home.[8]

The proofs that Danby sought were soon provided by Tonge. On 3 September he located letters with the Windsor postmaster from Thomas Bedingfield, the Duke of York's confessor, which when opened, were found to contain 'observing some mischievous expressions'. These were given to Sir Joseph Williamson (1633-1701), Secretary of State for the North, and then were examined by a committee of lords. They noted spelling errors therein and thought that the writings were genuine. Dr Tonge referred to certain individuals such as Thomas Whitebread and thought they ought to be seized. However, he admitted the limits of his knowledge, 'of his own knowledge he knew little or nothing, he had his information from one Mr Oats and was thereupon willing to become instrumentall in writing down the things in some order'.[9]

On 6 September Oates and Tonge, being taken by Kirkby, met Sir Edmund Berry Godfrey (1621-1678), a renowned and veteran Middlesex magistrate. Godfrey, according to Burnet, 'was esteemed the best justice of the peace in England'. He was a successful businessman, a zealous magistrate, and an Anglican. He had been conscientious in his work during the plague and fire in London in 1665-1666 and was knighted for his services. He was a believer in religious toleration and so did not press the laws against either Dissenters nor Catholics.[10] Oates swore to the truth of a Catholic conspiracy. He told the magistrate about 'the fire at Southwark & that Grove was one of the incendiaries'.[11] Several months later, Oates stated in public, 'I did go before Sir E.W. Godfrey and there upon oath, gave several depositions and after that I had made oath of those depositions we took the record along with us home again'.[12] However, there is another account which states that Tonge and Oates would have made a deposition on oath but that Godfrey refused to take it without knowing the contents of their papers. The two men left the papers with Godfrey on the following day. Tonge wanted a copy of them 'in case Oates should either fall back from his information, or be intercepted by any of the parties'.[13] North thought that Oates going to Godfrey with this news was unnecessary and superfluous.[14]

Matters came to a head on 27 September when Thomas Lloyd, a servant of Danby's who ran messages for his master, visited Tonge, Kirkby and Oates and said that they were needed to come before the Privy Council. They came with him but found that the council, business for the day over, had dispersed. Attendance at 10 am on 28 September was then required.[15] Also on that day, 'after we [Oates and Tonge] had taken two or three copies of this record we went before Sir E. Godfrey again and swore all the copies we had taken and so made them records'.[16] Later Oates allegedly told a confidante about Godfrey, 'He was a cowardly Rascal, for when I went with my deposition to him, he was so frightened, that I believe he beshit himself: for there was such a stink, I could hardly stay in the Room'.[17]

On the same day, Oates, Tonge and Kirkby were examined before the Privy Council. The council met in the palace of Whitehall. There is no verbatim record of what Oates said, and this was not recorded until he went before the House of Lords several weeks later. What follows next is the record from the contemporary Privy Council registers.

This was an 'extraordinary meeting' of the Privy Council. With the King were the political elite, including his eldest illegitimate son, James Scott, the Duke of Monmouth (1649-1685), his elderly cousin, Prince Rupert, the Lord Treasurer, the Archbishop of Canterbury and others. He told them that the meeting would concern 'a conspiracy of the Jesuits against the life of His Majesty'. A summary of what had gone on before was given. Dr Tonge was given encouragement and was offered lodgings to ensure his safety. More was needed of him, and 'he was directed to find out Mr Oates with all the speed he could'.[18]

That afternoon the Privy Council reconvened, but without the King, perhaps indicating his lack of interest in the matter as a serious topic. After the letters from Bedingfield were read out, the star performer made his debut entrance as was recorded, 'Dr Tonge attended with Mr Oates'. The account then read:

> Mr Oates was called in and being examined what he could say, he desired that he might speak upon oath and was sworne accordingly, and thereupon he did in a very particular manner, as to persons, places, and times, set forth his knowledge of the matters concerned in the papers already read at the Board.[19]

Sir Joseph Williamson made notes of the meeting. Oates said that Catholic priests and lords, with help from abroad, were to bring about a rebellion in Scotland, by nonconformists, and in Ireland. Weapons were to be bought for a rising there by 25,000 men. The Lord Lieutenant, James Butler (1610-1688), the Duke of Ormonde, was to be murdered and the Roman Catholic Archbishop of Armagh, Oliver Plunket (1625-1681), was a leading force in the campaign. Charles II was to be murdered in St. James' Park by being stabbed. Earlier attempts to shoot him, with silver bullets, had failed because the pistol's flint was faulty. After all these failures another method was to be tried. Francois la Chaise (1624-1709), Louis XIV's confessor, was to provide money to pay £15,000 to Sir George Wakeman, the Queen's physician, to poison Charles. Agents were to be spread throughout England to incite people to anger against the King. Oates named many Catholics who were involved in the plot.[20]

When Oates was shown the letters from Bedingfield 'he did particularly affirm the writing to be one of Nicholas Blundel, another of John Fenwick's, another of Dr [William] Fogarty's...another the writing of Thomas White and another the writing of William Ireland'. Sometimes he only read a few lines of each letter before he could make a correct identification of the author and 'This added to the particularity of his narration'.[21]

The council wanted to know how Oates came to such knowledge: 'Mr Oates having been required at his first coming to the council to set forth the matter of his information, the contrivers that were engaged therein, the reason of his knowledge'. He was more than ready to launch into such. Oates also provided a brief and selective account of his career which stressed his respectability. He was a minister of the Church of England and had 'had a small parsonage near Sittingborne and had been a chaplain at sea and in the Dutch Fights and lastly with Sir Richard Rooth after wch being in some leisure'. The reader will recall that England's involvement in the Dutch War ended in the year prior to Oates' brief time in the Royal Navy and that the previous war was from 1665-1667 when Oates was still in formal education. He then entered the Catholic Church, 'hearing much talk of the Jesuits policy and contrivances, he was willing at any rate to dive in to their secrets'.[22]

Oates said he met one Basil Langworth, confessor to Lord Petre and this was 'upon very easy terms'. He had been accepted into the Catholic church on Ash Wednesday, 1677. He was then asked to go to Valladolid to accompany the corpse of Lord Cottingham to England. He was deemed trustworthy to be charged with responsible missions at home and abroad, often taking secret letters, because 'they regarded him as one entrusted by the fathers in England, so had an unsuspected trust and confidence reposed in him'. And he 'showed himself such a master of the secrets he brought'. He opened letters 'having made himself master of all the secrets and contents thereof closed the wafer again'. In conclusion, he did all these 'That so he might be instrumentall in revealing the same as he had accordingly done, adventuring in the design, thereof both soul and body to serve His Majestie'.[23]

Having named names, the Privy Council, with the King in attendance again, ordered, on 29 September, that 'the messengers should go with a strong guard and Mr Oates to conduct them to find out the parties mentioned'. Those to be first arrested were Conniers, John Grove, Thomas Pickering, John Fenwick, William Ireland and Dr Fogarty. All but the first were rounded up and sent to Newgate prison. Conniers managed to escape.[24]

That afternoon, there was another meeting and Oates expounded at length, repeating much of what he had already said, but:

> in a very particular manner, but speaking of a great sum of money furnished at Madrid and paid before Don John of Austria. His Majesty asked him what kind of a man Don John was to wch he answered a tall man as he took it. But being told that Don John was a very short man, he replyed that it was one they called Don John and could say no more than as he was told.

Don John of Austria (1629–1679) was the foremost illegitimate son of Philip IV of Spain and had a distinguished military record and was head of state on 1677-1679; Charles had met him in Brussels in 1656 and so knew what he looked like; there is no evidence that Oates had ever seen the man.

On the next day, 30 September, Oates provided more information. He told that Wakeman had received a down payment of £5000. He told of a meeting of Jesuits in April. He said that several Irishmen had been paid to create the fires at Southwark in 1676. Oates knew all about this because he had heard the conspirators talking and had seen some of the letters written.[25]

Oates then stated that there were 500 English Jesuits who were abroad and 300 in England and that he knew about 200 of the latter. One Mr Wood arrived; he was a cutler and Oates had previously claimed that he had trouble recognising him as he was wearing different clothes to those he wore previously. Wood denied making the dagger that Oates alleged he had and furthermore, said he was a Protestant. Oates then said that one Kealy's servant would know about the dagger that had been made to kill the King. Finally, Oates told that Edward Coleman, secretary to the wife of James, Duke of York, had been in correspondence with La Chaise 'and that if his papers were well looked into there would appear that wch might cost him his neck'.[26] This was to prove the most critical accusation that Oates made as we shall soon see. The information about Coleman's correspondence had been provided by Danby.[27]

That afternoon, the council was reconvened. Oates repeated evidence against John Smith. Oates said that Smith brought treasonable papers to the home of a Mr Sanders; these gave the time and place for the King's death, following the consultation at Ireland's rooms in May. Oates 'knoweth the contents of the same', so he said. Oates had attended the consultation and Smith told him the contents of the letters that he was the deliverer of. Oates had also been at Connier's rooms and brought him information to Fenwick, who then sent it to St. Omers, where all such information was translated into French to be read by La Chaise. Oates said that Smith was a lay brother, but he replied that he was married with children.[28]

Smith left and Oates began to make allegations against Ireland, for conspiring to kill the King. Ireland had attended a meeting of Catholics at the White Horse tavern on the Strand in May 1678 and at later meetings discussed the shooting of Charles II. It was recorded 'The Deponent's case of knowledge is that he was one of the persons employed to go from company to company with the result of their consultations'. Ireland said that he had only seen Oates once or twice before. Oates said Ireland had sent a letter to Bedingfield at Windsor, written on 1 August and from Flamstead. Ireland said that Flamstead usually meant St. Omers and flatly denied writing the letter. It was not in his handwriting and to show this, he wrote a few words and these looked different from those in the letter.[29]

Oates then reasserted that the letter was in Ireland's hand and explained why:

> that Ireland can write a secretary hand with a great Deale of art, and as to the ill spelling of names of such like defects, that is industriously practised by all, to vary their hands and to write so, as they may discount their letters if need be, as also to antedate and post date their letters for the same end.

Ireland stated that he was not at St. Omers but at St. Alban's where Sir John Warner could vouch for him, but undeterred, Oates persisted with saying that Ireland was the treasurer of the Jesuits and had written to Rome about money.[30]

Sir Robert Southwell, diplomat and state official, noted that Oates 'went on for two or three hours very doubtfull as to his credit…his prodigious memory, confidence and unexpected answers at several times, were in great paine and surprise'. He deemed Oates' papers were 'such palpable matters of forgery…the handwriting of all appearing to be counterfeit…he at a glance could name all the hands, and adding that it was practised by them all to write counterfeit hands, which they might disown, if their treasons were discovered. This very thing took like fire soe that what he said afterwards had credit'.[31] Sir Thomas Bramston (1611–1700) wrote 'The narrative of Oates amazed every man' and 'putt the kingdome into great heates and jealousies'.[32]

Having arrested a number of suspects, under Oates' direction, these men were brought before the council for Oates to then cross examine. This took place on 30 September, the morning after their arrest. Fenwick was accused by Oates as being the leading Jesuit, the Procurator himself. He said that he attended the meeting at the White Horse tavern on the Strand in May 1678, gave his vote for the assassination of the King and in July he was visited by Richard Ashby from St. Omers with instructions for that murder and using the code number '48'. In June Fenwick had arrived from France to Dover with treasonable letters and a box of Catholic regalia, which had all been seized at Customs. In August, Fenwick had told Oates that he had received letters from the Catholic Archbishop of Dublin, Peter Talbot, about four assassins who were to kill the Duke of Ormonde or that Dr Fogarty would poison him.[33]

Fenwick replied that he had seen Oates only twice previously, though he knew both Grove and Ireland. He had not received the letters that Oates said he had, he did not know the code number 48 and had never heard of the meeting at the White Horse. He admitted to carrying a box of regalia but not the treasonable letters. He had met Ashby before the man travelled to Bath but no more. He had sent students to St. Omers but the only letters from them that he had handled were those of the students writing home. He denied any knowledge of the alleged Irish rising.[34]

Dr William Fogarty was next and Oates said that he had said 'if he had the interest in this court, wch so Sir George Wakeman hath, he would have undertook the poysoning of the King'. Apparently he hired four 'Irish Ruffians' to kill the King at Windsor. They had been employed on 21 August and were paid £80. Furthermore, the doctor had been seen at the Benedictine chapel at the Savoy reading the letter from Talbot already referred to in Fenwick's case. He added that he had much interest at the Irish court and so did not doubt that Ormonde would be poisoned. Oates added that Dr Fogarty was harbouring a banished Irishman and paying him 9s 6d per week for food. He was also writing under a pseudonym Crimson Blush, had a close correspondence with Talbot and had paid 'three Irish Ruffians' to burn Southwark two years ago.[35]

The rebuttal was similar to Fenwick's. Dr Fogarty knew Oates and once had provided him with medicine at the behest of some Jesuits. He knew Conniers and Talbot and had indeed corresponded with the latter. Yet he knew none of the other alleged conspirators. He denied using the pseudonym Crimson Blush. He had let the Irishman, Ward, stay at his house but was not paying him food expenses. Lieutenant William Stevens of Killigrew's Foot said that the doctor had cursed the King's troops, 'Will these times never end?' but the doctor said he liked the current times well enough and did not desire a change.[36]

Thomas Jenninson, a priest, was another man accused by Oates and apparently he had said that the King would not have a long life. He had attended the White Horse consultation where the King's death had been discussed and in August had met John Keyne and offered him money to deliver a letter not for Protestant eyes. Jenninson stated that he did not know Oates, did not know the significance of 48, had not been at the White Horse meeting, though he did know Grove, Pickering and Ireland. There was then a heated exchange between the two antagonists. As to Jenninson:

> 'he exclaims against Oates with passion, crying out what is this fellow that brings in question the lives of so many men, if it be Oates, he is a lying Rogue and a renegade and was chaplain to one Oaky, one of the murtherers of the late Majesty'.

'Mr Oates replied that he was now but thirty years of age, that he never saw Oaky but once when he was hanged, wch is about seventeen years ago and if then he had been his chaplain, he had been a very young one'.

John Okey (1606–1662) was a religious radical and Parliamentarian who signed the death warrant for the execution of Charles I in 1649. Despite fleeing to the Dutch Republic on the restoration of the monarchy in 1660, he was brought back. He was tried and hanged, drawn and quartered in April 1662 on Tower Hill. Okey's religious denomination was that of Oates' father and if Jennison knew this he may have been happy to link the two to Oates' discredit.

Jennison uttered 'other passionate words of warning', one to the Lord Chancellor to take care how he proceeded as all must be accounted for on Judgement Day.[37]

Sir George Wakeman was brought before the council, but there was then no charge put to him as there was no proof. This was said to be an 'unhappy circumstance' and 'twas wished there might be no fire where there appeared smoke'.[38]

However, Oates said otherwise. A letter from White to Fenwick, received in the previous month, and seen by Oates, proved that Wakeman had promised to poison the King for £15,000. Coleman had already paid Wakeman £5,000 of this sum. Initially Ashby had proposed £10,000 but the sum had been increased.[39]

Wakeman protested that both his ancestors and he had shown their loyalty to the Stuart monarchy by past actions. Of himself, 'he was the King's servant, and eat his Bread and there appeared so little probability that he would be a man guilty of any such matter and he hoped he would have reparation for the injury'. He admitted to knowing both Ireland and Fenwick.[40]

Coleman, who had already been identified by Oates as one of the Catholic conspirators, was next. He was asked if he had been to France recently, had he seen the French King's confessor and did he have a pass to go to France. He said he had been to France but had not a pass and had not seen the confessor, though once he had done so by chance. Oates said Coleman had written a treasonable letter to La Chaise, in December to thank the Jesuits there for £10,000 to be used to facilitate the King's death. There was also a note about the hoped for expiration of Protestantism in July. Coleman's role in paying Wakeman to poison the King was also referred to here.[41]

Coleman denied all this 'with the highest protestation'. All that Oates had said about Wakeman and the others was wrong. The notes record 'His Majesty seemed to be so far satisfied, with what Mr Coleman said, to dispense with that part of the warrant for his carrying to Newgate and that he should remain in the safe custody of the messenger'.[42]

Busby was next. Oates had accused him of, in 1677, transmitting £11,000 from Father Swanson of Madrid to Michael Hore, a merchant of Bilboa. Busby agreed that Hore was a correspondent of his, and that they were in business together but he had never received more than £3,000 in seven years.

The reader has already made the acquaintance of Oates and is fully appraised as to his mendacious character, as had his former naval shipmates, fellow scholars at various establishments in three countries and his former parishioners. However, the great bulk of the nation were unaware of him up to this point. We shall now note their first impressions of the man.

John Evelyn, a courtier, wrote, some years later:

> I went to see & converse with him, now being at White Hall, with Mr Oates, one that was lately an Apostate to the Church of Rome, & now return'd againe with this discovery: he seemed to be a bold man, & in my thoughts

> furiously indiscreete: but everybody believed what he said & it quite chang'd the genius & motions of the Parliament, growing now corrupt & intrested with long sitting, & Court practices; but with all this Poperie would not go downe: The discovery turn'd them all as one man against it, & nothing was don but in order to finding out the depth of this & Oates was encourag'd & everything he affirmed taken Gospel.[43]

He later added, 'I am little inclined to believe his testimonie; he being so slight a person, so passionate, ill bred, & [of] impudent behaviour, nor is it at all likely, such piercing politicians as the jesuits should trust him with so high, & so dangerous secrets'.[44]

Burnet wrote that 'He was proud and ill natured, haughty but ignorant...He conversed much with Socinians and had been complained of for some very indecent expressions concerning the mysteries of the Christian religion'. It was known that he was a perjurer and had been dismissed in disgrace from his office as a ship's chaplain.[45]

A Catholic memorialist wrote 'Oates, a poor and despicable Clergieman, either touched with scruples about Religion, or with designs of doing what he after put into execution'. His supposed motivations were elaborated thus, 'either out of revenge to the Jesuits who he thought had used him ill, or to gain a subsistence, being in the last degree of poverty and contempt'.[46]

Physically he was unprepossessing as Francis North (1637–1685), first Baron Guildford, noted. 'A low man, of an ill cut, very short neck; and his visage and features were most particular. His mouth was the centre of his face, and a compass there would sweep to his nose, forehead and chin within the perimeter. Cave quos ipso Deus natavit [watch out for those whom God has marked out]'.[47]

Another contemporary description was as follows:

> his brow was low, his eyes small and sunk deep in his head, his face was flat, compressed in the middle so as to look like a dish or discuss, on each side, were prominent ruddy cheeks, his nose was snub, his mouth in the very centre of his face, for his chin was almost equal in size to the rest of his face. His head scarcely portruded from his body and was bowed towards his chest. The rest of his figure was equally grotesque, more like a beast's than a human.[48]

Shortly after the Privy Council meeting, Oates later stated that he met Godfrey again. This was on 30 September. Oates alleged that he 'did tell me what affronts he had received from some great persons for being so zealous in this business. And he told me that others, who were well inclined to have the discovery made, did not think that he had been quick enough in the prosecution, but had been too remiss, and did threaten him, and would complain to the Parliament'. Oates claimed that in early October, Godfrey told him he had been threatened by Catholic lords, 'he was in a great fright and told me he went in fear of his life by the popish party and that he had been dogged several days'.[49] Godfrey was initially unconvinced by the story, with Dicconson writing 'of which he made no formal discovery, but on the contrary treated it as a suspicious story'.[50]

Oates then suggested that Godfrey take precautions against being followed, 'why did he not take his man with him, he said he was a poor weak fellow; I then asked him why did he not get a good brisk fellow to attend him? But he made no great matter of it he said, he did not fear them if they came fairly to work, but yet he was often threatened and came sometimes to me to give him encouragement and I did give him what encouragement I could that he would suffer in a just cause and the like, but he would often tell me he was in continual danger of being hurt by them'.[51]

The plot was generally believed. Arrests were being made of Catholics almost as soon as he began to make his revelations to the Privy Council. Those accused were being imprisoned, prior to potential trial. William Smith, Oates' former teacher, was another man arrested and he said that one Sarracoal and twenty others came to his rooms at 1am, broke his door, rifled his house, frightened a five year old to death [it is uncertain if this is meant to be taken literally] and took him to a crowded prison where he was almost smothered.[52]

Richard Baxter (1615–1691), a leading nonconformist, wrote, 'The parliament took the alarm upon it; and Oates was now believed; and indeed all his large confessions, in every part, agreed to admiration'.[53] Sir John Reresby (1635-1689), baronet and MP for Aldborough, noted, 'It is not possible to imagin what a ferment the artifice of some, and the reall beliefe and ſear of others, concerning this plot, putt the two Houses of Parliament and the greatest part of the nation, into'.[54] Burnet wrote, 'The whole town was all over inflamed with this discovery. It consisted of so many particulars, that it was thought to be above invention'.[55] L'Estrange wrote, 'At the first opening of the Plot, almost all Peoples hearts took fire at it, and Nothing was heard but the Bellowing of Execrations and Revenge, against the Accursed Bloudy Papists'.[56] Sir Thomas Ailesbury (1656-1741), a strong admirer of the King, wrote 'The credulous all over the kingdoms were terrified and frightened'. He wrote that ladies carried small guns in their muffs, and others were convinced that their throats would be cut by Catholics.[57]

Others were less certain. Sir John Biggs, writing to Major John Braman on 8 October, noted:

> Some say Titus Oates and Dr Tonge are not at in all circumstances very good witnesses, but then, methinks, their discovery would not have produced such a general affect as the disarming a party in a nation. I am much amazed... The discovery of a popish plot makes me exceedingly desirous to know the nature and extent of it...Some people are of opinion it is all sham, others cannot see what can be attain'd by such a false alarm...As far as I can see it must do good.[58]

Others were less certain. It was reported that after Oates had given his testimony:

> that he had lain under several discouragements as for instance (the Earl of Danby) Mr Oates being in ye privy Garden, the said Earl passing by said there goeth one of the Saviours of England that I hope to see him hanged within a month, he accused Sir John Robinson to have had knowledge of the plot or part of it four or five years, by one Everard Sackville said sons of whores who said there was a plot & that he was a lying Rogue.[59]

Sir Henry Goring (1622–1702), MP, told Oates that 'he was a rascal and a lying Rogue' when Oates called the recently bailed Sir John Gage 'a traytor'.[60]

Whether this is with the benefit of hindsight or not, L'Estrange wrote in 1686, 'I contracted a horror for this villainous chief of a Plot from the very spawning of it'.[61]

Sir Henry Coventry (1619–1686), Secretary of State for the South, wrote on 1 October:

> if he is a liar, he is the greatest and adroitest I ever saw, and yet it is a stupendous thing to think what vast concerns are like to depend upon the evidence of one young man who hath twice changed his religion – if he be now a Protestant.

He was still uncertain, writing three weeks later:

> The discovery made by Mr Oates is of that nature that it is equally difficult to believe it and not believe it...The accuser is so positive in his charge, so exact in all circumstances, so agreeing with himself in the whole, and each particular, and swear it with just assurance, that it seems impossible to be fiction.[62]

Oates was seen as being 'a former country curate, but for the preservation of the King and Country did among the rest counterfeit a villain, that he might detect them'.[63] His past was largely unknown and he was seen as trustworthy. Yet one of those arrested and placed in the Marshalsea Prison, one Netterville, 'said Oates was a villain. That he was always wanting money from the superior when he was a Jesuit'; Netterville had refused him.[64]

In 1687 L'Estrange wrote that 'From one end to the other of this history, of the Protestant Popish Conspiracy, the weight of the proof still rests upon Oates' Probity and Reputation: and the whole Frame has nothing to support it, than Flourish and Noise. The proof and Character of a Licentious and Habitual Dissolution of Manner, through the Entire course of Oates' conversation'.[65] There was more to it than this, however.

We now need to step back a little because it is important to understand why Oates' fantastic allegations should have been believed by many. It is therefore necessary to discuss the mindset of the Protestant majority in late seventeenth England, especially as regards to the Catholic minority. Without this context Oates' revelations will seem unquestionably and blatantly preposterous and this was not so then. In 1990 the author's supervisor set his class an essay asking why the Popish plot should ever have been believed and more recently a grammar school history master stated that his students found it difficult to comprehend the same, so removed is anti-Catholicism to the bulk of today's population. It is not enough to assert, as some authors have, that 'a wave of irrational credulity warped the nation's judgement'.[66]

England in 1678 was particularly receptive to tales about Catholic conspiracies. This was in part because of the country's longstanding anti-Catholicism which lost nothing in the retelling. There was the burning of Protestant 'heretics' during the reign of the last Catholic monarch; Mary, in 1553–1558. There was the attempted murder of James I and VI (Charles II's grandfather) and his Parliament in 1605 by Guido Fawkes and others. In the lifetime of many there had been the civil wars, when King Charles I's wife was Catholic and there had been massacres of Irish Protestants by Catholics in 1641 (this was real but numbers were highly exaggerated by propagandists). More recently there had been the Great Fire of London of 1666 which was allegedly begun by Catholics (this was without foundation in fact). Finally, since the beginning of the decade, it was known that the heir to the throne, given that Charles II's (Catholic) Queen was childless, was his openly Catholic brother, James, Duke of York (1633-1701). He had married Mary of Modena in 1673 and so the prospect of Catholic heirs was ever present, if a son were born. This second marriage of the Duke of York was objected to, with Evelyn recording 'This night the youths of the City burnt the Pope in effigie after they had made procession with it in greate triumph; displeased at the Duke for altering his Religion, & now marrying an Italian Lady'.[67] As Baxter wrote 'Londoners had before a special hatred against the duke, since the burning of London, commonly saying that divers were taken casting fireball and brought to his guards of soldiers to be secured and he let them go'.[68]

At the onset of the third Dutch War in 1672, Charles II granted toleration to all Catholics and Protestant nonconformists. In 1673 Baxter recorded that Parliament was concerned about 'the dangers of Popery and popish counsellors' and that a day of humiliation be held because of the growth of Popery' and wanted 'the powder plot' to be solemnly remembered. Dr Edward Stillingfleet (1635-1699), dean of St. Paul's and a royal chaplain, who wrote on this topic, was asked to preach on it. This led to an end to the previous year's toleration and to the passing of the Test Act, obliging all office holders to make an oath denying the tenets of Catholicism, which flushed out the Earl of Clifford, a leading politician, and the Duke of York, who resigned their commissions. Preachers 'greatly animated them and all the nation against popery'.[69]

It could be said that Catholics only formed about one per cent of mainland Britain's population, but the faith was proportionately stronger in some parts of the country, such as London and Lancashire (which had large numbers of Catholic gentry and their relations and dependants), and more numerous among the gentry, nobility and at court, and therefore some Catholics were socially prominent. Despite being a minority of the population, their potential for insurrection was viewed as being disproportionate, allied with Catholic powers just overseas. Some believed that their numbers were far in excess of what they were in reality. Looking across the Channel it was easy to point to the absolutist Catholic regimes of Spain and more so, France, with its increasingly beleaguered Protestant minority. France was the most powerful and successfully aggressive of the Continental powers as well as being nearest to Britain, with a formidable army and had been at war with the Protestant Dutch in 1667–1668 and 1672–1678.

Nor was Charles II seen in the same light as he had been at the restoration of 1660. His popularity at that time was now no more. Instead he was suspected of being sympathetic to Catholicism, with a Catholic wife, who had established a Catholic conclave at Somerset House, and having made a declaration of indulgence in 1672, granting a degree of tolerance to those not professing the Anglican faith. According to Evelyn, 'Papists & Swarmes of Sectaries now boldly showing themselves in their publique meetings' and later that year he wrote of 'such liberty had the Roman Catholics at this time obtained'.[70] Furthermore, in 1672, England had allied with France against the Protestant Dutch Republic, for two years of warfare and the court and ministers had been in receipt of French money. An army had been raised to take part in the war. As Baxter stated, 'The Parliament grew into great jealousies because of the prevalency of Popery...They said that so many of the commanders were Papists as made men fear the design was more. Men feared not to talk openly that the Papists, having no hope of getting the Parliament to set up their religion, by law, did design to take down Parliaments and reduce the government to the French model, and religion to their state, by a standing army'.[71] Evelyn wrote that their purpose was 'to invade Holland, or as others suspected, for another reason'.[72] Despite the war's end in 1678 the army had yet to be disbanded, due to a lack of money to pay arrears of wages. Standing armies in peacetime were viewed as the potential tools of tyranny and the military rule of the Commonwealth was only too near a remembrance.

Therefore there was a ready and willing audience for anyone who could provide evidence, however tenuous, that a Catholic conspiracy was afoot. A recent publication, now known as the work of Andrew Marvell (1621–1678), MP, poet and satirist, was published in 1677, titled *The Growth of Popery and Arbitrary Power*. It highlighted both the doctrinal follies of the Catholic Church and the political dangers that it posed in aiding the imposition of tyranny as seen in France and Spain, in contrast to the Parliamentary monarchy of Britain in which royal power was limited and every man had liberty. The pamphlet began:

> There has now for diverse Years, a design been carried on, to change the lawful Government of England into an absolute Tyranny, and to convert the

> established Protestant Religion into down-right Popery, than both which, nothing can be more destructive or contrary to the Interest and Happiness, to the Constitution and Being of the King and Kingdom.[73]

It has often been written that in 1678–1679 the bulk of England's population was 'credulous' in believing the outrageous stories invented by Oates. This is a harsh judgement by those who have the wisdom of hindsight denied to contemporaries. The context provided above gives evidence for a willingness to believe in a plot. The reader might also wish to note that many people in their own age are often all too ready to believe the worst of a minority of the population to which they do not belong; one of a different nationality, religious belief, social class, political creed, occupation or skin colour. All that is needed is for a small minority of that group to misbehave, whether orally or physically or even stories being spread about them, and a belief may well arise among others that the bulk of that group is involved in a major threat to the country. Conspiracy theories provide simple explanations to those who want to blame someone or some group for a particular problem and there are usually others who are quite happy to fan the flames of such views. Long before the phrase 'fake news' was employed, Sir George Clark observed, 'Once a false charge is made, uncritical people will always find circumstances which seem to point to its truth. They will do so the more readily if it is a charge against those whom they already hate and fear'.[74] Late seventeenth century England was not, therefore, uniquely credulous, but was suffering from a crisis of an unfortunate universal human condition.

A recent historian, Mackenzie, has a number of cogent remarks about this. She writes (in 2022) 'We can no longer consign conspiracy beliefs and the persecutions they give rise to a safely bygone age, one more barbaric, emotional and irrational than our own' and that such were a 'product of a divided society in which trust in authority was contested or had broken down, and in which rumours and speculation were often seen as more reliable than official information'. These theories were and are in order that some can understand, control and create a positive image of themselves and their group at the expense of a demonised other.[75]

The method of the revelations made by Oates was not then unusual either. It should also be noted that informers were commonly employed or used to unmask dangers to the state. In the absence of any state employed domestic espionage or detective forces, they were essential. Williamson was responsible for surveillance and as well as using the General Post Office to intercept and decode mail, informers were used, 'an army of mainly social misfits, criminals and turncoats who were prepared to risk their lives supplying information about the internal enemies of the state, in return for the grant of a royal pardon for past delinquencies or simple monetary gain'.[76] Oates thus fitted in very well to the genus of informer that the state's agents were accustomed to dealing with. Baxter referred in 1674 to being the victim of one such, denouncing him to the magistrates for his nonconformist preaching in

London. Once a magistrate was aware of an offence and offender, he could then put the law into action and deal with the accused.[77]

Furthermore, plots and rebellions were very much the stuff of fact in the Restoration era. Despite a wave of popular acclaim for the restored monarchy in 1660, there remained a hard core of Republican sympathisers who had supported the Cromwellian regime. Some former Parliamentary soldiers preferred their ideal of a Godly republic to the hedonism as espoused by the court of Charles II. Then there were the Protestant Dissenters; Presbyterians, Anabaptists and Quakers who suffered under the 'Clarendon Code' of 1662 and the Conventicle Act of 1664 which penalised any who failed to attend an Anglican church on Sundays or who attended a Dissenting conventicle. Furthermore, there were grumblings about the moral failings of the King and court and the competence of the royal government, as well as its intentions. In 1661 there had been the short lived Venner rising in London and then there was the Yorkshire plot of 1663 (one of its leaders being Captain Thomas Oates who was hanged – no known relative of Titus). In Scotland in 1667 and 1679 there were uprisings by the Covenanters, extreme Presbyterians, which had to be put down by the army and militia. Others were also investigated; many came to nothing. After all, Charles II's father had been overthrown and executed in the 1640s. Conspiracies were, then, to be taken seriously. It is worth noting that all these real risings were from Protestant nonconformists not Catholics.

There were additional reasons why Oates' story was believed. Credence was strengthened by two unforeseen events taking place rapidly after one another. Burnet wrote, 'A few days after this, an extraordinary thing happened that contributed more than any other thing to the establishing belief of all this evidence'.[78] Firstly, on Saturday 12 October, Sir Edmund Berry Godfrey disappeared, two weeks after Oates had made his second deposition to him and 13 days after Oates had spoken to the King and Privy Council. Rumours abounded that he had left London or was staying at a relative's house or was secretly courting a lady. Such speculation ended and more began when his dead body was found on Thursday, 17 October. It was on Primrose Hill near Hampstead. Although his sword was found run through his body, there was no blood. Instead there was a livid circle around his neck so strangulation seemed the likely cause of death. Suicide was deemed an unlikely possibility. Robbery was ruled out as a motive as his watch and money remained in his body. The King announced a £500 reward for the apprehension of his murderers.[79]

It might seem strange that Oates chose Godfrey to reveal details of the plot for he was no staunch persecutor of Catholics. Oates saw him on the day before he spoke to the Privy Council and made the discovery on oath to him. Burnet wrote, 'This seemed to be done in distrust of the Privy Council, as if they might stifle his evidence, which to prevent he put it in safe hands'.[80]

To some this was clear proof that Oates' story was correct; the magistrate had been killed by Catholic plotters who wanted all those with knowledge of their plot to be eliminated. Of course, such a supposition could not be proved, but it is the nature of conspiracy mongers to state that as it cannot be disproved it could (at least) be true. As Burnet wrote, 'All Oates' evidence was now so well believed that it was not safe for any man to seem to doubt of it'.[81] He added 'that the murder 'put the whole nation in a new fermentation against them', that it 'did so exasperate, not onely the Common; but all the nation' and 'men were now very angry with the papists, & violently transported, by reason of the late plot, & especially by the Murder of Sir E. Godfrey, which so exasperated'.[82] Clarke wrote, 'The credit of the plot, which had hithertoo but the support of one witness, and that a blasted one, too, seem'd very much to abate, people began to lay things togather and made use of their eyesight…but the death of Sir Edmond Bury Godfrey was so well menaged, as not only to revive, but highten the fury of it to a great degree…the people sufficiently disposed to charge the Papists with whatever was amiss fail'd not to credit the rumour industriously spread a broad'.[83] Oates, however, said to Smith, about the likelihood that the Catholics had killed Godfrey, 'I believe not a word on't, but my plot had come to nothing without it; it made well for me; I believe the council would never have taken any further notice of my else, if he had not been found'.[84] Ironically, James thought likewise, writing to his son in law, William of Orange 'This makes a great noise, and is laid upon the Catholicks also, but without any reason for it, for he was known to be far from being an enemy to them'.[85]

Then there was the case of Edward Coleman. Burnet wrote that Oates 'accused Coleman of a strict correspondence with P. de la Chaise (whose name he had not right, for he called him Father LaSheed and he said in general that Coleman was acquainted with all their designs)'. What was important was that when Coleman's rooms were searched, correspondence dating from 1674-1676 was found – though none for the last two years 'He left enough to give great jealousies'. Yet 'When Oates and he were confronted, Oates did not know him at first; but he named him when he began to speak'. [86] An examination of the surviving letters seemed to give additional proof, 'it got a great confirmation, since by these it appeared that so many years before, they thought the design for the converting of the nation was very near its being executed'.[87] In the papers there was a reference to Flamstead and Oates said that this was a codeword and so 'this too confirms Oates'. Lord Arundel's grandson at St. Omers also confirmed Oates' story.[88] Evelyn wrote, 'he gained Credit upon Coleman'.[89] Ailesbury concurred, later writing 'I own that Mr Coleman's papers were of a pernicious nature, and I do not wonder he underwent the hand of justice'.[90] These papers did not support the murder conspiracy allegations but did refer to the use of French money to bring about a Catholic restoration in England.

These letters were significant because the papers found in the rooms of other suspects were wholly unincriminating as Sir Robert Southwell wrote on 10 October, 'the truth is in all their papers, nothing as yet appears as evidence thereof'.[91]

On 20 October the judges gave their opinion on Oates' veracity. Could one man be convicted on the testimony of just Oates, and if not, what supporting evidence was needed:

> we are all of the opinion that the testimony of one witness alone, without further evidence, is not sufficient alone to indict or convict any person for encompassing the death of the King, but if one witness fully swear in the point with one or more other witnesses concurring in material circumstances to the same fact, it is sufficient to indict or convict for such treason.[92]

Charles II was noncommittal, stating on 21 October, 'I shall forebear my opinion, but I should say too much or too little, but I would leave the whole matter to the law'.[93] Privately he was sceptical about Oates, saying, 'Nay, he is a lying knave… Watch me catch him out in another lie'.[94] He told Paul Barillon (1630–1691), the French ambassador at great length and several times that he was convinced that Oates had been suborned to do what he had done in the hope of deriving some advantage to revenge himself on the Jesuits with whom he was displeased. He said likewise on a later occasion.[95] Unlike many Englishmen Charles was not anti-Catholic. Catholics had fought and died for his father and himself in the civil wars and had helped him escape after the battle of Worcester in 1651; he rather feared nonconformists.

On 23 October Oates was ordered to give his testimony before the bar at the House of Commons. He told of certain Benedictine monks who resided in the Savoy.[96] An account of what he told MPs ran as follows:

> He begins his account in King James' Reigne [James I and VI, 1603–1625], tells that he & his sonne prince Henry [died 1612] were very sent out of ye world before there time, by wt meanes & by whomee he gives an acct how they began ye villainy & wt the Jesuits were concerned in ye death of ye late King [Charles I] he tells them further how active they have been all along in introducing popery, how they fired the city in 66, what persons manadged every street, what ingredients there fireworks were made of, where they were usually & in greater quantity made of ye fire of St. Katherine, Southwark & yt more recently neare Limehouse & several other places in ye Country…this conspiracy hath been hatching ever since King James' time, only ye measures & ye instruments have been altered according to ye several ages.

The alleged plot was being managed by the rector of St. Omers and behind him was the Pope. The French had landed troops in Ireland and these were to be increased to 25,000 men, to be joined by Catholic Irishmen in order to massacre the Protestants and to burn Dublin. Apparently 'this parte of ye conspiracy was managed by

Coleman. There was also a plan to burn London, 'to 'begin a fire without Temple Bar, wch was to be carried on to Charing Cross'. The Duke of York was apparently to be offered the Crown once Charles was killed and if he refused he would die. Meanwhile, in Holland, Jesuits there were in conspiracy against the Protestant ruler, William of Orange.[97]

He gave evidence the next day with the result that the Middlesex JPs were to issue warrants to arrest the Catholics named by Oates. He attended the Commons on the next day to give more information and again on 28 October.[98]

The evidence on the 24th concerned a meeting at the White Horse Tavern on the Strand in May 1678, before then going to various other places to plot to kill the King. Pickering and Grove were named as the assassins and Jesuit priests organising it were Bedingfield and Symons.[99]

On 28 October he told the Commons that the Duchess Mazarin (a French mistress of Charles II), 'was a spy here on pretence of being in a difference with her husband for France, and for this assertion, gives this reason, that all agents here, resort unto her, and Mr Coleman can, if he will, say as much as I have done'.[100]

Official measures were taken against the Catholics and this can only have served to give credibility to Oates' allegations. On 30 October all Catholics were ordered to leave London, to reside no nearer than 10 miles from the capital, and on 20 November there was a reward of £20 per Catholic priest or Jesuit apprehended. Orders were given for the arrest of six named Catholics all deemed to have been involved in the plot. On 30 November it was ordered that no Catholic could sit in Parliament. In Dublin Archbishop Peter Talbot was arrested.[101]

On 31 October, Oates gave his story before the House of Lords; all 81 statements, based on letters, which dates Oates could recall exactly and some were in Latin that he had read, from the alleged Catholic conspirators he claimed he had seen or conversations he said he had overheard or had partaken of with them. Many of those named were men who he had met in recent years. A number of themes emerged. Chief among them was were the assassination of Charles II and possibly that of his brother; referred to in 30 of these statements. Then there was the work of gathering Catholic support in England for an armed rebellion, but more so, also in Scotland among the Presbyterians opposed to the restoration settlement, and in Catholic Ireland, using money from France (these are both mentioned in eight of these statements). There was talk about stirring up dissension between England and Austria and between William of Orange and his people in Holland. Finally, there was some alleged personal experiences of Oates in recent days. Lists of Catholics involved in the conspiracy were also given. They were not given thematically but in the chronological order which Oates claimed he learnt them. Much that was said had already been related. This is very much an abbreviated version of what Oates related.

1. Letter by Richard Strange, John Keines, Basil Longworth, John Fenwick and Mr Harcourt, Jesuits, concerning a Jesuit plot to contrive a Presbyterian rebellion in Scotland against episcopal rule and referring to Charles II as being too pleasure loving to care for Scotland. Matthew Wright, William Morgan and John Ireland were to go there to preach sedition.
2. Oates told how he was paid £10 to carry the above letter to Father Suiman to Spain; he opened it and read the contents.
3. St. Omers College to send 12 students to Spain to study. There is a sermon where the Oath of Allegiance to Charles II is denounced as 'Heretical and Anti-Christian and Devillish'. His illegitimacy proclaimed; 'his father was a black Scotchman, not Charles I'.
4. Letters refer to the deposition of Charles II and that of James if he does not carry out their plans.
5. Father Suiman writes 'that the King of England was poisoned, to the Great Joy of the English Fathers'. His brother will be killed if he does not root out Protestantism in England and return the county to Rome.
6. Letter concerning the murder of Charles II. Richard Strange, John Keines and Father Gray 'to procure some persons to despatch the King'.
7. Letter from English Jesuits lamenting that 'their man William, being faint hearted, could not then do it, though he had one thousand five hundred pounds promised' to kill Charles II.
8. Letter from the Provincial of Spain to Strange and Keines 'that if the Business of despatching the King of England could be effected, they should have ten thousand pounds for their pains'.
9. Letter from the English plotters that 'they had an Intent to procure on to stab him [Charles II] in his Court at WhiteHall and if that could not so conveniently done, they would employ one of his physicians to poison him, and for the Work they had Ten thousand pounds'. Father La Chaise is to procure the money for this.
10. Letter thanking La Chaise for his help in propagating Catholicism and in trying to destroy those who oppose it.
11. Letter stating that there could be 20,000 men to rebel in Scotland and if France breaks with England and lands troops in Ireland, there would be 40,000 arms given to the rebels there.
12. Thomas Whitebread is the new Provincial in England. He and Coniers to preach at St. Omers against the oaths of Allegiance and Supremacy.
13. Jesuit fathers meet to contrive 'a happy Disposal of His Majesty the King' and likewise his brother if he disappoints them.
14. Richard Blundell to visit condemned prisoners in Newgate to convert them to Catholicism and to teach youths in the City of London likewise.
15. Advises the Spanish King to seize English property in Spain.

16. Edward Nevill and Thomas Femour claim 'they would not let this Black Bastard [Charles II; his Commonwealth foes in the 1650s referred to him as 'a black man'] go to his Grave in peace' as he has cheated them often; they will kill James if he is unsupportive of Catholicism.
17. Letters to the Habsburg Emperor about Charles II aiding the Hungarian Protestant rebels and that Charles is supporting William of Orange's ambitions.
18. Letter concerning Archbishop Talbot of Dublin's support for an Irish rebellion in the event of a war between England and France.
19. Account of 'one Pickering, a lay Brother, that waits upon the Jesuits lying at Somerset House, to shoot the King as he was walking in St. James' Park, when he was at some distance from his Nobles and Attendants, but the flint of his pistil being something loose, he did defer his action till another opportunity'.[102] He was promised 30,000 masses if he succeeded, but was caned 30 times for his failure.[103]
20. Confessor tells Oates that Charles I was not a martyr but a heretic and an illegitimate son of Queen Anne and a tailor.
21. William Morgan has been sent to Ireland with £2,000 to raise 4,000 armed men.
22. Fathers journey to Berkshire, Oxfordshire and Essex to persuade Catholics there to pay for a rebellion in Ireland and letters from Scotland that concern a rebellion there.
23. Letters concerning the deaths of Charles II and his brother.
24. Letters concerning that though James is a good Catholic he has a tenderness for his brother and therefore will not be part of a plot to kill him and so he must not be told about this.
25. Letters stating that the Catholic lay clergy are not supportive of a plot to kill Charles II at Whitehall.
26. 'That there was an Attempt to make an assassination on the person of his sacred Majesty in the Month of March, several days, as he was walking in the Park, and once as he was going to the parliament House, by this honest William and Pickering, but opportunity did not offer itself'. Pickering was caned 20 times for failure.
27. Letter concerning an imminent Irish rebellion of 20,000 infantry and 5,000 cavalry who will cut Protestant throats and if the French arrive there will be an additional rebellion in the north.
28. Letter concerning the meeting at the White Horse Tavern on the Strand in May 1678 in which there is discussion to kill Charles II, 'five or six in a company did contrive the death of the King'.
29. Whitebread tells Richard Ashby, in Oates's company 'That he hoped to see the Fool at Whitehall laid fast enough' and likewise James if he is not supportive.
30. Letter concerning the killing of Dr John Stillingfield because of his writing an anti-Jesuit pamphlet.

31. Richard Ashby wrote of the Earl of Clarendon's deathbed conversion to Catholicism, made to Father Warren.
32. Oates is to go to London to meet the Fathers there with further orders for them. He travels with John Fenwick who takes Catholic artefacts with him.
33. Ashby to go to London with £10,000, 'to treat and agree with Sir George Wakeman, about the poisoning of the King, and that if he would undertake it, he should have the Ten thousand Pounds'. The bishop of Hereford is also to be killed.
34. Richard Strange tells Ashby that the Catholics paid £14,000 to have London set on fire in 1666; an attempt in February 1665 failed.
35. Further messengers are to be sent to Scotland to provoke rebellion there.
36. Ashby is asked to canvas Catholic support in Somersetshire when he goes to Bath for his health.
37. Whitebread tells John Fenwick 'if Ten Thousand Pounds would not do, he would give Fifteen Thousand Pounds should be proposed to Sir George Wakeman, if he should refuse Ten Thousand Pounds'.
38. Whitebread tells Fenwick to send 12 Jesuits to Holland to stir up the people there against William of Orange.
39. Letter concerning Whitebread's annoyance of not having news of the progress of the assassination attempts on Charles II.
40. Whitebread writes to Fenwick, 'If poison would not take the King away, Fire should'.
41. Fenwick tells Oates that the Jesuits have £60,000 in annual rents and £100,000 saved.
42. Oates is told of a planned rebellion in England and Wales.
43. Two preachers to be sent to Scotland in the guise of nonconformist ministers to stir up rebellion.
44. Information about Charles II's secrets are being sent to La Chaise by one Smith from Coleman.
45. Jesuits to learn the value of landed estates and so learnt the strength of the nation.
46. Letter from Whitebread, 'did rejoice very much that Sir George Wakeman had taken the Business into his Hand; and if he did it Fifteen Thousand Pounds would be paid, but ordered Pickering and his companion honest Will should not desist in their Endeavouring to assassinate the King's person'.
47. William Berry, a secular priest, to be killed for advocating Catholics comply with Protestant laws.
48. Richard Heath and Fenwick discuss with Oates 'some Discourse of the Design of killing the King…that the Bastard should not trouble the world long'.
49. John Grove told Oates about how Irishmen were paid £1,000 to begin a fire in Southwark in 1676.
50. Letters concerning the work in Ireland of Jesuits to depose Ormonde.

51. Oates hears about the progress of the planning of the insurrection in Scotland and Ireland and of the attempts to separate William of Orange and his subjects.
52. Keines is to go to Windsor 'in order to settle the Business there in and towards the dispatching of' Charles II.
53. Jenninson declares that the Catholics could kill 100,000 Protestants in London. Payments are given for court intelligence to be sent to La Chaise.
54. A group of men in Islington, including William Smith and Matthew Medbourne, are being paid by the Jesuits to stir up the people against the House of Commons and the bishops.
55. Jenninson says he shall continue his work of making men disaffected to Charles II and if he does not become Catholic will not reign much longer.
56. Letters to say that 12 Jesuits have gone to Holland to stir up the people there.
57. 'Honest William' is to attend the court at Windsor.
58. John Keines preaches to 12 men that it is lawful to depose heretical monarchs as it would have been to oppose Cromwell.
59. Keines and Fenwick tell a gentleman in Westminster to leave London or be destroyed with the other sinners there.
60. Keines tells Oates about 'it was endeavoured to despatch the King at Windsor' and suggests Oates 'would undertake to assist in despatching the King he should be well rewarded, if not here in Heaven' and 'That he could not do such a thing for all the World'. On the King's death, 20,000 Catholics will rise and take over; if James resists he will die.
61. Keines asks the Dominicans to help financially in killing Charles II but their poverty does not allow them to do so.
62. Oates hears that 'Honest William' is unwell so cannot go to Windsor to kill Charles II.
63. At a Jesuit meeting in London, news comes from Archbishop Talbot about the plan to kill Ormonde and raise a rebellion in Ireland.
64. Fogarty is willing to kill Ormonde if Talbot allows him to do so and that Fogarty 'That himself and Coleman were in Council when Wakeman was contacted withal to poison the King' He added 'That he had hired four Irish Ruffians, whose names he did not tell…and these Irish Ruffians were to mind the King's postures at Windsor'.
65. Sir William Godolphin, Ambassador in Spain, is in correspondence with Suiman and is supportive of the plans.
66. Money is sent to 'supply the Expenses of the Four Irish ruffians…who were gotten to Windsor …and the sum so sent was Eighty Pounds'.
67. Letter from La Chaise to ask for a progress report; 80 letters sent to Jesuits in England.
68. Coniers tells Oates that he plans to kill Charles II, 'he did Laugh at the Means the Fathers intended to use, videlict [namely] by shooting him. Then the said

Coniers…shewed him a Dagger or Knife, Two edged, with a very sharp point, and it was broader and broader towards the haft, which was of Bucks-horn, being a foot long in the blade, and nearly half a foot in the haft. With this, said he, the villain will fall to the ground'. He would buy it for 10s at the old cutler's shop in Russell Street. He would stab the King through his coat and then would be pardoned if he were not knocked on the head.[104]

69. Blundell tells Oates that he has a bag of fire balls with which to burn Westminster.
70. Blundell told Oates that the Catholics will try and bring about Charles II's death.
71. Blundell shows Oates a rolled paper plan as to how Westminster is to be burnt down.
72. Oates said that the Pope has issued a Bull allotting senior positions in a new Catholic Church of England to various individuals; Whitebread is to be bishop of Winchester and Napper bishop of Norwich.
73. In a letter to John Grove there is reference to 8,000 Catholics in Scotland joining with other Scottish rebels.
74. Oates sees letters written by Whitebread to give £1,000 from France to the 12 Jesuits who are in Scotland creating dissension there; and that a French army might invade Scotland.
75. Letter to Blundell from St. Omers to reveal that the plot has been discovered, but that it should not be desisted with.
76. Oates is ordered to wait on Whitebread who is now in London.
77. Whitebread accused Oates of treachery and assaults him, but he tells Oates that he can be forgiven if he can divulge the name of the clergyman who has informed on them.
78. Pickering says that Coniers has gone to Windsor.
79. Oates hears Whitebread and others are discussing kidnapping him and torturing him as a traitor.
80. At Oates' lodgings he met one Grigson who warned him to move lodgings because he was to be killed there by one Stratford.
81. On 8 September Nevill tells Oates when he is on his way to church on Sunday morning that there is a Catholic plot to kill him. Oates tells of how Catholics have been allocated to various posts in Church and in a rebellious Catholic army. Richard Langhorn was to be Attorney General, John Lambert the Adjutant General and Lord Stafford was to be given high rank. Lists of conspirators are then given; 43 Jesuits (15 are not of England); 23 monastic priests (four outside England); seven were secular priests, there were three English Jesuits in Scotland, twelve unknown Jesuits in Scotland, four secular persons, including Wakeman, Coleman and Fogarty, six assassins; the four unnamed Irish ruffians, Pickering and Smith, Archbishops Talbot and Lyne, Jerome Suiman and Sir William Godolphin.[105]

He swore on oath the veracity of what he had said:

> 'That the information set down in these papers, containing 81 articles, written and subscribed by his own hand, are true in the whole and every particular thereof, that is
>
> 'I say, that such particulars as he has set down, to be seen, heard, done or known by him, he knows to be true, and what he has set down only to be heard by him, were so heard and related.[106]

It was noted that he only accused 'priests and inferior persons'. This was largely so as to not startle the court and so make prosecutions of these people more likely to occur, against people 'for whom no man would have regrett'; in particular James was exonerated.[107] Yet Oates had been caught out by the King in another error by being not able to correctly tell where the Jesuit college in Paris was, yet this did not seriously dent the story.[108]

One point should be made about the above claims that Oates had made. It crucially does not state who would be King following the murder of Charles II. There are several references to his brother James being slain if he did not go along with the plotters' aims. Next in succession after James was William of Orange and Mary, eldest daughter of James, both stridently Protestant. It does not, therefore, make sense as a Catholic plot. Possibly the son of the radical Samuel was implicitly seeing this as a republican plot to replace the monarchy with a republic. The inclusion of the imprisoned Parliamentary general Lambert as being in the plot also suggests a similarly radical overtone, as did the puritanical critique of the pleasure loving 'Merry Monarch'. It could also be argued that a Catholic plot against Charles II did not make sense because he was tolerant towards Catholics; with the 1672 Act of Indulgence, the fact that no Catholics, despite the draconian laws against them, had been executed in his reign (so far) and that the anti-Catholic legislation had largely been in abeyance in this period. Yet for most such analysis was unexplored territory.

After Oates had given his lengthy statement, he desired that he should be guarded because it was dark and he might be in further danger. The Lord Chancellor announced, 'That the House takes very well what he hath done, and to the end, he may be freed from those persons who may come to discourse with him, purposefully to undermine, so as to invalidate his testimony in this business, he is not to discourse…with any person on this matter…the Duke of Monmouth to take care of the safety of his person…'

He was also to be provided with better accommodation by the Lord Chamberlain and a set income by the Lord Treasurer.[109]

There was no evidence for any of the above allegations, yet as it was a sworn statement it was taken as being true. However, for reasons noted earlier on it was in no way laughed out of court or even seriously doubted. Parliament soundly backed Oates' testimony:

> 'Resolved Nemine Contradictine "That upon the Evidence that has already appear'd to this House, this House is of opinion, that there is, and hath been a Damnable, and Hellish Plot, contriv'd and carry'd on by Popish Recusants, for assassinating and murthering the King, for subverting the Government, and Routing out, and Destroying the Protestant Religion"'.[110]

and therefore:

> Ailesbury blamed Danby 'by his wrong advice, the pretended plot was laid before Parliament...I cannot but say that he made a very false step'. This was because Parliament was 'consisting of so vast a number of inexperienced persons, whereas a thing of that high nature should rather have been committed to a competent number of both houses'.[111]

Once Oates was given living quarters in Whitehall, he asked to see Dr Gilbert Burnet, an Anglican clergyman. The latter recorded, 'Oates came in and made me a compliment, that I was one that was marked out to be killed'. Burnet asked why Oates had so much animosity towards Catholics and:

> He broke out into a great fury, against the Jesuits, and said he would have their blood...He upon that stood up, and laid his hands on his breast, and said, God and his holy angels knew that he had never changed, but that he had gone among them on purpose to betray them. This gave me such a character of him, that I could have no regard to anything that he either said or swore after that.[112]

A recent historian has said of the palace that was to be Oates' home for the next two and a half years:

> 'Whitehall was not just a royal residence and seat of the executive; it was like a vast overpopulated and slightly shabby hotel with some 1,500 rooms, occupied by officials and household servants'.

The King and Queen each had a suite of rooms there, as did his brother James and his wife, Prince Rupert, as well as senior ministers and a whole host of others. Government business was conducted there and the Privy Council met there. It had recently been renovated by Christopher Wren.[113]

On 1 November, Oates was again called to the bar of the House of Lords and asked about five men who were in custody. Oates looked at one, Mark Preston, and said 'He was a Romish Priest'. On being asked how he knew this, he replied, 'He had been at confession with the said Marke, at Wylde House, and that he had confessed to the said Marke Preston, as a priest'. On being told that Preston had been married for 11 years, had children and was certainly not a priest, Oates said 'He knew him not, but had heard by a gentleman (Kirkby) of the Guards, that Preston had spoken very unseemly words against the King's Person. The next prisoner was Dennis Glisson, of whom Oates said, 'That he heard, by Dr Tonge, the said Glisson, being a school-master, did instill ill principles into children, and he said that there is no learning in Cambridge, and nothing but debauchery in Oxford'. Glisson explained that he was a Protestant and had the bishop of London's licence as a schoolmaster.[114] Mr Moore was then charged by Oates as being a seller of Catholic literature, 'That he had five hundred pounds of Popish books in Somerset House'. He added 'Moore sold to him one of Goodwin's books against Dr Stillingfleet, and told him, he had four hundred of them'. Matthew Turner was next and of him, Oates said, 'That upon a search for Popish books, he and his brother Mr Moore, had been too nimble for the Searchers'. Preston was sent to Newgate and the others were dismissed.[115]

Finally, Richard Langhorn, a Catholic lawyer, came in and denied he knew Oates. Oates said to the contrary, 'That he brought him letters in 1677, to his Father, from his sons in Spain, and this Richard Langhorn told him, when he knocked at the door with the said letters, that his father was at dinner and desired that he meet his father in his chamber that night'. He added 'that this Richard Langhorn received a commission from his father Mr Langhorn, in Oates' presence, to be carried to Lord Arundel of wardour, that the said Richard longhorn did put into his pocket, but whether he delivered it or not, Oates does not know'. Langhorn junior was sent to Newgate, to join his father who was already there.[116]

Oates did not always identify those who appeared as suspects as participants in the plot. On 7 November 1678 John Blundell appeared and Oates was asked if he was a relative of the Blundell he had mentioned in his account. He said no, he did not know him, and the man mentioned was Nicholas Blundell, not John. He was discharged.[117] Ormonde wrote, following the arrest of Richard Butler, that 'if Mr Oates had been well informed, he would have rather named my cousin Ned'.[118] Yet another man that Oates informed against was one Barton, a Lancashire Catholic. John Carroll was identified by Oates as yet another plotter and was sent to the Tower.[119]

Oates was deemed an important part of the plot, 'that inexhaustible fountain of invention' and 'the foundation of the whole Fabrick, is Otes' consult at the White Horse in the Strand...Oates' plot is the Ground-work of the whole'.[120]

However, Oates was not the only informant. A new figure who emerged at this time was William Bedloe, from Bristol, and whom Oates had met in Spain in the previous year. He had a poor reputation, being described by Burnet thus, 'He had led a very vicious life. He had gone by many false names, by which he had cheated many persons. He had gone over many parts of France and Spain as a man of quality, and he had made a shift to live on his wits, or rather by his cheats so a tenderness of conscience did not seem to be that to which he was very much subject'. He told magistrates in Bristol that he knew the secret of Godfrey's murder, having seen the body at Somerset House and having been offered £4,000 to help in disposing of it. Later he claimed he knew of a Catholic plot, albeit a different one to that as expounded by Oates. According to Bedloe, 40,000 men were to be shipped from Spain to England, although he knew not how.[121] Bedloe's importance is that he reinforced Oates's stories. As a contemporary biography of the former stated, his account 'not only confirm'd the Dr [Oates]'s Evidence, but made further Discoveries'.[122]

Bedloe was brought to London and gave his story to the House of Lords. Charles thought Bedloe had been given the information about the alleged plot as he only spoke about it after the Godfrey murder. Burnet reasoned, 'he now not only confirmed the main parts of Oates's discovery, but added a great deal to them… Here were now two witnesses to prove the plot, as far as swearing would prove it'.[123]

Oates' revelations had largely been believed, in part due to the findings among Coleman's papers and the strange death of Sir Edmund Berry Godfrey. It now remained to be seen what would happen to those unfortunate men arrested for their alleged part in the conspiracy and Oates' further involvement in it as he took centre stage in the ensuing tragedies.

Chapter Four

The First Trials, 1678

So far, despite Oates's talk, no one Catholic had been physically punished. This was to change. To conspire against the state was high treason and this was a capital offence. Two men were to be hanged this year for such. The first was William Staley, a Catholic goldsmith of London. He was tried at King's Bench on 20 November for entertaining the King's death. Apparently in an eating house six days previously he had been overheard by William Carstares saying 'The King of England was a tormentor...a great heretic, and the greatest rogue in the world...here is the hand that would kill him'. He was found guilty and hanged on 26 November. Oates was not directly involved in the trial nor had he named Staley in his earlier pronouncements, yet it is hard to think that Staley would have been tried and hanged without the atmosphere created by Oates' revelations and subsequent events.[1]

More importantly there was the trial of Edward Coleman, once secretary to the Duke and Duchess of York, which took place on 27 November at the King's Bench Court, a court reserved for cases of High Treason, not ordinary civil criminals. Judge Sir William Scroggs (1623-1683), who was Lord Chief Justice from 1678-1681, presided over the trial which lasted from nine in the morning to five in the afternoon. Coleman pleaded not guilty. Chief among the witnesses against him were Oates and Bedloe 'who spoke very fully'.[2]

It should be noted that at this time the odds were very much stacked against the defendant. He or she was allowed no defence counsel and the contest pitted the defendant against the court's witnesses and they could cross examine the witnesses. The judge was a government appointee and so was naturally on the side of the prosecution, though in theory was meant to be neutral. Trials were very short and rarely lasted more than a day, even in capital cases. Juries usually sided with the prosecution.

Burnet wrote that the two 'swore flatly against him'. Coleman denied that he had ever seen either of them. He asked Oates when it was in August of that year that he had seen him allegedly hiring assassins. Apparently 'Oates would fix on no day', though he was very punctual on matters of less moment'.[3]

Coleman was accused of rebellion and plotting to kill the King, and of conspiring to use French resources to do so. The first witness was Oates and Serjeant John Maynard (1604-1690), prosecuting, described him thus, 'Mr Oats was the first man, that we hear of, that discovered this treason, he was the single man that discovered so many agents…he being found to be that single'.[4] Sir William Jones, the Attorney General, later produced Oates and addressed him thus:

> Mr Oates, we leave it to yourself to take your own way, and your own method: only this we say, here's a Gentleman that stands at the bar for his life, And on the other side, the King is concerned for his life, you are to speak the truth and the whole truth, for there is no reason in the world that you should adde any one thing that is false…let him be condemned by truth, you have taken an oath and you being a minister know the great regard you ought to have for the sacredness of an oath.

Oates stated that last November, Coleman entertained one John Keines, a confessor, in his house. Oates was introduced to Coleman as a recent convert and was about to go to the seminary at St. Omers. Coleman then asked Oates to take some letters there for him. He did so and on reaching his destination, he opened them. 'In this letter of news there was expressions of the king, calling him Tyrant'. It was directed to the Rector of St Omers and was giving news of England.[5]

There was also a letter addressed to La Chaise, thanking him for the £10,000 sent to propagate Catholicism in England and 'to cut off the King of England'. This letter, unlike the first, was written in Latin (a language, it will be remembered, that Oates lacked even basic knowledge of). It was written by Coleman. Although Oates had not seen him write it, he recognised the handwriting as his.[6]

Oates was then asked by the judge about a meeting of Jesuits in April 1678 at the White Horse Tavern. This was where Pickering and Grove were spoken of about killing the King for 30,000 masses and £1,500 respectively. Coleman was then told about all this in Oates' hearing at Wild House, the Spanish Embassy. Coleman then wrote of this to Father La Chaise. Justice Sir William Wilde then asked for confirmation:

> 'You did positively say that Mr Coleman did consent and agree to what was consulted by the Jesuits, which was to kill the King, and Pickering and Grove were the two persons designed to do it. Did you hear him consent to it?'
>
> 'I heard him say at Weld House that it was well contrived'.[7]

Oates then talked about another meeting, in August, where Coleman was present and a rebellion in Ireland was being discussed 'and was mighty forward for Father Fogarthy sent to Ireland to despatch the Duke [of Ormonde] by poyson'. He also heard Coleman say, in Fenwick's rooms in Drury Lane, that he knew of a way to send £200,000 to Ireland to arm the Insurgents and to kill Ormonde. Four Irishmen were to be given £80 to commit the crime. Furthermore, Ashby, Rector of St. Omer's, had met Coleman in London and had instructions, in case Pickering and Grove should not succeed in killing the King, that Sir George Wakeman should do so instead, for a rather higher fee. There were also letters sent to potential donors, the principal Catholic gentry of England, of the necessary money for such.[8]

Oates talked of other matters not directly concerned with Coleman, but he accused others of being involved in the plot. Eventually Coleman was allowed to speak in bis own defence and he addressed Oates:

> 'this man who now gives in evidence against me there told the King he never saw me before, and he is extreamly acquainted with me now, and hath a world of intimacy…I never saw Mr Oates since I was born'.

Oates replied, 'he saieth I said there that I never saw him before in my life. I then said I would not swear that I had not seen him before in my life, because my sight was bad by candle-light, and candle light alters the sight very much, but when I heard him speak I could have sworn it was he…I cannot see a great way by candle light'.

He was then asked why he did not emphasise Coleman's role more highly when speaking to the privy council and Oates replied:

> 'I was so weak, being up two nights, and having being taken Prisoners, upon my salvation, I could scarce stand upon my legs'.[9]

He was asked a similar question and replied similarly, adding, 'the Council apprehending me to be so weak, that one of the Lords of the Council said that if there were any occasion to further examine Mr Coleman, that Mr Oates should be ready again, and bid me retire'. He was asked why he had not talked more about Coleman, and answered, 'Because I had spent a great deal of time accusing other Jesuits'. There was another question about Oates identifying Coleman, to which Oates answered, 'I spoke little of the persons until we came face to face'. But Oates had provided a detailed description of Wakeman, said the Lord Chief Justice; so why could Oates not provide one of Coleman?

'For want of memory; being disturbed and wearied sitting up two nights, I could not give that good account of Coleman, which I did afterwards, when I consulted my Papers, and when I saw Mr Coleman secured, I had no need to give a further account'.

Coleman had additional questions about how Oates did not recognise him after claiming to have been in his company on several occasions. Oates gave additional reasons why not:

> 'He was much altered by his periwig in several meetings, and had several periwigs, and a periwig doth disguise a man very much, but when I heard him speak, then I knew him to be Mr Coleman'.

This ended Oates' contribution. Further witnesses were called, including Bedloe and a boatman; Coleman's letters were read out in court. Oates was recalled to tell again of the meetings of Jesuits in April and in August; Coleman not being at the first but showed later that he knew of the resolutions there and approved of them. Coleman asked Oates when was the meeting in August and after prevaricating Oates said it was the 21st. At which Coleman claimed he was in Warwickshire on that date. Coleman again swore he had never seen Oates at the places where Oates claimed to have met him.

It was not only the witnesses' evidence that was used against Coleman. Some of the letters he had written in 1675 were also read out in court. These were then summarised for the benefit of the jury:

> The expiration of the Protestant religion, and introducing of Popery and the subverting of the government. And this appears by a letter written by Mr Coleman, dated 29 Septr. 1675, and sent to Mr La Chaise, the French King's confessor...he does also assert the true way to carry on the interest of France and the promoting of the Popish religion in England was to get this Parliament dissolved, which he says has long been since affected if £300,000 could be obtained from the French King.

There were letters to other prominent Catholics on the Continent including phrases such as 'the converting of these three kingdoms and the utter subduing of a pestilential heresy'. These letters (admittedly not referring to a plan to murder the King) were undeniably written by Coleman and backed up by the evidence of Oates and Bedloe who swore to Coleman's part in the assassination plot seemed strong evidence indeed against Coleman. Yet the lack of reference in the letters to a murder plot was explained away that such evil conspiracy would not be committed to paper. The jury must find the defendant guilty or Oates and Bedloe must be stated as being perjurers.[10]

The jury found Coleman guilty and on 28 November he was sentenced to death. He protested about the validity of Oates' evidence, how it was so precise in some matters and so vague and inexact in others. This was unheeded. He maintained his innocence throughout. Coleman was the first man that Oates' perjured evidence helped to send to his death, but it would not to be the last in the year 1678. He was taken from Newgate by sledge, hanged, drawn and quartered at Tyburn on 3 December.

Oates made another and far more serious accusation. On 13 November he had told the King, Williamson and Coventry that the Queen had given sums totalling about £4,000 to English Catholics and that Father Richard Strange, a Jesuit priest, had acknowledged these. However, he did not say that this necessarily had any connection with the 'plot'. It was not until 24 November that he was more explicit about the Queen's rather more direct alleged involvement in it. Initially he was vague and could not recall the time that the meeting he claimed he saw occurred. When he was asked about why he had not mentioned this earlier, he claimed 'That he had nothing more to say against any great persons' and that 'If he had, must crave their lordships' pardon, for he did not understand the question'. Did he have any relevant papers, he was then asked, 'No, durst not trust this to paper'.[11]

Most dramatically and controversially, he took a further step when he stated 'I do accuse the Queen for conspiring the death of the King', he told the Commons on 28 November. He had apparently seen a letter written in May from Sir George Wakeman, the Queen's physician and a Catholic, to Ashby, a Jesuit in which he 'liked well the proposal of killing the King, if it could be, and the Queen had engaged him in that work'.[12] This was a big risk. Oates had been believed so far and now went a step further. The Queen was the leading Catholic in the country and he may have believed that the King's flagrant adulteries meant that he had no regard for his wife.

The King's Catholic wife was now named as a plotter. He explained to the House of Lords on 29 November what he witnessed:

> 'In July last he saw a letter from Wakeman, to Richard Ashby, alias Thrimbleby. In this letter he gave an account of the proposals made for destroying the King; and declared his liking thereof, provided his reward might be answerable; and told him; the Queen Consort did approve of them; which were, to poison the King'.

On being asked if he knew the doctor's handwriting, Oates replied:

> 'No, but Thrimbleby told me it was Sir George Wakeman's letter'.

He then proceeded with his tale:

> 'In the same July, a messenger came with a letter to William Harcourt, for him, and John Keynes, Basill Longworth and John Fenwick, to attend the Queen at Somerset House, which they accordingly did, taking him with them; Harcourt telling him he must go. When they were there, having passed by the presence, he was left in an Ante-Chamber, and they went into another Room. But the door not being quite shut, he heard a woman say "That she would no longer endure the Affronts but would revenge the violation of her Bed, and assist in propagating the Catholic Religion"'. He heard these words spoken; and when the Fathers came out, he, being desirous to see the Queen, was introduced, either by Longworth or Fenwick, and saw no woman there, but the Queen with these Fathers.'[13]

He added:

> 'That the Queen had given several sums of money to Colker, a Benedictine, under the notion of charity, which he believed was only to pervert the King's subjects in their Religion' and that £5,000 had been doled out, and that the Queen was in correspondence with the Pope and the Jesuits'.

Apparently Oates had seen Wakeman write a letter to Ashby 'advising him, for his Health, being troubled with the Gout, to take a pint of milk in the morning, and a pint at night and also an hundred strokes of the pump, every day when he continued at the Bath. That in the same Letter, Sir George Wakeman did declare, his liking of the good proposal about poisoning in the King providing good terms be had'.

Apparently this method of murder was chosen because the previous attempt had failed. This was when Pickering was to have shot the King with a gun loaded with silver bullets. So he was disciplined with a beating. This was to occur in April 1678. Oates was then asked why he had not told this before and he replied, 'he had much Distrust in himself, in his Judgement, in the discovering of it, and that once he intended to disclose it, upon Sir George Wakeman's business on this Board, but was willing His majesty should know it first in private…as to the question of being so long in silence, in a matter of Dangerous Consequence That he was willing to communicate anything about the Queen in a public court, but only to the King in private, to prevent the Danger, she being the wife of his Bosom. He cannot remember the precise day when these words were spoken, but that it was on a week-day, not a Sunday, and a day of some solemnity, just before High mass'. He added that the plot had been laid in 1670, or 1666 or 1660.[14]

As to the room in question, Oates said he was never there before nor since and thought he could find it again. He was then asked why he had not told of this before as he had said 'he had nothing more to say against any person of quality' and answered 'he had nothing more to say against any one of that House' and asked that he not be asked about it any more. He was then asked about what he had any more details about this aspect of the plot and he replied that he had not dared to put down anything else in writing. Oates was asked if he knew Bedloe before and he said not, though he had seen him, and said that Wakeman had not attended the Jesuit meeting on 24 April because he had been too unwell.[15]

On 24 November, Oates had accompanied Lord Thomas Butler, sixth Earl of Ossory (1634–1680), heir to the Duke of Ormonde, with Howard and other men in a search of Somerset House. He was shown the main door and was asked if he had been in that way before and said yes. He then took them to the guard room and said he had been there and then went to the Presence room and there he said 'he remembered the canopy'. On reaching the next room he was doubtful. So they retraced their steps to the guard room and then the presence chamber where Oates thought that there had been some stairs. These could not be found, so they opened other doors, went to the Queen's bedchamber and several small rooms. The Galley door was opened and Oates said 'he had never seen before and those little rooms were none of them the room he looked for'. They went to the stairs that went to the garden by the chapel but he insisted these were not those. Returning to the guard room he insisted he knew that room. As to the stairs, 'the stairs he sought for were a light pair of stairs and the rooms they went to had great folding doors and were large high rooms'.[16] Apparently, according to Dicconson, 'this inexhaustible fountain of impudence as well as invention, was not dejected, nor out of countenance at all these disappointments'.[17] Ossory later wrote 'We found him in a manifest lie'.[18]

Oates was questioned about his allegations. He first claimed that he did not remember the day on which he heard the Queen in conspiracy, but that it was a weekday before mass was heard, and that he thought he would remember the room if he was shown it again. As to why he had not told this story earlier, 'he had noe more [information] against any one of that house before whom he now was', adding that on the previous occasion in September, 'he was at that time faint and weake, and had been up two nights together'. This was the same excuse he had made in the trial of Coleman as to why he had not previously recognised the man he had claimed he had seen previously. He added that he did not feel he could have addressed a public body 'but onely the King in private to prevent the danger, she being the wife of his bosome'. On the next day he suddenly recalled that his overhearing the Queen was on St. James' day [25 July] or a day or two afterwards.[19]

In the Commons, Colonel Silius Titus (1623–1704), a courtier and MP, said that he did not believe the story because Oates had told it but because he thought it probable. Other reactions were far more sceptical, to put it mildly. Apparently Oates 'putteth His majesty into no little resentment, being entirely confident of the loyalty of the Queen'.[20] Sir Thomas Bruce, whilst stating that the King 'never believed a word of all their plot, but dissembled it...when that audacious villain, Oates should have brought the Queen into their plot, that roused the King out of the state of lethargy and he resented it highly with high expresses of tenderness and affection towards the Queen'.[21] The King told Dr Burnet, 'She was a weak woman, and had some disagreeable humours, but was not capable of a wicked thing'.[22] As her brother in law, James, told William of Orange, 'That great villain, Oates did Sunday last accuse the Queen of her having designed to poison His Majesty...and yesterday had the impudence to say the same to His Majesty in full council. Oates is so well secured that he cannot get away with it he would. The King was willing to give Oates line enough...and seemed to give way to it'. Oates claimed that the Queen summoned certain Jesuits to her apartments at Somerset House. He followed them and listened behind a door of a room which they had gathered. He claimed that he heard a woman's voice therein saying that she would help them in killing the King. Oates was then presented to the throng on entering the room and he later said that the only woman there was the Queen. However, Oates denied that he was explicitly accusing the Queen as being a party to plotting a murder, for he had not actually seen her. The implication, though, was obvious.[23]

Another contemporary opinion was, 'his reception was not so cheerful there as formerly it had been, and seeing that so many of the Lords were favourably disposed towards the Queen it is very possible that matter may sink and vanish'.[24]

John Evelyn, courtier and diarist, and no friend to Catholicism, found this suggestion shocking and wrote:

> '*Oates* on this grew so presumptous as to accuse the *Queene* for intending to Poyson the *King*, which certainly that pious and virtuous Lady abhorred the thought off, & *Oates*, his Circumstances, made it utterly unlikely in my opinion: Tis likely he thought to gratifie a more, who would have been glad his Majestie should have married amore fruitfull Lady: but the King was too kind a husband to let any of these make impression on him'.[25]

On 18 November, the Lords stated that Oates should be guarded by two men. On the next day he was told he could have £200 as reward for his information already rendered; though he had had £120 to date.[26] Meanwhile, Oates claimed that he was having problems of his own from Sunday 24 November. 'I have an unjust Restraint on me and my papers have been taken from me contrary to the known laws of the kingdom'. He thought the alleged protection of him was next to useless, and that if this was all that could be offered he could do better left to his own devices. 'If they intend by it the security of my person, I undervalue it. I can secure myself better in another place'. He claimed that his friends were denied access to him, his writings and his servants had been taken from him and he had been robbed of money. He even found Yeomen of the Guard smoking their pipes in his rooms. He feared he might be taken to Newgate.[27]

He later continued in this vein, claiming that initially he had been allocated three servants to see to his needs and to protect him. Apparently he was fearful for his life, as he said, 'I am in some danger of being poisoned as I was before in being stabbed'. He wanted his lawyer, his father and Tonge to be allowed to see him in his rooms. 'I will endeavour to save three kingdoms' he boasted.[28]

Meanwhile, some of those MPs assembled there flattered him. Sir Christopher Musgrave (1632–1704) an MP for Carlisle, said, 'We owe much to this man'. Sir Thomas Meres (1634–1715), an MP for Lincoln, was more fulsome: 'After King and Kingdom have so great a deliverance by Mr Oates discovery that he should be used like a rogue'. Sir Thomas Clarges (1618–1695), an MP for Southwark, said 'I would have £200,000 given him. The saving the King's life by the discovery of this plot, is above the Restoration of the King. He cannot be too well rewarded'.[29]

Oates' security was seen as paramount. Sir Thomas Littleton (1647–1709), a lawyer, argued that he could be lodged in the Abbey Church Yard and have two or three men to guard him. There was also a company of militia stationed nearby. He was to be allowed liberty but must be kept in Whitehall.[30]

At the end of November, Oates was granted a pardon for all offences that he had committed up to that day's date. This was to be important in later trials as no one could now refer to his criminal past with any legal validity.[31] He had already been given such a warrant on 10 November, as well as that of 28 November.[32]

On 2 December, Oates was in the Commons again and the issue of his personal security was discussed. He said 'The Guards that I have annoy me'. He desired them to be neither in his chamber nor to follow him when he walked in St. James' Park. He pointed out that until November he had none such and had been unharmed. It was pointed out to him that there were those who would seek to injure him because of his revelations about the plot. 'I fear nothing' he added. He then repeated what he had said about the Queen's complicity in the poison plot and that she had smiled at him when he had seen her there.[33]

There was subsequent discussion in the House, four days later, as to whether Oates should be prevented from seeing people or not. Members were divided. On one hand, it would be useful for those with information, such as Catholics with consciences, should do as they could to supply useful information to him. On the other, following Oates' revelations about the Queen, there were those who would willingly cut his throat. It was decided to remove the complained restraints from him except the guards outside his rooms.[34]

Yet, as well as the steps taken by the magistrates against Catholics in London and elsewhere, there was more to come. The Test Act was rigorously enforced and so those Catholic peers who sat in the House of Lords were now barred from doing so; 'a mighty blow' wrote Evelyn and he and other Protestants were shocked by this. Catholic servants in the royal household were banished. Meanwhile the clergy preached against 'the Conspirators against The K: and Government' and warning about 'the heavy Yoake of Popish bondage'.[35] Such actions can only have reinforced Oates' view that he was being taken very seriously and very importantly.

A later pamphlet which was hostile to Oates imagined his superior status at this time:

> 'Whenever I came to Westminster House, or to the Old Bailey, or to any well affected coffee house in the City, the people ran in shoals to view my person, and made a lane for me as I passed along. One cry'd, "Make room for the King's evidence there". "How, says his Neighbour, is the Gentleman there with his mouth in the middle of his face, he that sav'd their wives and daughters". I had my Guard of Beefeaters to protect me from being insulted or assassinated, my 10 pounds per week duly paid without deductions, venison pasties and Westphalia hams flew to my table without sending for. I was as much stared at, at the Amsterdam coffee house [on Bartholomew Lane, near

to the Royal Exchange] and in Dick's [a coffee house on Fleet Street, near Temple Bar], as a foreign Ambassador.'[36]

Oates next appeared at a trial on 17 December, this time at the Old Bailey, the assize court for the county of Middlesex usually reserved for the great mass of criminals who were being tried for capital offences. Thomas White alias Whitebread, William Ireland, John Fenwick, Thomas Pickering and John Grove, all Jesuit priests, were taken from Newgate to the Sessions Hall. They were to be tried for high treason for plotting to kill the King. All pleaded not guilty. The charges were then laid out in detail.[37]

Oates was called as the first witness against them after swearing on the Bible. He declared that in December 1677, Whitebread received his orders from Rome and then these were sent to St. Omers that a sermon be preached there on St. Thomas' day to encourage the congregation that they need not heed their oaths of loyalty ('anti-Christian and devilish') to Charles II. Next month Whitebread sent instructions to kill the King. In February there were orders for the Jesuits to hold a meeting in London on 24 April. Was Whitebread at that meeting, Oates was asked?[38]

Oates told how Whitebread was in London and there was a second summons on 5 April. Nine men were summoned, some from St. Omers, and they met at the White Horse on 24 April. They later went to other houses, including those of Grove and Ireland. They drew up a resolution. This was, Oates said, 'as near as I can remember the words', 'That Thomas Pickering and John Grove shall go on in their attempt to assassinate the King'. Grove would be paid £1,500 and Pickering received 30,000 masses. Whitebread, Fenwick and Ireland signed the resolution, which Oates passed around to each of them. Whitebread asked if Oates saw him sign it and he said he had. Where did he sign it? Oates said that each man signed it in his own rooms.[39]

Whitebread asked him if he were at all these places and Oates said he was. Whitebread then said, 'You were not in all these places, and saw them sign there, were you?' Oates replied: 'Yes, I did see them sign it in all those places'.

He added that in May, Whitebread went to St. Omers to meet with Cary and to tell him what had been decided in England, what money had been gathered, their supporters and told Oates to return to England. He was told to murder Tonge and arrived back on 23 June. He met Mr Fenwick at Dover and on their coach journey to London, they opened a box for Richard Blundell which contained Catholic regalia. On 27 June they were in London. Meanwhile, Whitebread met Ashby from St. Omers. There were instructions drawn up; that Wakeman be paid £10,000 to poison the King, that the bishop of Hereford and Dr Stillingfleet be murdered, and that Pickering and Grove should persist in their attempts to kill the King. These instructions were copied out and distributed by Coleman. Wakeman refused the sum, but on Whitebread's orders, he was offered £15,000 and accepted that.[40]

Oates did not witness Wakeman's accepting this new offer, but he did see it on 'their entry books' and in a letter. Whitebread 'did show a great deal of joy' at the doctor's acceptance. There was another meeting of the Jesuits in August when Dr William Fogarty attended and also present was Fenwick, Harcourt and four paid assassins. Fogarty had recommended these men and Fenwick consented. They were to be paid £80 in gold. Whitebread also told what he had done in Scotland and sent two agents there. Whitebread questioned him on this and Oates replied 'they went to prosecute and carry in the design which Fenwick and Ireland plotted, of a rebellion amongst the disaffected Scots', pretending to be presbyterian ministers who hated the episcopal party there.[41]

Oates was asked if he knew all the prisoners at the bar and he named them. He was asked if Pickering and Grove accepted the terms. Yes, at Mrs Saunder's house where Whitebread lodged, he was there then. They took the sacrament from a Jesuit called Barton. Whitebread then stated that there were many witnesses from St. Omers who could swear that Oates was there when he now claimed to be in London seeing their alleged conspiracies take shape. 'I take to God my witness that I was not' said Whitebread. Oates swore otherwise. He then talked of seeing Pickering and Grove in St. James Park, with long pistols loaded with silver bullets. They had been specially sharpened for increased deadliness. Oates had seen these in May and June.[42]

Oates was asked if he knew if Pickering had done any penance:

> Yes my lord in March (for these persons had pursued the King for several years); but he at that time had not looked to the flint of his pistol, but it was loose, and he durst not venture to give fire. He had a fair opportunity as Whitbread said, and because he missed it through his own negligence, he underwent penance and had 20 or 30 strokes.

This had happened in March and then Oates was asked about the four ruffians who went down to Windsor in September, but he know nothing of them. He only knew a little because a letter that Bedingfield sent was to Whitebread, whose rooms he was in. Oates said Whitebread read it to him when Whitebread berated him for having apparently been seen with the King. Oates said that it was another man who had done so, not him, but another whom he had given drafts of his evidence.[43]

Oates then said that because Whitebread suspected him of betraying them, 'I was beaten and affronted and reviled and commanded to go beyond the sea again…I had my lodgings assaulted, to have murdered me if they could'.

'By whom?' Whitebread asked.
'By Mr Whitebread and some of them'.
'Who beat you?'
'Mr Whitebread did'.

Serjeant Baldwyn asked

> 'Was it Pickering or Grove who had the flint of his pistol loose?'
> 'Pickering'.

Pickering said

> 'My lord, I never shot off a pistil in my life'.

Baldwyn then asked about the £80 and Oates explained that this was to be given to the four ruffians who were to shoot the King at Windsor. He had heard about this at Harcourt's rooms in Duke Street. Harcourt was to send the money to a messenger, name unknown to Oates, to the four men, whose names were also unknown to him. Coleman was also present at the time of this transaction, as was Fenwick. The latter asked when this happened and Oates said that it was at the end of August. Harcourt stated

> 'I never saw you there in all of my life; are you sure I was there when the money was there?'
> 'Yes you were'.[44]

The judge shut Fenwick down and asked Oates about the order to have Grove and Pickering carry out the murder. He replied that over 40 men had signed the order. These included Whitebread, Fenwick and Ireland. He claimed he had been attendant on them since 1666. He had carried it from lodgings to lodgings after the meeting of 24 April, for the men to sign. He knew the contents; viz that Pickering would receive £1,500 and Grove 30,000 masses for the killing. The resolution was made after the White Horse tavern meeting; at the meeting the resolution had been made but it was not written down until later that evening in Whitebread's chambers.[45]

Oates went on to say that the men had mass that afternoon after some of them had signed the paper. Whitebread protested his innocence: 'we are to prove a negative and I know it is much harder to prove a negative than it is to assert an affirmative, it is not a very hard thing for a man to swear to anything, if he will venture his soul for it…there have not been three true words spoken by this witness'.

Whitebread was then told that the Catholic faith allowed men to lie if necessary. Oates then provided additional fuel to the fire: 'This Whitbread received power from the see of Rome to grant out commissions officers military. And my Lord, here are the seals of office in court, which he has sealed some hundreds of commissions'.

Whitebread was asked by the judge if he was the provincial of the Jesuits and when Whitebread said that was true, the judge stated, 'Then there are more than three words he hath spoken which are true'.[46]

Oates was then asked by the judge about the army that was to be raised and he said: 'My lord, they were to rise upon the death of the King, and let the French King upon us. And they had made it their business in Ireland and Scotland, to prepare for the receiving of a foreign invasion'.

The army's general was one Johannes Paulus de Oliva. Sir John Gage of Sussex was one of the men to be commissioned as an officer, but many of the commissions were blank. Oates delivered the commission to Gage. Oates then told that he had more to say, and that was that Grove and Smith were to gather money to fund the conspiracy and that Grove had already been engaged in this. Grove asked Oates about this and Oates said it had occurred in Cockpit Alley (near Drury Lane), when Oates lived there. Unlike others, Grove admitted that he had seen Oates before, perhaps on three occasions, but never by Whitebread, 'as I hope to be saved'.[47]

Oates refuted this. He said that before he left for St. Omers in December 1677 he went to Whitebread's and saw Grove there. And arranged to meet at Grigson's on Drury Lane next day, where Grove lent Oates the 8s fare to Dover. Grove agreed that he had lent Oates the money, which he never had returned. Then, the Lord Chief Justice said, the two did know each other. Oates said that when notes were made about the doings in Parliament they sent details of such to Louis XIV. He recalled meeting Grove on one of these occasions, too. Oates said he had drunk with Grove and that Grove confessed to him that he started the Southwark fires in 1676. Apparently Grove was paid £,1000 to do so, and paid three Irish ruffians £200 each to assist him.[48]

Grove was not allowed to answer these allegations, but Fenwick was next turned to and asked about his connection to Oates. Fenwick agreed that he knew Oates and the latter said that Fenwick was his father confessor. This Fenwick denied having ever received a confession from Oates. He agreed that he had met him several items and repaid the 8s for him, for the coach journey. Asked about this unrepaid loan, Fenwick admitted he had been foolish and that 'he came to me once in a miserable poor condition' and as he was starving he must return to the ministry and then Fenwick gave him 5s. Oates denied he had ever been in such dire straits and that he had been ordered by the provincial to come to the procurator for orders. The sum that Fenwick had given him had been much larger than 5s, often 30 or 40s.[49]

Fenwick then asked about the alleged meeting on 24 April in London. Was Oates there?

> 'That resolve [document about the meeting's resolutions] I did then carry to your chamber'.
>
> 'Then was himself at St. Omers'.

The Lord Chief Justice suggested that the confusion may have been because of the difference of the British and Continental calendars, but Fenwick pressed the point:

> 'But my lord he hath sworn he was present at several consultations in April and May, but from September to June he was constantly at St. Omers.

The Lord Chief Justice said that if this was so 'what he [Oates] hath said cannot be true', but Oates had answer for that:

> 'in the month or December or November, I went to St. Omers. I remained there all January, February, March and some part of April, then I came over with the Fathers to the consult that was appointed the 24th of that month'.[50]

Oates added that he had returned to France in May. Fenwick said that he could prove 'by abundance of witnesses that he went not from St Omers all that month'. He could ask for witness statements in writing from the college that Oates was there but he was not told that that statement would not be sufficient. Witnesses had to be present in court and the signature of the town's mayor as to the genuine nature of the evidence was not enough. Oates decided to bolster his position by naming men from the college who knew if he was there and mentioned a fellow student called Hustle who later came to London with him, but none could actually be produced in court. Oates said that he stayed at Grove's house at this time he was in London but he denied this. The defendants were told that if they could prove that Oates was at St. Omers in April and May that was 'a great defence'. Oates then stood down, in need of refreshment and Bedloe then gave his testimony.[51]

After a while, the doubtless refreshed Oates decided to provide, as he often did, additional information: 'I did omit a consult wherein there was a design laid of taking away the duke of Ormonde's life, and of a rebellion that was to be raised in Ireland...That the Catholics had a fair prospect of effecting their designs in Ireland'.

This had been discussed in January 1678 in a letter from the Irish Archbishop Talbot and Fenwick, Ireland and Whitebread all knew of it. The three then informed the fathers at St Omers. Oates had seen the letter and he recalled that it referred to 'they would not leave a stone unturned to root out that abominable heresy out of that kingdom'. At a meeting in August Fenwick consented to the murder of Ormonde and the rebellion in Ireland. Four priests were to do the deed and if they failed, Fogarty was to go to Ireland to see the archbishop in Dublin. There was also a letter from Whitebread when he was in St Omers agreeing to all this. Oates was asked if he had that letter, but he had not, but he referred to an accounts book which would list payments made for postage. Whitebread denied the book existed but Oates and Bedloe both said it did.[52]

Then there was an alleged letter sent from one Peters about issuing invitations to the consult of 24 April. Oates said that Whitebread asked Peters if he had sent out invitations and apparently these had gone to men in Warwickshire and Worcestershire. He had heard these words on 23 April and when Whitebread questioned him in this he repeated himself. He knew Peters' handwriting. The letter was read about, followed by witnesses stating that Ireland was absent from London in early September when Oates said he was in the capital. He got round that by stating that it was common practice for the conspirators to date their letters for a day after they were in London. Ireland denied this.[53]

Sir Dennis Ashburnham, an MP for Hastings, was produced as a witness to cast doubt on Oates' reliability. He was from Hastings and told the court of the episode from Oates' past that had occurred there, but was doubtful whether Oates was unreliable on this present occasion. 'I do think truly that nothing can be said against Mr Oates to take off his credibility'. Yet he was pressed to give details of the past and he consented:

> 'It is set forth that he did swear the peace against a man, and at his taking the oath did say, that there were some witnesses that would evidence such a point of fact, which when they came, would not testify so much, and so was foresworn'.

The Lord Chief Justice dismissed Ashburnham's evidence and said that the evidence against the five defendants did not just come from Oates but also from Bedloe and so as it was corroborated it was strong enough. The defendants pleaded that their recent ancestors had died for the King against Cromwell, and that they had other witnesses, but these were all dismissed as being Catholics and so unreliable.[54]

The Lord Chief Justice then began to summarise the evidence against the three defendants, as Whitebread and Fenwick had been removed from the list of defendants, because of the lack of evidence against them. He said it was undeniable that Oates knew Ireland and said that the defendants' main defence was that of denial. But much of his summing up was directed against Catholics and Catholicism as about the evidence, that it was a wicked religion and its members bloodthirsty and untrustworthy. The jury brought in a verdict of guilty against Ireland, Grove and Pickering, and were commended. 'You have done gentlemen, like very good subjects, and very good Christians, that is to say, good Protestants and now much good may their 30,000 masses do them'. They were sentenced to death on the next day and all protested their innocence. Grove and Ireland were hanged at Tyburn on 24 January 1679; Pickering on 25 May of that year; Whitebread and Fenwick were to be tried again later that year.

Another informer appeared, who was 'a more composed and credible person… that had been the Lord Aston's bailie, and lived in a fair reputation in the country' compared to Oates and Bedloe. This was one Stephen Dugdale, who had been in prison for refusing the oaths of allegiance and supremacy. He claimed that his master's priest, one Evers, was in correspondence with the Jesuits in London, as part of the plot to kill the King. He said that Whitebread had written a letter for Evers and that one Govan was also involved. Lord Stafford had offered £500. He seemed more reputable and although Charles 'had very little regard either to Oates or Bedloe' he thought that Dugdale might be credible.[55]

Finally there was one Miles Prance, a Catholic silversmith, who made a discovery about the Godfrey murder. He implicated three men from the Queen's household in the killing. Jenninson was another witness.[56]

Oates and Bedloe were often asked to work in tandem. In December of this year, they were asked to identify one John Gerrard. Neither could do so. However, Oates claimed that he thought he had seen Gerrard's face near an altar and so was a priest. Gerrard was gaoled.[57] Making money was important for Oates. So much so that on 4 December he asked for permission to print a record of the trials that he had been involved in 'on account of the late plot discovered by him'.[58] The penultimate day of the year saw Oates accuse one Anthony Ballinger as being a Jesuit and a Dominican involved in the conspiracy against the King.[59]

Sometime towards the end of the year, Oates sent word for his brother Samuel to visit him in London. He did so, hoping for help in advancing his naval career, but found that Oates was 'backward in his sollicitations' and so Samuel's career faced a setback.[60]

1678 had been, by its end, a most remarkable year for Oates. After the unprofitable months at St. Omers, he had, again returned to London and this time he had given rein to his talents. Working with Kirkby and Tonge (who both faded out of the picture by the year's end), and a degree of good luck, he had been propelled to the centre of national politics. For many, this was to have fatal results. Yet on the last day of the year he announced that it was his life that was in danger whilst he lived at Whitehall.[61] This is standard fare for those involved in alleged conspiracies as it both boosts the ego of the speaker as well as it being an attempt to convince others that their claims are true.

Chapter Five

The Course of the 'Plot', 1679

The new year opened with belief in the plot, for many, undimmed. A letter from one Mr Busbridge, a gentleman of Cublington, Sussex, on 3 February referred to 'The greatest of God's goodness is causing a discovery of a most wicked and bloody design against our religion and government, and against the life of our sovereign Lord King'. He noted that what was even more impressive was that it had been exposed before it could be carried out and that it was revealed by men who were hitherto involved in it.[1]

It was this year, in February at the latest, that Oates decided to promote himself – he who had not even a BA or MA – to doctor of divinity (DD) and chose Salamanca University as his alma mater. Perhaps he chose this university because it was an ancient seat of learning and because it was relatively distant and so his fantasy could not be easily exposed. Thereafter he expected to be called Dr Oates, as he styled himself. This gave rise to his opponents then and in following years referring to him derisively as the Salamanca doctor, once his duplicity was exposed. However, it was not unknown in the seventeenth century for some to award themselves higher titles than they had actually merited. Thomas Blood never gained a higher military rank than lieutenant but referred to himself as Colonel Blood and William Bedloe who had never served in the army or navy was known as Captain Bedloe.

Oates was very much an important part in the investigation of the plot in the year after his initial disclosures. On 17 January 1679 he began to accompany Sir William Waller (c.1639–1699), a London JP, and other magistrates, in visiting all of London's prisons to ascertain whether any of the prisoners there were involved in the plot. Twelve days later the privy council ordered that no one was to be discharged from prison if there was the slightest suspicion that they were involved in the plot until the gaolers 'do first send for Mr Oates, to see what hee hath to testifie against the parties concerned before he consent to let any be discharged upon bail'.[2] Oates found one Lewis, said to be at the alleged meeting in 1678, there.[3] Another of the many that Oates saw was one John Sidway, on 12 April; Oates identified him as being a Catholic.[4] In May he was to go to Newgate with Bedloe and Dugdale to question priests there for further evidence about the plot and Oates went by himself to another prison that month to speak to three men.[5] He was thus seen as critical in the investigation.

He also gave other information, not previously disclosed by him, to the House of Lords committee to investigate the plot, that he felt was germane. On 19 February he told how 1,000 Spanish pilgrims had been seen arriving at Milford Haven, as noticed by travellers there and that even more were expected from Spain, presumably as part of an invasion force.[6] Naturally this was entirely fictitious, and was soon discovered to be such, but it did not seem to blunt Oates' credibility.

Oates continued to address the privy council with allegations against Catholics between January and May 1679. Lionel Anderson was identified as a priest, as were Father Skinner and Mr Sharp. Numerous other men were accused of being priests. Some were noted as being without money but had that 'skill and interest' to push the 'plot' forward. Sir William Andrews of Essex was accused of collecting money for the Jesuits, to the tune of £500, with £1,000 to come, to carry on the plot with instructions coming from London and St. Omers.[7] Oates initially gave his information about Andrews to Sir Edward Warcup, JP, and then before the Lords on 28 April.[8]

He and Bedloe were concerned about the published versions of the trials in which they had featured prominently as witnesses. The account of the Coleman trial gave them worry, 'it is in some places mistaken and they sense somewhat of the misfortune of it to be true as they have that the trials of Ireland, Grove and Pickering are also preparing for the press' and 'for those tryals are intended for the press that Mr Oates and Mr Bedloe be first consulted as to the evidence they gave'. Oates also wanted to vet any second edition of the Coleman trial and the privy council agreed to this.[9] When Bassett, a printer, made errors in publishing Oates' own narrative of the plot, Oates decided, in April, to take the matter in hand personally by writing his own works. There were also errors in a book published about Godfrey, and Oates found these injurious to himself, especially as it had wide coverage.[10]

Oates was treated by most as being the fount of all knowledge about the plot. The Attorney General went to see Oates to ascertain what information he had about James Colker, a London priest. Oates was asked to write down a list of all 'considerable' English Catholics in seminaries abroad so that they could be encouraged to return. Danby asked him if he knew George Johnson. Yes, said Oates, he was a Dominican monk. On being asked about Gerard Ireland from Lancashire, Oates said that he had come from Rome. Yet when Oates and Bedloe questioned Valentine Harcourt from Shrewsbury, neither recognised him and so he was returned whence he came. He also complained that the Earl of Castlemaine and Captain Spalding had been released from Newgate into the custody of King's Messengers.[11]

Other information was provided by Oates. He claimed that a recent fire in the Temple was a contrivance and would be proved 'in a little tyme'.[12] He told of a nobleman's house in London in which there was Catholic regalia and books. Catholics met there.[13] This could have been the house that he told Waller about and a warrant was given to Waller and Oates to search it.[14] Yet when Oates asked to peruse the papers found by Warcup on one Mr Jolly, he was only given permission to take some of them.[15]

Oates did much to keep himself in the public eye in 1679 after his dramatic revelations of the previous year in other ways, too. One method was to preach to the public, and as he was believed to be an Anglican clergyman, this was no difficulty for him to be a guest preacher in churches. As was common in the seventeenth and eighteenth centuries, he had some of these sermons published and so reached an even greater audience. They also provided the author with another income stream.

The sermons were not just designed for the attention of the great mass of the public, as important as they were. They were also designed to remind those among the political elite of his continued value to them. A sermon preached at St. Michael's church in Wood Street on 30 January was dedicated to the King's cousin, Prince Rupert, who had fought bravely in the civil wars and had been a pillar to Charles II as well as his father before him, and of course as a member of the privy council, had heard his revelations first hand last year. Yet by 1679 Rupert was mixing with members of the Opposition and so it is significant that Oates sought his approbation. Oates wrote of Rupert, 'to whom…is chiefly owing a very considerable Temporal Deliverance of this Nation'. He added more compliments, 'great zeal and interest and generous Example…to support the evidence [of the Plot]' to avoid 'a dismal deluge of Blood and Slavery upon the Nation'. He also referred to 'the merits of your Highness, and your renowned Courage'.[16] St. Michael's on Wood Lane in the City of London was the church for which Dr Tonge was the vicar and so Oates would have had no problem in preaching there.

Another sermon was dedicated to the Earl of Shaftesbury. Again there was flattery, with reference to 'the obligations that your lordship laid upon this kingdom' and finished with 'God Almighty bless your lordship'.[17] There was also a pamphlet published in this year written by him that was dedicated to Shaftesbury. At its outset it stated, 'your lordship appearing to stand by the Evidence with all Candor becoming a Person of your Worth', Oates wrote that 'I thought it my Duty to pray your Patronage and Protection'. More praise for Shaftesbury, 'this Nation hath reason to bless the most High God for your care for her Peace and establishment in the Profession of that Religion'.[18] As noted in a previous chapter, it has sometimes been surmised that Shaftesbury was behind the plot but on this evidence it would appear that it was Oates, in this year, who was reaching out to Shaftesbury as an ally.

Oates also used the dedications and prefaces to promote himself directly. In one he drew attention to the alleged danger he was in, with reference to 'some exceptions raised against me, by some open and some secret enemies' and 'the danger I am in, from so many enemies'.[19] In the other he referenced 'I have had nothing but Affronts and Afflictions'.[20] There was no doubt who his enemies were, with phrases such as 'Rome's Tyranny and witchcraft', 'Rome and France', 'Rome's detestable practices' and the necessity for all to resist 'the Romish interest against our Religion and Liberties', 'to the great confusion of Prince and People'.[21]

More positively, Oates inflated his efforts. 'I appear more loyal to my Prince'.[22] Yet the Almighty protected him, as he claimed, 'God in his goodness has delivered me' and that he had had 'blessings from God upon my labours'. In the secular world, Oates spoke of 'My Fidelity to my King and Country'. That God was with him, he claimed to have no doubt, 'And that God would stand by me' and signed off, 'I am thy Brother and Servant, in our dearest Redeemer'.[23]

Anti-Catholicism made up the bulk of these and other sermons, as would be imagined. In one he attacked Catholic practices, including holy bread ('the stinking leaves of papistical Pharisees'), holy boughs ('conjured, bewitched and charmed'), made references to sorcery and the Devil and noted, 'The Papists are very busy-bodies, and love to meddle with all kinds of matters'. He ended with a comparison with the Catholic and Protestant churches, 'Such blasphemous Baggage…Christ alone is our wisdom, Righteousness, Sanctification and Redemption…To whom all honour and Glory, both now and forever. Amen'.[24]

One sermon may well relate to himself, using the text from Matthew 18, 11, 'The Son of Man is come to save that which is lost'. He told the congregation that Christ came into the world to save it, making His will known to men. He highlighted the following issues, why Jesus was called His Son, why was he also called the Son of Man and why he came into the world, to 'save what was lost'. He concluded, 'Let us love one another, for seeing it is apparent that Christ came to save us, and did manifest the love of the most high God to carry into the world, and dying for our sins'. To take the sermon at face value could be seen as a straightforward plea to take up the Christian message or it might be Oates likening himself to the saviour of the world.[25]

He was quite an effective speaker. One North wrote of an ancestor of his 'He once heard Oates preach at St. Dunstan's [Stepney, London] and much admired [was astonished by] his theatrical behaviour in the pulpit'.[26] The 'theatrical' tag might be a backhanded compliment about a sermon that is meant to be instructional in nature but a comment made two decades later about the effectiveness of Oates's sermons supports this comment being made at face value.

The pamphlet he wrote about the Jesuits was for 'every true Englishman and Protestant…that they may detest all such Practices, and protest against them'. The author was to 'give the People of England such an Account of the Villainies of the Jesuits, as will I hope make them and their Votaries to be an Abomination to every sober and judicious Protestant'. The account relates how the Jesuits aimed to distil suspicion of all other Christian denominations into the minds of rulers. They also aimed at political influence and were directed by the Pope. Jesuits did not serve any ruler except the Pope and manipulated those they were in contact with in order to serve their own interests. The methods of the Jesuits were claimed to include murder, oppression of the poor and the deception of rulers. They created dissension between countries. When they had returned England to Catholicism the Jesuits would be the rulers. The solution to these woes was 'that they be utterly Rooted Out of all Christendom'.[27]

Secular rewards came Oates' way and were doubtless most welcome. He had been complaining on 2 January that 'he has been now serving His Majesty three months and has spent much money of his owne'.[28] On 13 January, Oates was granted a weekly allowance of £10 from the public purse.[29] He thought this was insufficient, complaining that he was in 'a very great debt', borrowing money from friends and needing advances of money.[30] By March he was receiving a weekly allowance of £12.[31] Apart from such generous regular payments, he was also sometimes given one-off lump sums. On 4 April a sum of £107 10s was awarded to 'our trusty and well beloved Titus Oates, Dr in Divinity'.[32] Other such payments include a free gift of £50 and also £150 for helping to apprehend one Richard Prince.[33] Yet in 1685 Oates claimed he had been given £100 for the discovery of the 'plot', another £100 for writing an account of it for publication and between £50-60 for having played a part in arresting Jesuit priests.[34] An enemy wrote in 1683 that Oates 'wears Good Cloaths; He drinks Good Wine and keeps Good Company'.[35]

It should be noted that money was certainly a matter close to Oates' heart; from being almost a pauper he now had wealth. We should recall that this is pre-decimalisation and so twelve pence made up one shilling and twenty shillings was a pound; twenty-one shillings being a guinea. Incomes varied considerably; in the 1680s the archbishop of Canterbury enjoyed an annual revenue of £4,317 whilst the bishop of Bristol's was £350 (less than Oates', it will be noted). Lesser clergy, as Oates had been at Bobbing for example, had to exist on a tenth of that of the latter.[36] And most of the population enjoyed even less. The income that Oates was now receiving was that enjoyed by many country gentlemen and for a man who was penurious in the previous year this was a vast improvement in his finances, to say the least.

There were some indications that Oates was under attack as early in January and February 1679, though it was then at a low ebb. William Brookes said that one Netterville told him that if they could vilify the characters of Oates and Bedloe they would be paid handsomely.[37] One Phillips said that a woman brought to him in a pub by Mrs Medbourne offered him money to say that Oates suggested paying him for his testimony.[38] There was the idea put forward that Oates and Bedloe should be examined together and if there was any variation, the whole plot should be invalidated.[39] From Paris, a Catholic sympathiser pointed to Oates' bad character and the improbability of the plot and his errors over Don John and La Chaise. There was also evidence from St. Omers that Oates was there not in London in May witnessing the Jesuit meeting there.[40]

The veracity of Oates and Bedloe was being questioned in other quarters. There was a suggestion that Louis XIV, by the medium of Danby, might try and bribe witnesses to speak against either. There was also a report from the magistrates at Hastings that Francis Norwood, a churchwarden there who had known Oates in his campaign against the Parkers in 1675, said that for £1,000 or £2,000 one could swear that Oates was perjured. This was of concern to the privy council because such statements could be scandalous and so would 'weaken ye King's evidence'. Norwood was thus to be arrested.[41]

He also took a part in politics, during the election in March 1679. Oates went to Southwark in a coach, with many flocking to see him. Apparently 'he made speeches to the rabble, desiring them to choose who he would recommend'. This was for Thomas Smith, an anti-court candidate.[42] He was not successful in the election, however.

Oates and Bedloe were before the Commons again on 21 March. Here he took the opportunity to attack his political enemies. Firstly there was Danby who had been critical of him in the previous year. Then there was Sir John Robinson, whom, he claimed, had known of the plot for four or five years, from one Everard, but had chosen not to reveal what he apparently knew. There was Sir Edward Sackville who had verbally abused Oates as 'a lying Rogue' and for claiming that those who believed in the plot were 'sons of whores'. Goring was accused of wanting bail for Sir John Gage (accused of being a Catholic plotter) and when Oates said no, Goring called him a 'rascally lying Rogue'. Oates complained that the guards on his apartment caused him hardships. He was given until 24 March to substantiate his claims. One MP, Pilkington, was sympathetic towards Oates, stating that they owed much to hm and that anyone who spoke against him ought to be made an example of.[43] Oates denounced Sackville (who claimed that anyone believing Oates and Bedloe was foolish) in the Commons on 25 March; the majority of the MPs backed Oates as being truthful and Sackville was sent to the Tower for a week; he was also asked to give evidence against Robinson but never did.[44]

Although Oates' message was widely approved of in the Commons, his language was not. Oates apologised, 'I am sorry I gave offence to the House in what I said, but it was my conscience and it was the truth'. When he then left he was the subject of discussion. Garroway said 'Oates is a passionate man, and none of the best mannered men'. Others agreed, with Coventry saying 'This language is like a woman indicted for being a whore'. Yet his message, if not the manner of its delivery, was generally approved of. Oates was reprimanded.[45]

The next major trial was of the three men who had been accused of being Godfrey's murderers by one Miles Prance, a Catholic silversmith, at the end of 1678. They were tried at the Old Bailey on 10 February 1679. The men were all servants of the Queen's household at Somerset House. Their names were Robert Green, Henry Berry and Lawrence Hill (two Catholics and a Protestant). They were accused of killing the magistrate on the night of 12 October when he was on his way home and concealing the corpse at Somerset House for several days.[46]

Unlike the case with Coleman and also the priests in the previous year, Oates had a relatively small part to play in the trial, but even so, such was his stature, he was the first witness called. He recounted his meetings with Godfrey in September and October 1678 as have already been related, telling how Godfrey was in fear of being murdered by Catholics. But that was all: he had never said that he had any knowledge of the murder and did not alter that stance now by recalling previously forgotten 'facts'. Instead, it was Prance who was the main witness, for he had claimed he had seen the murder and the body. Bedloe also provided a great deal of testimony as well and referred to Oates a couple of times in his statements. In the summing up to the jury, the Lord Chief Justice referred to Oates' evidence as showing that Godfrey was fearful of being killed by Catholics; two of the defendants were of that denomination. They were all found guilty and sentenced to death.[47] They were executed at Tyburn on 21 February (Hill and Green) and 28 February (Berry). As with those executed in 1678, all protested their innocence to the last.

Not all those put on trial were found guilty. On 11 February, Samuel Atkins, a clerk to Samuel Pepys at the Admiralty, was on trial as an accessory of the murder of Godfrey. Oates was not present as a witness. Atkins was found not guilty due to having a strong alibi. It probably was in his favour, too, that he was a Protestant.

When Charles II's leading minister, Danby, fell from power, following allegations of treason with the French, and lodged in the Tower in April 1679, there were calls from the Opposition to have him put on trial for treason. Oates produced one John Lane, who had become his servant, as a witness who could state that Danby had offered him a reward if he could persuade Oates to withdraw his depositions of the previous year. Oates' friends abused Danby 'as one that spoke the basest and most contemptible words of the King himself, and he associated himself with none but whores, rogues, pimps and panders' and that the King never went sober to bed.[48] Charles refused to sacrifice his former minister, however and Danby never stood trial.

Political circumstances certainly favoured Oates at this juncture. Charles II dissolved Parliament on 24 January and a new election occurred. This was probably unwise and had unfortunate consequences for the court, because it resulted, on 6 March, in a House of Commons which was largely opposed to the royal court, far more so than previously. It was also generally supportive of the idea that there was a plot, which was widely mostly believed, and because of this, in May, put forward a Bill to exclude James from the succession. Charles was heartily opposed to his brother being excluded from the hereditary succession. Yet he was in a weak position and was forced to play for time. He prorogued Parliament. Principal among those calling for exclusion was Shaftesbury, once a republican, then a royalist and having lost his former political pre-eminence in 1673 was desirous of a return to high office and all the fruits that entailed. Oates had thus strong political supporters, more so than in the previous year.

Whether the exclusion campaign, which was to gather steam throughout 1679 and 1680 would have occurred without the anti-Catholic allegations of Oates and others is a moot point. It had already been known since at least 1673 that James was a Catholic and as the Queen was childless, he was next in line to the throne. Yet the exclusion campaign was given more credibility and impetus because of Oates et al and its inception. The onset of exclusion following the anti-Catholic allegations was surely no coincidence

Oates' next appearance in court was not until 13 June when Thomas Whitebread, William Harcourt, John Fenwick, John Gavan and Anthony Turner, all of whom Oates had identified as being involved in the plot in the previous year, were on trial at the Old Bailey. They were all allegedly at the meeting on 24 April where the death of the King was plotted. This time, Oates was principal witness. He told the court that Whitebread was made Principal (ie senior Jesuit priest in London) in December 1677 and that he instructed Father George Conyers to preach against the oaths of allegiance and supremacy. In January or February 1678, Whitebread wrote letters to St. Omers about the state of Ireland, as Archbishop Talbot said that as soon as the blow was struck in England, thousands of Irishmen were ready to rise.[49]

Oates clarified that the phrase 'the blow' meant the murder of the King. Whitebread, so Oates said, sent over two Jesuits to Ireland in January to see how matters stood and they came back in April. After the alleged meeting on 24 April Harcourt, Whitebread and Turner all signed the resolution in their different rooms. He was asked about Gavan but said 'I cannot be positive' about him but would reveal evidence about him later. Oates then told that he went abroad with some of the others, returning in June 1678 and sharing a coach from Dover to London (14–17 June) with Fenwick. The latter had a box of Catholic regalia to be delivered to the Fountain tavern near Charing Cross. Fenwick told Oates that he had on his person some letters about the plot.[50]

In July Ashby had allegedly received papers from Whitebread who was still abroad, about paying Wakeman to poison the King as well as enclosing a commission, signed by Whitebread, for Sir John Gage as an officer in the supposed Catholic army. Whitebread then asked Oates about the letter that was allegedly from him. Did he order it and when exactly was it sent out? In July, Oates said, 'the beginning or the middle'. Are you sure, he was asked, and Oates replied 'I am not sure, but I think it to be in July'. Who was present? Ashby, Ireland and Harcourt, Oates replied.[51]

He then said that Fenwick and Harcourt advised Ashby to go to Bath to discuss the plot with allies in Somerset. Fenwick was insistent that Oates give a date for this conversation. Late July or early August, Oates suggested. Fenwick reminded the court that earlier Oates had said it was early or middle July. Oates then moved onto Gavan, who he said he had not recognised from previously because he was disguised 'he was under that mask…under an ill favoured periwig and being a man I knew had a good head of hair of his own, I did not understand the mystery of it and so spared my evidence at that time from informing the council against him. He now recalled that in June 1678 Gavan was writing letters about the state of play of the Catholics in Staffordshire and Shropshire.[52]

Gavan asked from where the letters were sent. Oates replied that it was not customary to give a place of sending in these letters, but that it was in July. Gavan asked him to be more precise. He could not be so. Gavan replied 'I am as innocent as a child unborn'. Oates said that Ashby gave an account of the two said counties to Ireland. Gavan asked Oates what he had written and Oates said it was about the state of the Catholics in the two counties. The letter also mentioned Lord Stafford's activity but Oates pleaded to be excused any statements needed for another trial. When pressed as to content he said: 'He gave an account of how prosperous things were in those counties, and did say there was about two or three thousand pounds that would be ready in that county for the carrying on of the design'.

He added that Ireland departed between 8 and 12 August to go to St. Omers. He left his chambers in Russell Street. On 21 August, Harcourt and Fenwick, with others met at Wild House. There was gathered the £80 to pay the four assassins. Coleman gave the messenger a guinea to take the letter to the four. A day later, Fenwick and Harcourt met to discuss news from Ireland from Archbishop Talbot about the plot to kill Ormonde and asking about the state of play in England. They asked for a commission to raise forces and for money; Fenwick sent commissions via Chester. On 26 August, Fenwick left to take some students at St. Omers.[53]

Oates continued that on 1–2 September, a letter arrived announcing Whitebread's return and on the 3rd Oates went to his chambers to meet him. Next day 'he did revile me, and strike me' for Oates' treacherous behaviour. Whitebread had been told that Oates was passing information to Dr Tonge. Oates said that the man they had seen wore similar coloured clothes to him and so they had mistaken him for Oates. After he had explained himself, Whitebread showed Oates a letter from Bedingfield to state that the plot had been discovered as letters to Windsor had been intercepted. Whitebread also offered Wakeman an additional £5,000 to poison the King and when he accepted, 'Whitebread did greatly rejoice'. Did I tell you so? asked Whitebread; no, said Oates, you were in Flanders but I read it in a letter.[54] It was now time for Oates to turn to Turner. Oates began thus, 'I speak to him as being at the consult in April, and signing the resolve of the death of the King'.

On being asked if Gavan was at the consult, Oates said that there were 40 men there and he could not be sure, but his name was on the list of signatures. Oates was then asked if he was sure about the handwriting and had he seen samples of Gavan's previously. He was uncertain. Yet he was adamant that Gavan wrote the letter about the state of Shropshire and Staffordshire. The lord chief justice moved onto the question as to whether Whitebread, Harcourt and Fenwick were at the consult and he said they were. Was Turner also there. Yes.[55]

Gavan then began to ask Oates questions. He wanted to know about the letter which had his name on it. To whom was it written and where was the money to be received? Oates said it was sent to Ireland and the money was to be given to Grove as an assassin. The Lord Chief Justice said of Oates, 'I perceive your memory is not good' and Gavan replied, 'I perceive his memory is very good'. Gavan asked when and where was the letter written and Oates said it was in London in early or middle July. Gavan replied, 'Just now, you said it was at the latter end'. Oates complained: 'My lord, I beg this favour, if the prisoners at the bar ask any questions, they may be proposed to the court, for they are nimble in their questions and do abuse a little the evidence. They put things upon them that they never say'.

Gavan was told to do so and said 'I would do so my lord, in whose honour I have more confidence, than in whatsoever Mr Oates says or swears'.

The judge, springing to Oates' defence, said 'Do not give the King's witnesses ill words'.[56]

Whitebread then asked Oates if he was at the consult on 24 April and he said he was. Whitebread then asked how long was he in England on that occasion and he began to be vague, but thought it was about 20 days. Nor could he be sure with whom he travelled to England. There were discrepancies in his statement of the previous year to what he said now, but the Lord Chief Justice was sympathetic towards him and said that such differences were not important, though the defendants emphasised that they were. Gavan tried to press Oates as to when he saw him in London, was it July or August and if the former, what part of it. Oates could not be precise and the Lord Chief Justice again came to his defence, 'Really, I believe there is scarce one in all this company, able to give account of a particular time of a passage so long ago'. Gavan said 'No doubt he has an excellent memory'.[57]

Although Oates claimed to have met Gavan twice on a day in July in the company of an apothecary called Walpoole, Gavan stated:

> 'I never saw Mr Oates before the day in January, when he says I had the periwig on, and he does not know me: as to July, I call God to witness, I never saw him then'.
>
> Turner then asked Oates if he had ever seen him before and Oates answered:
>
> 'You were then in a disguised habit and a nasty periwig and I did not know you so well'.
>
> 'You, at Whitehall, were pleased to say I went by another name'.
>
> 'I do not value names, but your person; you are the man'.

Turner asked Oates if he saw him at the consult and Oates said he thought not but that he had seen him after at Fenwick's chambers. Turner said that earlier Oates had said that earlier he had seen him at Wild House instead. Oates answered because much of the meeting was there he referred to all of the meeting as having happened there. When a juryman asked Oates where he saw Turner he replied that it had been at Fenwick's chamber, where 'I saw him sign the resolve of the King's death'. Other witnesses against the defendants were then called, beginning with Dugdale, followed by Bedloe and Prance.[58]

Later in the trial, Whitebread attacked Oates' integrity as a witness. He said that witnesses in cases of life and death should have good characters, 'That Mr Oates is not any such person'. He maintained that Oates claimed to have been at the consult on 24 April:

> Now I desire your lordship would be pleased to consider whether this was probable, and whether I had not been very much a mistaken man all this while, to trust a man with such a business, and whether I ought not to be sent to Bedlam than Newgate for trusting such a man as he, whom by his own confession I never saw till that time. It is not rational that a man should trust him.[59]

There were many reasons why Oates was untrustworthy. He was not a good Catholic, he led a debauched life, he never repaid loans, and so 'to trust him with such a great intrigue as this was…had been a madness'. Furthermore, Whitebread then went on to produce witnesses from St. Omers to show that Oates had been at the seminary in France when he claimed he was at the meeting in London in April. Fenwick added that Oates had no evidence against them, 'I have had a thousand letters taken from me, not any of these letters had any thing of treason in them…All the evidence that is given come to this, there is but saying and swearing'.[60]

Mr Hilsley was brought by the defendants to prove Oates was a liar. Oates was asked if he came to England with Hilsley or not and he said

> 'That one Mr Hilsley did come over with us when we did'.
> 'My lord I did not' said Hilsley.
> 'How can you tell?'
> 'I left him at St. Omers.
> 'What do you say Mr Oates?'
> 'It is true, Mr Hilsley did leave me at St. Omers because he went out on a Sunday morning and I came out of the Monday morning, but I overtook him at Calais'.
> 'My lord that is false and I have a great many here that can prove it'.

Hilsley was then asked if he was a Catholic and eventually he confirmed this. William Perry, another from St. Omers, came to state that Oates was there, eating and then in the infirmary. Oates denied it and played the anti-Catholic card, 'this gentleman is not only a votary of the Jesuits, but has been one of the sodality several years. And they have dispensations, and are bound by an implicit obedience to say what the Jesuits bid them, who are their superiors'.[61]

To muddy the waters, Oates made the point about Old style and new style dating, which was ten days different and the latter was in use in France and the former in Britain. Parry affirmed that Oates was at the seminary from December to June and never left it for more than a day. Oates said that those leaving wore secular clothes but that the instant he returned he donned his habit and so he stated that it 'did not appear that I had gone out of the house, nor did I know if it was known that I had gone out of the house'. Whitebread said that this was irrelevant because he was very noticeable among the students on account of the separate table at which he sat for his meals and the fact that he was much 'ancienter' than the others. Another student, Doddington, stated that Oates was not absent from the college for any length of time. Many others came forward to say that Oates was at the seminary.[62]

There were people who claimed to have seen Oates in London in April 1678. One such was William Walker, an elderly priest, who said that he saw him in late

March or April 1678. He was in disguise, in a grey serge coat and a grey hat. Walker spoke about Oates to a woman whose name he did not know and she told him that Oates 'he is an undone man…he has changed to the church of Rome'. Walker did not speak to Oates. The second witness was Sarah Ives, who kept a chandler's shop, and she had spoken to Walker about Oates. She had seen him before and then saw him in disguise in St. Martin's Lane. It was last April that she saw him but did not know the exact date. Mrs Mayo, Sir Richard Barker's housekeeper. said that a servant of Sir Richard Barker's told her that he had seen Oates and she later saw him in the garden of Sir Richard's house. All this was in May. Philip Page, one of Sir Richard's servants, claimed he also saw him there, as did Sir Richard, seeing him in June or July but had been told by others that he had been there in May. A servant of Sir Richard also claimed to have seen Oates at the property, in May.[63]

Burnet commented about this stage of the trial:

> By this the credit of the St. Omers scholars was quite blasted. There was no reason to mistrust those who had no interest in the matter, and swore they saw Oates about that time; whereas the evidence given by scholars bred in the Jesuits' college, when it was to save some of their order, was liable to a very just suspicion.[64]

Whitebread was asked what he had to say about this evidence of Oates' accuracy and he said that at his previous trial Oates had mentioned none of these witnesses who now appeared to vouch that he was indeed in London in April 1679. Lord Chief Justice North defended Oates, arguing that no one could be precise as to recalling dates of a year ago and that 'Oates stands a good witness' and was 'upright and good'. Gavan poured scorn on Oates' testimony; there were sixteen witnesses from St. Omers who declared he was there, but Oates' witnesses clashed with his own statement of arriving on 20 April and staying six days. Yet one of Oates' witnesses talked of seeing him in disguise and another of seeing him in May. He said that Oates' testimony could not be reconciled either by the witnesses of the defendants, and even if they were discounted, by the ambiguity and conflict of Oates' witnesses.[65]

Gavan attacked Oates' credibility again:

> 'As to the honesty of Mr Oates' life, you heard that he was disgusted by the Jesuits, esteemed not a person of that diligence or fidelity to be intrusted by them, was turned out of St. Omers.

When asked how this affected his views on Jesuits, he added:

> 'It might be a ground of hatred and malice in him against them'.

Turner also attacked Oates' character:

> 'whether it is reasonable that Bedloe and Oates should be looked upon as good witnesses, that these persons who have been such scandalous people should be admitted to oath, who were debarred from sacrament for according to the Church of England, no man that is publicly scandalous can be admitted to the sacrament'.[66]

The summing up discussed the credibility of the evidence against the five accused. It was pointed out that there were three witnesses against Whitebread and Fenwick, four against Harcourt, two against Gavan and Turner. Oates had testified against all five. As to there being more witnesses testifying to Oates having been at St. Omers than there were for him having been in London, this was not of any weight because they were not, and could not be on oath, but also because they were Catholic and so 'because they are of a religion that can dispense with oaths, though false, for the sake of a good cause'.[67]

There was more said in defence of Oates; witnesses and their being credible, as well as more said of an anti-Catholic nature. The jury returned after a quarter of an hour with guilty verdicts against all five men.[68] All five were hanged, drawn and quartered at Tyburn on 20 June; as with others hanged, all pleaded their innocence of the charges for which they were to die. Later that year apparent confirmation of Ireland's guilt was announced and Robert Jenninson confirmed Oates' and Bedloe's stories as a gentleman 'of a very considerable estate' supported their case. As he was in 'no want of a livelihood' he was seen as being independent and so trustworthy.[69] Later that year, papers found at an address in Duke's Street, Lincoln's Inn Fields, of receipts and payments by Jesuits, were claimed by Waller to confirm Oates' story.[70]

On 15 June, Richard Langhorn, a Catholic lawyer, was tried at the Old Bailey for allegedly being part of the plot; he had been identified by Oates in the previous year. As ever, he pleaded not guilty before the charges were read out. Dugdale gave some evidence and was followed by Oates. He began with his first knowing Langhorn's sons in September 1677, 'but I will not be positive as to the time of their coming' in Spain, the two boys being students one at Valladolid and the other at another Spanish college.[71]

They gave Oates some letters to give to their father and when he was in London, he went to Langhorn's house in Sheer Lane. He was there directed to Langhorn's chambers in the Temple and did there deliver the letters to the lawyer. Langhorn said that his sons would become secular priests and 'they would suddenly have great promotion in England: for he said things would not last long in this posture'.

In November, Langhorn gave Oates letters to deliver to St. Omers as he was travelling there in the next month. These letters made reference to a plan carried on by Coleman and also correspondence with La Chaise. Later ones referred to 'the carrying on of the designs of the Catholics and several expressions there were in it were bad enough…but they were to this effect, The parliament began to flag in promoting the Protestant religion and now they had a fair opportunity to begin and give the blow'.[72] Although Langhorn was not at the consult on 24 April, Oates said that he had been given orders by the Provincial to tell Langhorn what happened there. He did so and on later hearing of what happened there, Oates said that 'Mr Langhorn lifted up his hands and eyes and prayed to God to give it good success'. Langhorn asked Oates when this happened, 'Do you know the day of the month? You have asserted the day of the month formerly, pray do so now'. The judge told him to hold the question until later. Meanwhile Oates told how he had seen parchments in Langhorn's office which were commissions to various Catholic lords in the Catholic army to be formed.[73]

These papers were from the authority of the papacy and were directed to the Jesuits. Langhorn had let Oates see them because he believed he was an agent in the plot. There was one commission for Langhorn, to be 'a judge in the army or an Advocate General, so they called him'. There were also letters there and one was from la Chaise, giving the assurance of the support of the French King in the Catholic endeavour in England, by providing men and money. These were given to Oates by Langhorn to deliver. Some letters referred to Coleman. Furthermore, Oates told that Langhorn was employed as solicitor to the Jesuits and accompanied Harcourt, Fenwick and others as they visited Benedictine monks desiring support and money from them. Apparently £6,000 was promised and given and collected by Langhorn in July or August. Oates added that Langhorn was disgusted that Wakeman wanted so much money for his part in the assassination of the King, calling him 'a covetous man', 'a narrow spirited and a narrow souled physician'.[74]

Oates was then shown some handwriting under a Jesuit seal and he said he recognised that from the writings he had seen in Langhorn's office. Langhorn then said to Oates that they had met in late November 1677. Oates confirmed this and went on to say he was at St. Omers in the next month. The Lord Chief Justice, doubtless recalling similar lines of defence in the previous trials, came to Oates' aid by saying 'All their defence lies in catches upon a point of time, which no man living is able to be positive'. Langhorn then had Oates admit that he had been at St. Omers from December 1677 to April 1678. When exactly did Oates return to England, asked Langhorn. 'I came about the middle of April, or the latter end, I will not be so positive in that, and I was in England under 20 days'.[75]

Who came with him, asked Langhorn. Oates said that about 9-10 men did so. These were fathers Williams and March, the rector of Liege and Sir John Warner. He did not recall the others. Langhorn said that Oates had named them all in his statement to the House of Lords. He was asked where he stayed in London and Oates said it was at Mrs Groves' house. He agreed he stayed elsewhere and that he returned on 6 May but was unsure on details. He was asked if he knew Langhorn's handwriting and said he did. Langhorn said that Oates was an Anglican minister and then converted to Catholicism and wanted more details. Oates was unhappy about such past history but thought he converted in February or March 1677 and had been at Bobbing parish as a vicar but left for health and other reasons.[76]

Langhorn asked Oates if he was a Jesuit but after some debate he was told he need not answer an incriminating question such as that. Langhorn instead asked Oates when he saw him in 1678; apparently on four occasions; in April or May and in July or August. Langhorn had done with Oates at present and he was replaced as a witness by Bedloe.[77]

As in the previous trial, Hilsley was brought in as a witness for the defendant and he previous day, refuted Oates' statement that the two men had travelled to England from St Omers together in April 1678. Other witnesses backed up Hilsley in adding that Oates did not travel from St Omers to England. One said he saw Oates in the seminary garden on 1 May. All this went against Oates' statements about being in England at this time. Others said that Warner was on his travels in April and May. As the Lord Chief Justice noted 'if he be to believed, and that he doth not speak falsely, or more than he knows, it is impossible that Oates' testimony and his can stand together…the question is whether he is to be believed'.[78]

Another dozen witnesses gave evidence that Oates was at St. Omers all the time or that those he claimed to have travelled with were elsewhere. Mrs Groves was another witness and was asked by Langhorn if Oates stayed at her house as he said he had done in April 1678, which was for three or four nights. She said that she had never seen him before but on it being stated she ran a lodging house where many people have stayed in the last year, was unable to say that she recalled all the temporary lodgers there. However, she thought she would have known him. She mentioned others that had stayed there. It was suggested that Oates might have been in disguise. Mrs Grove's maid was asked who stayed there in April or May 1678 and she said it was only family members, Mrs Fitzherbert and a Master Strange.[79]

Langhorn then asked Oates how many were at the consult on 24 April and he believed there had been 18-20 in two or three rooms. The tavern's proprietor at that time was asked if she recognised Oates. She did not. Langhorn reminded the court that previously Oates said that there had been 50 at the meeting. She added, 'It is a small inconsiderable house there is not a room in that that will hold more than a dozen. I never remembered so great a company at one time, but once in all my seven years, and that was a Jury of the parish'. Three unidentified witnesses came into assert that the house had been known to cope with from 12-30 people.[80]

Langhorn had more questions for Oates. Oates had claimed he was poor but that he had spent £600-700 on his investigations currently. He said that no one would entrust one so impoverished as Oates with such a sum of money unless he was given it as a reward for giving evidence. He then asked Oates about his alleged dispersal of commissions. He replied he did not know who distributed them nor to whom, except one was to the Earl of Arundel's son. Langhorn said that earlier he had accused him of dispersing these commissions. The witnesses that Oates had previously called, including Sir Richard Barker and others, came forward again to testify that they had seen him in and out of disguise in London in March, April and May 1678.[81]

Langhorn gave a summing up speech in an attempt to demolish Oates' case, beginning with the fact that the St. Omers students all testified that Oates was there from December 1677-June 1678, to which the Lord Chief Justice replied, 'They are all papists and speak in a general cause'. Langhorn thought that this was very hard indeed. He added that it was fairly proved that Hilsley or the others mentioned did not come over with Oates, that he did not lodge at Groves' as he said he did. Therefore, 'if any of these points are clear to me, I think his testimony ought to be set aside'. He also attacked Bedloe's evidence.[82]

The Lord Chief Justice announced that the evidence against Langhorn 'depends upon the testimony of witnesses. The testimony that Oates gives against him amounts but to thus much'. Oates could not affirm that Langhorn was at the consult but that shortly afterwards he received news of it and praised their endeavours, and that he had commissions for a Catholic army in his office, one of which was for Lord Arundel's son. There was some doubt cast about Oates, 'if Mr Oates says true, all our lives and liberties, our King and religion, are at stake…the Plot is proved, as plain as the day, and that by Oates, and further than that, Oates' testimony is confirmed by that which can never be answered'. The jury made their decision; that Langhorn was guilty and so was sentenced to death.[83]

On 20 June the five Jesuits Fenwick, Whitebread, Gavan, Turner and Harcourt were hanged at Tyburn; Langhorn was hanged on 14 July, the King being reluctant to sanction his death. The 'plot' had claimed another six victims. Oates and the others had not had their testimonies doubted to the extent that judges and juries were unconvinced by their lies. Yet all this was to change very soon. The first seeds of doubt as to the veracity of Oates and others may well have been planted at this stage. Burnet wrote, 'These executions, with the denials of all that suffered, made great impressions on many…the behaviour and last words of those who suffered made impressions'.[84]

Oates and Bedloe reattested his allegations against the Queen on 24 June; those he had already provided the previous November.[85] One of the key trials of alleged plotters took place at the Old Bailey on 18 July 1679. Four men were on trial. Principal among these was Sir George Wakeman, physician to Queen Catherine of Braganza. Evelyn wrote of him 'whom I was well acquainted with, & take to be a worthy gent'.[86] There were three others, described by Evelyn as Benedictine monks. These were William Marshal, William Rumley and James Corker.

The trial was well attended. Evelyn wrote that he went early to it and noted that both the Bench was crowded and that there were 'innumerable spectators'.[87] The main charge was that they had conspired to murder the King, subvert the government, raise an army and to introduce Catholicism.[88]

The main witnesses against the accused men were Oates, now styling himself Dr, Bedloe 'a man of inferior note', Dugdale, Prance and Jenison. Unusually,

Dugdale was the first witness to give evidence, followed by Prance. Oddly, Oates was the third witness and he provided a lengthy testimony about Wakeman. He claimed that his knowledge began in July 1678 when Ashby, being ill, was given written instructions on how to recover. The writer of this medical advice was Wakeman, advising him to drink plenty of milk on a very regular basis. But he also wrote more:

> 'In this letter, Sir George Wakeman did write, that the Queen would assist him to poison the King'.

A group of fathers went with Oates to the Queen's chambers at Somerset House, and he heard the Queen say 'she would assist them in the propagation of the Catholic religion...and she would assist Sir George Wakeman in poisoning the King...' and later was present when Wakeman was offered £10,000 to kill the King. Oates said that Wakeman refused it, saying it was 'too little for so great a work'. So Whitebread authorised offering another £5,000 more; Wakeman accepted and this was recorded in an entry book.[89]

Wakeman had been seen by Oates in the transactions described above, but Wakeman reminded Oates that in the previous year he had told the council that he had never seen him before. Oates tried to explain this contradiction:

> 'I had been up two nights together, and the King was once willing to excuse me from staying for any further examination, and being so ill in respect of my intellectuals...but now I have a proper light whereby I may see a man's face I can say more to him'.[90]

Wakeman said that this was exactly the same as Oates had said in the Coleman trial. Oates now said that he had seen Wakeman in conjunction with the letter about poisoning and that 'he cannot deny it'. To which Wakeman replied:

'Cannot deny it! Yes, I hope you will be able to prove it. You said you never saw me before in my life, before you saw me in the council'.

Oates insisted he saw Wakeman at Ashby's chambers. Harcourt, Fenwick and Ireland had all been present with them. So Wakeman made the obvious reply, 'You will be sure to name those that can never be witnesses for me nor against these'; all three named witnesses having been recently executed.[91]

Oates said that he knew all of this prior to the Privy Council meeting of the previous year. Wakeman pressed him on if this was true then why did he not tell all on that occasion. The Lord Chief Justice also needed an answer from him and Oates replied:

> 'I can, by and by, give an answer to it, when it is proved by him, what I did say'.

He went on to accuse Corker of having a patent from Rome to be bishop of London and that he was privy to the plans by Langhorn and the Benedictine monks to raise funds for the conspiracy. As part of this, he went to Lampspring in Germany, in the summer of 1678. Further, whilst there he consented to the raising of such money and then went to Paris to meet with Louis XIV's confessor and English Catholics there. Oates knew this because he had read it in a letter addressed to either Father Hitchcot or Howard in London. He also saw Corker and Fenwick exchange money in London in June. Corker also distributed money given by the Queen to further the plot's aims.[92]

Oates was asked about the alleged meeting on 24 April. He said that Corker knew of it but opposed the selection of Pickering as the assassin. This was because Pickering was so often at mass that he might miss an opportunity to kill the King and so a layman would be a better choice for the role.[93] He was then asked about the two other defendants. He said that Marshal was present at another meeting when the £6,000 was agreed to be paid but was not turned over until a letter from Corker arrived. Marshal was not present at the alleged meeting but he did know about Pickering being selected as killer and agreed with Corker's view of his ineligibility.[94] Finally there was Rumley. Oates stated that 'He is a Benedictine monk or at least a lay brother'. He said that he knew of the £6,000 being raised and he did 'pray God it might have good success and that the Catholic cause might flourish once again in England'. On being asked if he could remember anything more about the prisoners, Oates said that he could not do so 'at present'.[95]

It was now time for the defendants to ask him questions. Rumley made Oates confirm that he (Rumley) was at the meeting about the money in August. Corker asked Oates where Lampspring is and how once there could he have met La Chaise. Oates replied that he only knew that Corker said he was going to Lampspring whereas he was going elsewhere and that this was common practice among Catholics to say one thing and go elsewhere. He asked about the patent for bishop and Oates said he did not know who gave it to him but recalled that he was jubilant about it and said he hoped it would come soon. He also recalled Corker being at a meeting when a joke was made about the King not seeing another Christmas. Marshal was also laying a bet about this.[96]

Marshal asked Oates how long he had known him and when he had seen him. Oates said he had seen him several times and had seen him officiate in Catholic services. He claimed to have known him for two years, but Marshal said he had never spoken to him. I only knew him by sight, Oates protested. He could also not be sure when he had last seen him, only that it had been at a Benedictine community in August. Oates added that he had been at another meeting there on 21 August in which Corker had approved the sending of commissions for the army of men in Ireland and approved of the murder of Ormonde. Rumley asked Oates which consults he was at in August and he replied he had been at two but not the last one. Oates was clearly flagging under the pressure for he declared

> 'My lord, I desire I may have leave to retire, because I am not well'.
> 'You must stay, Dr Oates, until after their defence is over'.
> 'If you desire any refreshment, you shall have it got for you'.[97]

After Bedloe was cross examined by the defendants, Oates had to answer additional questions. The first was from Wakeman, about the letter he allegedly wrote about the assassination plot. Ashby had read it and said there was nothing there about any plot. The letter was shown in court and Oates denied it was the one that he had read. Oates said that Ashby did not go to Bath for another ten days; other witnesses said that he had gone on the day after he received the note. Wakeman queried why Oates was adding more compared to what he had said about him in the previous year:

> 'I was so weak by reason of being up two nights together, one whereof was so very wet, and being hot, wet and cold all in a few hours' time, so that I thought it would cost me my life, not being used to such hard services, I did not charge Sir George so fully'.[98]

Wakeman asked Oates if he knew his handwriting concerning the letter he allegedly wrote about the poisoning and whether he wrote it. Oates was uncertain whether he knew this at the time of the House of Lords meeting. Nor could Oates be certain that he saw Wakeman sign it. He thought it was the same handwriting. Sir Philip Lloyd said that on 30 September, Oates had talked about a letter in which Wakeman had been nominated as the poisoner, but Wakeman denied it. It was also noted that at the earlier meeting, when Oates was asked, 'No, God forbid I should charge him with anything further I know no more against him', in contradiction to what he now was alleging. Oates protested that he was too weak at that earlier time but was told that it did need not much effort to say 'I saw a letter under Sir George's hand'.[99]

Wakeman attacked Oates' knowledge of him, as Oates once claimed he had never seen him and Oates had said that he had heard Wakeman named as the poisoner when Oates was at St Omers. Corker said that Oates and the others were men of disreputable backgrounds using lies that could not be proved or disproved. Both stressed that Oates once claimed not to know either man. Marshal said likewise, 'Mr Oates is a perfect stranger to me, and consequently hath nothing against me'. Marshal brought witnesses to show he was 50 miles away from London, at Tunbridge, when Oates said he saw him in London, so he could 'disprove Oates in his positive testimony'.[100]

Marshal added

> 'Mr Oates did not know me, neither as to my calling, conversation, words nor actions. He can bring no person, no man nor woman, that ever saw him in my company, nor took notice of our meeting together'.

The Lord Chief Justice went through the evidence. There was general evidence about the plot that was provided by Dugdale and Prance. Then there was specific evidence. This included Oates witnessing the letter written by Wakeman to Ashby. The judge was very sceptical about this, and indeed about the evidence against the others. He said, 'it is a very strange thing, if Dr Oates knew this of us, why did he not tell us before?' Oates' excuse about non recognition due to his weakness was also scorned, 'a man could not be so weak but he could have said, he saw a letter under his hand'. The jury was told to be very careful in their forthcoming decision.[101]

Their evidence was unimpressive, thought Evelyn, 'their testimony were not so pregnant, & I fear much of it from hearsay, but sworne positively to some particulars, which drew suspicion upon their truth, nor did circumstances so agree'.[102] The charge against Wakeman was that he had been hired for £15,000, £5,000 of which he had already received, to poison the King. Initially the witnesses were asked what they knew of the plot in general, and they gave the same evidence that they had given against Mr Langhorn. They then claimed no great acquaintance with Wakeman, but that his name had been seen in a book with such a proposal and his answer in it. There was also a letter, allegedly written by Wakeman to Ashby, and after giving medical advice, it then referred to the plot. Yet neither of these were seen as being good evidence and the writing in the former piece of evidence was not proved to be that of Wakeman.[103]

The defendants were given plenty of time to make their cases and to bring witnesses to testify on their behalf. Neither the lawyers nor the jury were convinced by the prosecution evidence and after 'a long & tedious trial of 9 hours' the jury brought in a verdict of not guilty.[104] A near contemporary historian wrote, 'the jury reflected that Sir George Wakeman must needing be very indiscreet to entrust him [Oates] with so great a secret'. They had taken an hour to discuss the matter so clearly it was not a straightforward decision to reach. Thomas Bramston, a chancery clerk, wrote 'But by this time the world began to understand Oates and the rest soe well that the jurie acquitted him'. But this is not so, because of the reception the jury and judges received once the news was known:

> 'But the common people would have all the papists hanged with more ado, and were much enraged against the Jury and Judges, and swore they were all turned Papists'.[105]

There was also much criticism of the witnesses. In particular the trial was not thought to have reflected well on Oates and Bedloe. Evelyn wrote, 'For my part, I do looke on Oates as a vaine, insolent man, puff'd up, with the favour of the Commons, for having discovered something really true'.[106] Burnet gave another reason for the verdicts, 'this was looked upon as the Queen's trial as well as Wakeman's and now the witnesses saw that they were blasted and they were enraged upon it, which they vented with much spite upon Scroggs'.[107]

Oates provided valuable evidence at the trial, 'swore he had brought him a commission, signed by the Pope, to be the paymaster of the army to be raisd against the King'. Along with his fellow informants, Dugdale and Turberville, 'they seemed soe positive in this and other dangerous evidence'.[108]

A man who attended the trial, on leaving it, was arrested, accused of being a priest. He was brought before Oates, who claimed he was one Dormer. As a priest of this name had been previously mentioned in a royal proclamation, he was sent to Newgate.[109] He was presumably released for later that year Oates claimed that he had seen Dormer talking to the Catholic Countess of Powys, though she denied this, but Oates' word carried sway over a member of the Catholic nobility and so Dormer was once more seized and imprisoned.[110]

He was not particularly effective in court on occasion. In November he was before the Middlesex Grand Jury in a case against Sir Thomas Preston, Peters and several priests. He quarrelled with the court's officers that one Ward had stolen the Bill against Lord Howard. He then said that he did not know the accused priests.[111]

Oates was seen as being relevant in other ways. When Sir Philip Lloyd, clerk of the court, was doubting Oates' validity, and whether the plot was even real, Oates accused him of complicity in it. He was backed up by four witnesses and a hostile commentator declared that Oates 'had got ready four shrewd coffee drinkers' and so Lloyd was suspended.[112] These four witnesses were probably cronies of Oates who would lie on his behalf.

An early biographer noted that at this time, 'This business, however, a little mollified the Doctor's arrogance' as he had spoken of Wakeman and others slightingly to men of distinction.[113] Despite the rebuff at the Wakeman trial, Oates was still seen as being useful. In early August he was given leave to go into the country apparently for his health's sake, and though he may have been suffering from the shock of the Wakeman acquittal there was another reason for his leaving London. He was given a commission to work with the sheriff and JPs of an unnamed county, but presumably one near to the capital, and for them to provide him with a guard if he desired such.[114] In the said county a 'committee of council' was held and there Oates charged two people, one for accepting bribes and one for corruption. However, at least one more witness was required to make each charge hold. It is not known who the accused where and what the outcome was, but it does show that Oates was being trusted with more than rooting out Catholic plotters; or it may have been a tactic to remove him from London.[115]

By the end of 1679 national politics were still in a state of flux. Charles dissolved Parliament in July and writs for another election were issued. In August a new Parliament was formed and again passed another Exclusion Bill. Parliament was prorogued several times and did not sit again until October of 1680.

Although he did not stand as a witness at another trial until 1680, Oates was busy in other ways in 1679. He, and fellow informants Bedloe, Prance and Dangerfield, were present at the examination of one Mr Brill, a Catholic priest, for his alleged involvement in the plot.[116] One Daniel MacCaree, an Irish priest, was arrested by a constable and was taken to a coffee house at Charing Cross on 25 August. Oates and Bedloe were summoned to see the man. Apparently 'as soon as he [Oates] saw MacCaree, he called him by his name, assuring him that to his knowledge he was a priest'. The constable then took MacCaree to Sir William Waller.[117] In the next month both Oates and Bedloe were called for to be examined about 'recent discoveries'.[118]

One Anne Price visited Oates with information about James, Monmouth and others, and Oates passed this on to Edmund Warcup, a London magistrate. Oates had also conferred with Shaftesbury about the plot. They had discussed how to reveal their new information and thought it better to do so in private before going public. Shaftesbury wished to impeach James for high treason.[119]

In the autumn of that year Oates spent some time in Oxford. It seems there was a possibility of him being actually awarded a doctorate of divinity there, but Thomas Halton, the Vice Chancellor, and Dr John Fell (1625-1686), bishop of Oxford, denied him such. One John Lovelace took Oates to a horse race at Woodstock on 14 September. He had Oates preach on a Sunday and a Tuesday. Oates once sent word to Halton, 'he would come and wait on him, not surprise him, for his degree' and Oates and some of the city's residents accused Halton as being Catholic.[120]

Later that year, Oates and Bedloe 'were got into a balcony in Cheapside and a great rabble about them: and as the Duke of York passed by they cryed out, "a pope, a pope"'. Upon which, one of the Duke's guards cocked his pistol, and rid back, saying "what factious rogues are these". Upon which they cryed "No Pope, no Pope God bless his highness". So the King's worthy evidence (Oates and Bedloe) sneaked away'.[121] On another occasion, apparently 'Oates had said publickly the Duke was possess'd with a devil, and that for the love he bore the Nation, he would make no scruple to kill him with his own hand if he could come at him, yet no notice was taken of it'.[122] Yet curiously in this year, at the Cider House at Meadow Lane, there was a dinner in which Oates, Bedloe, Tonge, Sir William Waller and James were present and presumably it was amicable enough.[123]

Several payments made to Oates in the autumn of 1679 provide evidence of his activity outside the courtrooms. On 31 October he saw an increase in his weekly allowance to £12 for having assisted witnesses and taking them by coach to the courtrooms. He was allowed the £84 17s he needed to pay his legal costs in the prosecution of Knox and Lane, for which see later, and this was granted on 26 November. It was said that Oates had been accused of 'very dangerous crimes' and that the prosecution was necessary 'in order to validate his evidence'. He received £100 for having identified three men as being Jesuit priests. Finally at the end of November he was given three books of accounts for the College of Jesuits in London taken from Mr Harcourt of Chester. This was so he could read through them and report his findings therein to the King in Privy Council a few days later.[124]

Oates did not go uncriticised throughout this year of his greatest fame. On 21 April there was evidence presented by Dr William Jones, Bedloe's physician. He told that a month ago a Dr Smith came to his lodgings at The Ball, Charing Cross. Smith told Jones, after enquiring if he knew Oates and Bedloe, and when Jones answered in the affirmative, he replied 'God damn them both. Why do you not poison them? You may have more money for that service than you know what to do withall'. He added on another occasion 'The plot was no plot at all'. Smith pleaded that he knew nothing of any plot against the two men, but he was gaoled. Nothing more seems to have come of this, however.[125]

Likewise, on 12 May Richard Child testified that Henry Lawson, a lawyer of St. Clement's Inn told him that 'he could not imagine a death could be bad for them'. He disbelieved the plot and said 'he did not believe that there were not two such Rogues in the World'. He added that Oates had been branded on his shoulder and then had escaped from Dover Castle. As with Smith he was gaoled but there is no record of any trial.[126]

In early November there were witnessed two sides to Oates. He was noted as preaching on Foster Lane, presumably at the still fire damaged St. Vedast's, just to the north east of where St. Paul's Cathedral was being rebuilt, 'where greate crouds of people, more to see than to heare, for some tell me his performance is not Extraordinary'. The latter conflicts with other accounts of his preaching but clearly Oates was seen as being of interest as a sight. However on 5 November, usually a day for demonstrations of anti-Catholicism to celebrate the God given deliverance of Protestant England for the gunpowder plot of 1605, both Oates and Shaftesbury were burnt in effigy at Temple Bar.[127]

Oates was not always on the side of the prosecution. There was an instance when he was the defendant and his past caught up with him. On 19 November 1679, as the Earl of Rochester wrote to Henry Saville, 'Mr Oates was Try'd two days ago for Buggery, and clear'd: The next day he brought his action to the King's bench, against his Accuser, being attended by the Earl of Shaftesbury, and other peers, to the number of seven, for the honour of the Protestant cause'.[128] Oates was not actually on trial for any offence at this time, the accusation being made against him in print only, but he naturally took offence at it and so sought legal redress; he was the plaintiff not the defendant.

The trial in question took place on Tuesday 25 November as Thomas Knox was accused of suborning William Osborne and John Lane, servants of Oates 'with great sums of money' into alleging that Oates was 'a person of wicked and vicious life', and accused 'Dr Oates of that horrid sin of sodomy' and claimed that Oates had 'made an assault on the said John Lane'. In more detail, Lane told a magistrate that after Oates had sent the other servants away to the royal chapel in Whitehall, he had Lane begin to dress him in breeches, stockings and morning gown and took him into his bedroom:

> 'there he told the Informant, That he must take his Penance, whereupon he made the Informant lye down upon the Bed with his breeches down, and gave

> him nine lashes with a lash of three small Ropes with a knot at each end which he usually kept in his pocket for that Purpose (which usage the informant durst not deny lest he should call to the Sentinel take hold of him and say to the said Sentinel, That the Informant should have offered Violence to him, which was his usual way of threatening the Informant, if he durst at any time resist his Cruel Usage and after he had severely lash'd him, he took the said Informant by the hand, and clapt his hand eagerly about his Neck and kiss'd him, and put his hand into the Cod piece of the Informant's Breeches, and took him by the Privy-members, and said that he would be Friends with the Informant, and at the same time when Mr Oates' hand was in the Informant's Breeches, and held him by the members, the said Mr Oates unbutton'd the Informant's Breeches with the other hand, and commanded and forced with an angry Countenance with his hand the Informant to lye down upon his Belly upon the Bed, and the said Mr Oates lay'd down by the Informant's side, and told the Informant, that he had a mind to see whether his backside were flea'd enough, and when he saw that it look'd red, he took the Informant about the middle, and kiss'd him in a lascivious manner, and at the same time the said Mr Oates thrust his Belly against the said Informant's side, and did with his naked Privy-Members press the said Informant's Body hard: and that the said Informant doth further upon his Oath declare, had not a Woman that was sweeping the next Room heard a noise (which made him think the rest of the Servants were come from prayers) he would grievously have abused the Body of the Informant'.[129]

Oates took John Lane and Thomas Knox to court, to be there accused of perjury. Clearly, 'if he were such a one, of little credit could be given to such a man'. This is the first time that it is known that this formal accusation was made against Oates. Knox and Lane said that they were not guilty of perjury.[130]

There were other accusations. Oates was said to have insulted the Queen, by saying, on seeing her going past his windows, 'Where is our Gammer, or our Dame Short Arse [sic] going now?' On the other hand, Osborne claimed, contrary to Lane's allegations, 'he hath layen several nights with Mr Oates, but never found he offered the least lascivious or indecent action to this Examinant, but did exhort this examinant from time to time to live a good course of life'.[131]

Robert Radford told how Robert Lane, the servant's father, that 'Dr Oates did attempt his son many times to do such and such things to him that was in the way of Buggery'. Radford tended to disbelieve this statement, however, believing Lane to be a liar. It was also claimed that Lane had been bribed £1,000 to bring the story to the courts so as to discredit Oates' testimonies. When Knox and Lane were found guilty of perjury against Oates 'At which the people gave a great shout'. Oates' popularity was as yet undimmed.[132]

Knox had earlier produced evidence that Oates and Bedloe had met in Oates' chamber to discuss how they could bring about Danby's downfall. Mrs Blake recalled a conversation where Lane told her: 'I was Mr Oates' man and he would have buggered me. And he did make complaint for want of linen'. Mr Withins, counsel for Knox, said 'I think they have served the nation too well to be vilified here' about Oates and Bedloe. Mrs Lane said that her son told her than Oates 'used him uncivilly'. Her daughter Mary Lane referred to her brother talking about Oates' 'beastliness'.[133] Lane and Knox were found guilty of perjury and were fined (200 and 100 marks respectively) and gaoled.[134]

Indeed, a contemporary newspaper, on reporting the trial, concluded that its result had been to Oates' credit, 'The honour that Dr Oates got by his Tryal is of greater concernment than some may imagin: Next day he appeared at the bar and demanded judgement on those convicted and His majesty gave order for the Treasury to reimburse Oates' costs'.[135] Some believed Oates and concluded 'This matter highly reflects upon the late lord Treasurer, proofs being made yt my lady Danby furnished all the money & yt one of ye conspirators should say. 'We must stand fast for my Lord Treasurer unless his head in our hands'.[136] Danby was an enemy of Oates and had bribed men to speak against him. In the following year, when the Duke of Buckingham was accused of sodomy, a charge which looked as if it might stick, it was observed that if this were so, then it might cast a new light on the Knox and Lane case vs Oates.[137] This may have been the first time that Oates was accused of such practices, but it was not to be the last.

The informants and magistrates sometimes socialised together. There is a reference in October of this year that Oates and Dugdale, together with Warcup and others, having dinner. Warcup reported that there was no talk about 'matters', however. Even so, it is noteworthy that these men sought each other out and that at times may have discussed 'matters' as that mutual interest was what brought them together.[138]

Oates' true political nature became more into focus in October 1679; and he was not a staunch defender of the Stuart monarchy as he might have appeared to have been by his public utterances. His radical sympathies were already known to William Smith through his tavern talk of 1678 and may have been imbibed from his radical father. On 21 October 1679 it was reported that 'Mr Oates sayd it would never be well in England till monarchy were elective', which rather went against the grain of the Stuart monarchy, which claimed divine and hereditary right, as it now was and put him into sympathy with the likes of Shaftesbury and other opposition figures. This would become more apparent in the following years.[139]

Oates' mother visited him in December 1679 and stayed with him at York Buildings. Apparently 'The old woman, much unlike her husband and son, was look'd upon by all that knew her to be a very pious and vertous woman'. Apparently she said 'Indeed I do not like it well'.[140] This is presumably a reference to her son's situation in life.

Oates, as a classic nouveau riche, wanted to have for himself an impressive genealogy and coat of arms. One Major Fisher was employed by Oates with the heraldry. Messrs Wright and Black arrived and searched for records into possible high born ancestors and found none. Eventually a coat of arms of a chevron between three crosses was designed and a Sir Otes Swinford, husband of Lady Katherine Swinford, descended from John of Gaunt, Duke of Lancaster, were discovered. Apparently 'This the doctor believed, and joyfully received and most triumphantly engraved it on all his plate and in a large soul ring'.[141]

Yet despite all this and 'for he was rich, set up for a solemn housekeeper, and lived up to his Quality' and 'he lived in all the Plenty and Luxury, as before at Whitehall', his behaviour was less salubrious, as the hostile Francis North wrote:

> 'His common conversation was larded with lewd oaths, Blasphemy, Saucy, Atheistical and every way offensive Discourse. He delighted in occasions, such as respecting of others, to mouth out blasphemous speeches'.

In appearance he was described as follows:

> 'He put on an Episcopal Garb (except the lawn sleeves) silk Gown and Cassock, Great Hat, Sattin Hatband and Rose, long scarf, and was called, or most blasphemously called himself "Saviour of the Nation". Whoever he pointed at, was taken up and committed, so that many people got out of the way...The very breath of him was pestilential'.[142]

He was also seen as dangerous because 'Oates would never say all he knew; for that was not consistent with the uncertainty of events. For he could not foresee what evidence there might be occasion for'.[143]

It is noteworthy that, in light of his later denunciations of James, that in the September of this year, Oates claimed to be on his side. Sir Thomas Williams discussed this with him, and Oates said that James was innocent, as he had said in his statements of 1678, and was right to leave the country, claiming rogues would accuse James. It would be a 'dishonest thing' to have yet another attempt by the Commons to bring about exclusion 'designed only to breed confusion'. He offered to speak to James in person, but this was declined. Oates was also critical of his apparent ally, Bedloe, 'a beast of yt nature'.[144]

Yet there was further criticism of Oates. In a small and unnamed village in Dorsetshire, Catholics and Protestants discussed the whole case in a public house. Apparently they 'spoke with all scorn and contempt imaginable of Mr Oates and his evidence'.[145] Later that year there was published an apparently anti-Oates pamphlet, 'Ballad on Dr Oates', being sold by one Turner, as well as pamphlets supportive of Catholics.[146] More importantly, the King, always a sceptic when it came to Oates, told Warcup, 'bid Oates meddle with his own matters and speak truth'.[147]

Chapter Six

New Plots for Old, 1680-1683

Oates was called upon to take other action in the anti-Catholic campaign. On 3 January 1680 he and Bedloe were asked to attend Sir Creswell Levinz, the new Attorney General, in order to deal with priests. However, they did not want to have any dealings with the Lord Chief Justice, Sir William Scroggs, because of the way he had treated them at the Wakeman trial. They finally agreed to discuss this before a board. That meeting occurred two weeks' later, when Scroggs appeared alongside Oates and Bedloe. Scroggs was hostile towards them, stating that no one could doubt that either would do anything against anyone for money. Oates asked what Scroggs was paid and then laid 20 charges against the judge. He and Bedloe wanted to have Scroggs prosecuted in the King's name and to have the King's counsel to assist them in this. He even made an outrageous accusation, 'Dr Oates told ye Lds of ye Council yt he wou'd not positively say it, but he believed he shou'd be able to prove, yt my Ld Ch. J. danced naked'.[1] However, in the event, Scroggs was acquitted of any wrongdoing.

After several months from being absent from a trial, Oates was back on familiar ground and was required to provide evidence in another treason trial. This was on 17 January 1680 at the Old Bailey. The defendants were Lionel Anderson, William Russell, Charles Parris, Henry Starkey, James Corker, William Marshal, Andrew Lumsden and David Kemish. All were accused of being priests, which was a criminal offence, but was difficult to prove. They all pleaded not guilty and Thomas Dangerfield, another informant, was the first to give evidence against them as being involved in the plot.[2]

Anderson asked Oates a question; could he prove that he was a priest? He replied, 'My lord, I saw his letters of orders' and soon after, that Anderson had confessed as much to him, and that he was an Englishman and the son of a gentleman. Anderson said that it was not true that Oates had earlier heard him saying mass. Oates reiterated this, however.[3]

The court moved next against Corker and Oates was asked to give his evidence against him as being a priest. Oates said, 'My lord, he has said mass at Somerset House, and before the Proclamation and Declaration of 1674, made against the Catholics, he was one of the Queen's priests, he is a Benedictine monk… and I have heard him say mass at the Savoy'. He had seen him in a monk's habit giving the sacrament. He must have been a priest, said Oates because only priests can give the sacrament and further Corker was designated as bishop of London and only priests could be made such. Oates had seen the patent for making Corker so.[4]

Oates swore that he had heard Corker say mass in 1677 and 1678 and on other occasions. About a dozen times in all. Once he had heard him say mass at Somerset House to 'a church full'. He was asked by Corker, if he had any other witnesses who could corroborate what he had said. How could he do that, said the judge, with a whole church full?[5]

Marshal was the next defendant. Oates stated what he knew that was pertinent to the charge:

> 'I have heard him say mass in the Savoy, and I have seen him in that posture that the priests are in when they say absolution'.

He had seen him in Benedictine robes, consecrate the host and had known him as a priest since 1677. Marshal said that Oates was out by a year in his last statement. He asked Oates about where he had seen him. Oates said he had seen him at the Savoy and on a few other occasions. Marshal asked him to be more precise. Oates said he would and came up with 'several times last summer' and clarified that this was before he went to Spain and before the plot was discovered.[6]

He pinned this down to April 1678 when he was allegedly absent from St. Omers and also in the June of that year. Marshal said that from April to July 1678 he was not within 60 miles of London. Oates replied that he 'could not speak positively' but declared he had seen him officiating at mass in the past twelvemonth. This would have been after he returned to England in June and before he exposed the plot in September. He repeated that he had seen him in 1677 both before and after the Spanish trip. Marshal said that Oates could not prove that he had seen hm as priest at the Savoy. 'Let Mr Oates be positive in any one thing and we will disprove him', Marshal said.[7]

Marshal said that he could prove he was not in London in the summer of 1678, and then Oates became vague, 'I am not so positive in that my lord', but reiterated about seeing Marshal as priest in 1677. Eventually Oates said that he had seen Marshal say mass in the middle of August 1678 and that on that occasion he went along with Pickering to the Savoy. Marshal called Ellen Rigby, who was housekeeper to Corker and Marshal, as a witness and she testified to having seen Oates receive alms several times from Pickering in the summer. Oates said that if she was truthful then why did she not give evidence in Pickering's defence.[8]

Marshal claimed to have only arrived in London on 24 August 1678. He also said that he had been found not guilty in a previous trial and that Oates was not a credible witness. 'Now he pursues his malice' Marshal said. Scroggs said that both Bedloe and Oates gave positive testimony of Marshal saying mass. If you believe them, he addressed the jury, you must find Marshal guilty.[9]

Russell was the next defendant and Oates testified first against him, 'My lord, this is Russell, went by the name of Napper [mentioned in Oates' 81 articles of 1678 as a prospective bishop in the Catholic new order], and is a Franciscan friar and I heard him say mass several times at Wild House'. He was wearing a priests' habit and he heard him say mass twenty times in 1678 at that address. Oates recalled receiving the sacrament from him but Russell said he had never seen Oates before in his life, 'more know Jack pudding than Jack Pudding knows'. Oates added that he had heard Russell say mass at Wild House in November 1677. Prance supported Oates' evidence. Marshal said he never went there prior to 1678.[10]

Parris was the next defendant. Oates said of him, 'My lord, he is a reputed priest and hath said mass several times, I have heard him say mass at Wild House, not in the public chapel but in another room'. He had also seen him say it twice at Mr Paston's house and between 1677-1678. At Wild House it was on a Saturday. He was in a priest's habit and consecrated the host. Parry asked him about dates but again Oates was vague, 'I cannot confine myself to a month' and 'I knew him to be a priest but I had little acquaintance with him'.[11]

Oates was sure he was the man, however, but when he knew him he went by the name of Johnson. Parry denied he ever used that name. Prance said he knew him by the name, too, which Parry again denied. Parry asked Oates who was the ambassador at the time he knew him, a question which went unanswered. Parry also had witnesses who attested he was at Windsor in 1677-1678 when Oates said he saw him in London. He also pointed out a contradiction in Oates' statements about seeing him. Scroggs pointed out that two witnesses were positive against Parry.[12]

Henry Starkey was the next defendant before the bar. Oates was asked if he knew of Starkey being a priest and Oates replied, 'My lord, Mr Starkey is a priest, and I once heard him say mass at Mr Paston's. This was three years ago; he wore priest's habit, he received the sacrament and consecrated the host. Starkey asked him what exactly he wore and Oates said it was 'a thing about his neck, and a surplice, and a thing about his arm'. Starkey strongly opposed this:

> 'I know you not, and I perceive you neither know what a priest's habit is, nor the difference between his habit and his ornaments. A priest's habit is a cassock down to the ground and a side cloke. The ornaments of a priest are not a surplice but an albe that falls to the ground and other things besides it'.

Starkey also asked Oates how he knew he had said mass or how he knew that he was in holy orders. Prance then gave evidence against Starkey.[13]

Finally there was Andrew Lumsden. As ever, Oates led the way as prosecution witness when asked.

> 'I heard him say mass. He is a Dominican friar, as I remember. I heard him say mass 20 times at Wild House'.

Furthermore, he saw Lumsden consecrate the host, take the sacrament and heard confessions. He saw him in the summer of 1678 and 'Mr Lumsden knows me well enough'. Lumsden denied it all. 'Truly I do not know that I ever saw him or conversed with him in my life'. Dugdale and Prance gave evidence and Oates added 'He is the Procurator General of the kingdom of Scotland' and had heard him admit that he was a priest 20 times. Prance thought he was an Irishman but Oates said he was Scottish.[14]

More evidence was given, there was a slight summing up and the jury found each man guilty. They were all sentenced to death, but none of the sentences were carried out.[15] This was the second time that any of the defendants in a trial in which Oates was one of the witnesses escaped with their lives. Yet they still had all been found guilty and so despite the failure against Wakeman and the other three, Oates was still a lethally effective witness and credible to juries.

Oates was still a significant player. Robert Walsh, in February 1680, was in Sir Leoline Jenkins' presence, along with Oates. The latter ordered Walsh away 'saying that Walsh was a convicted papist'. Although he obeyed, he later complained that that behaviour had been 'an affront and a disgrace'.[16]

Oates was involved in other anti-Catholic activity. On being informed about Catholic activity in Mrs Beddingfield's house in Hammersmith, allegedly a private nursery to instruct the daughters of Catholic nobility and gentry into Catholicism, he went to the Lords of Council for them to provide him with a warrant, a magistrate, a Messenger and officers. He went with Waller and his own servants, armed. They broke three doors down and found an old lady teaching some girls. Oates took some Catholic regalia which was of value. As ever, monetary gain was always one of Oates' motivations, though under the sanctimonious cloak of higher motives.[17]

As in 1679 Oates was still in demand as a preacher. On Sunday 25 January he 'preached an Excellent Sermon at St. Botolph's Aldgate to great Satisfaction of a very numerous Auditory who were then present'. One month later he was at Tonge's church on Foster Street, preaching at the festival day of the Goldsmiths' Company using 2 Chronicles 26 verse 5 as his text 'As long as he sought the Lord, God made him so prosper'. Apparently 'he had a very numerous Auditory'.[18]

Oates was challenged again in this year. Oates accused the Rev. Adam Elliott, a fellow student from St. John's College, Cambridge and now an Anglican vicar in Ireland, of being a Jesuit spy, alleging that he was 'one of the most mischievous wicked men in the world...had more malice in him than all the Jesuits who were hanged...a Jesuit who is no Christian but a Turk'. He added that Elliott was a Muslim (he had actually been enslaved for a time by Muslims). On Elliott's being in London, Oates reported this to the King, who told him to obtain a warrant from Sir William Waller, which he did and then confronted Elliott.[19]

Yet Oates did not have Elliott arrested. The latter stated that this was not out of any change of heart but that he feared Elliott had powerful friends who would make life worse for him. So Oates took Elliott to his own house. Oates then recalled Elliott from their university days. Oates told Elliott that he had heard that he had said mass at Somerset House, but Oates now told him that he now believed this to be not so. He also said that he had heard in Rome that Elliott was a priest. Elliott recalled that this was 'a piece of such intolerable impudence'. Oates then contradicted himself and let Elliott walk free 'but of his cowardice and fear' and was not 'the effect of his Repentance or good nature'.[20]

Elliott stated his strong views about Oates, 'The most notorious Salamanca Dr Titus Oates, after having signaliz'd his prodigious parts, by the Destruction of several eminent persons and hazarding the lives of God knows how many more'. He later wrote that Oates was 'an indocile Blockhead, that could never be brought to turn three lines of English into tolerable Latin'.[21]

When Elliott was back in Ireland, he learnt that 'Oates' testimony was in so great credit then, that it was judg'd a crime equal to Blasphemy or Treason to call it into question: so that even my friends and intimate acquaintances were at a loss what to think of me'. Dissenters insulted him and a captain tried to arrest him as 'a popish priest and a Turk'. Elliott told him that 'Oates was a great lying Rogue' but was told 'do not blaspheme the venerable doctor' and he was arrested and in court was fined £200 and was gaoled.[22] Even after his release, Elliott claimed that Oates had told others that he was corrupt and debauched.[23]

This seems like the case reported as having occurred on 16 March 1680. The newspaper reported that a man had been indicted for alleging saying that Oates 'was a Rogue, and the priests that were executed on his evidence dyed martyrs or words to that effect'. There were two witnesses to this and one was a clergyman. Many attended the trial and the defendant was found guilty, fined £200 and not being able to pay was gaoled.[24]

Other priests were brought before the magistrates in London on Oates' evidence. On 25 March, Edward Turner was one, from the evidence of Oates and Stephen Dugdale.[25] On 3 May, Charles Parris was another and was later sentenced to death. On 11 May 1680, Alexander Lumsden was yet another such. Other priests, John Fleming, James Baker/Hesketh and Morrice Gifford/Baker, were brought forth likewise a week later, though Oates does not seem to have been a witness in any of these further three cases.[26] Henry Neville, a Catholic, was accused by Oates of carrying letters overseas for sinister purposes and so was sent to Newgate in early 1680. He was also accused by Oates as carrying £2,500 for the Jesuits.[27]

Oates took time to attack his enemies. In May 1680, he took his revenge on Norwood, whom he had clashed with in Hastings in the 1670s and thereafter. Apparently 'Oates complains of Norwood's having abused him and endeavoured to take away his reputation'. Oates tried to suggest that Norwood had been to see the five Catholic lords ensconced in the Tower since 1678 and thus to prove Norwood's confederacy with them. Norwood denied this and so he remained in the custody of a King's Messenger.[28]

Despite five Catholic lords being gaoled in 1678, the first peer to be tried, nearly two years later, was Roger Palmer (1634-1705), the Earl of Castlemaine, husband of one of Charles II's former mistresses. This trial took place at the King's Bench court on 23 June 1680. Oates, as often was the case, was the first to give evidence. He stated that he had returned from Spain to England in November 1677, with letters from the fathers there. One was addressed to Castlemaine and though Oates did not deliver it, he knew the contents of it, though he had not mentioned this previously in 1678. This was because the priests showed it to Oates. The contents of the letter were apparently:

> 'That the fathers in Spain were very zealous to concur with the fathers in England in the design; which was the subversion of the government, altering the religion and the destruction of the King'.[29]

When Oates went to St. Omers, later in that year, he claimed to have seen confirmation that Castlemaine had received the letter. He was further questioned and said that one Armstrong from Valladolid gave him the letter and he gave it in turn to the provincial in London. He was privy to the incoming letters at St. Omers and that is how he knew Castlemaine acknowledged its receipt. In it, Castlemaine expressed his pleasure that the fathers in Spain had every confidence in him. Oates added that Castlemaine was in London a few days after the great consult of 24 April. He hoped that an agreement could be made with the monks in Germany. He heard this from Castlemaine because he was seen as a trusted servant.[30]

Oates added that in June 1677 he was in London and saw Castlemaine and Langhorn together and he went with them to Fenwick's chambers (being dead neither could deny this and Oates had never hitherto mentioned this). The conspiracy was being discussed. They talked about killing the king and the advances to be made for the furtherance of Catholicism. In particular, Oates recalled what Castlemaine said, 'Now he should be revenged for the injuries done to him'. This was an allusion to the peer being cuckolded by the King taking his wife, Barbara, as a mistress and making her pregnant several times.[31]

Castlemaine was now allowed to question Oates and he first asked him to repeat his narrative. Oates told how he went to Valladolid in April 1677, returned to London in November of that year, was at St. Omers in December, at Liege in March and back to London in April 1678. Castlemaine quizzed him about precise times and Oates, as on similar previous occasions in court, became vague, 'My lord, it is now two years ago or better, and I can't remember every particular time'. He said he was in London a few days before the consult but did not charge Castlemaine as being at the meeting. Castlemaine then asked him about the meeting preceding the time spent at Fenwick's rooms. He asked Oates when it was and if Castlemaine had a servant with him and what form of transport the peer had with him, Oates said that he could not remember or did not notice. He was then asked about the two hour conversation at Fenwick's. Oates replied that it concerned college revenues and the attempt to contact Father La Chaise for funds.[32]

Oates declared that Castlemaine's letters were full of the need to reintroduce Catholicism. He said that many such passed through his hands. The Lord Chief Justice said, 'I wish you had one that was of moment' and Oates replied, 'It cannot be expected my lord, that I would have them'. Castlemaine asked Oates about his acquaintanceship. Oates insisted it began on the night at Fenwick's chambers. He could not remember if they ever met again after that night. Oates added that he had heard Castlemaine discuss divorce proceedings. He added that there were letters discussing the support for his divorce from Barbara. Oates then wanted to leave the court but was told no and to stay as Dangerfield gave evidence.[33]

Later Castlemaine brought Oates' activities in Hastings from 1675 to the court's attention. He said 'please to call Mr Parker, who will shew you what kind of a man Mr Oates is'. He repeated the case and after Parker could prove his innocence of the charge of buggery brought against him by Oates, the witnesses 'all looked upon Mr Oates as a detestable man'. This was evidence of Oates' malice, Castlemaine argued. However, the lawyers argued over whether this case was currently relevant to the proceeding trial. There was also reference to Oates' accusation against Parker's father and the ensuing hearing in privy council where the case was dismissed and 'the council sent Oates away with the greatest contempt'.[34]

Evidence was also brought against Oates about him being at St. Omers during the time he was allegedly in London in April 1678. Several recalled his presence there but Oates denied it. Castlemaine refuted that he had been seeking a divorce because, as a Catholic, it would have been virtually impossible. The attorney general finally summed up the prosecution case; that Oates and Dangerfield had testified against Castlemaine, and that 'What is said against Mr Oates signifies nothing'. The Lord Chief Justice stated that Oates' evidence boiled down to the letter to Castlemaine from St. Omers and the receipt from him, (neither of which could be produced) and the conversation at Fenwick's. Despite accusations against Oates' probity, nothing could be proved against him, but Dangerfield was another matter as he had a verifiable criminal record. He added that Oates' and Dangerfield's testimonies did not agree with one another. And, in a case of treason, two witnesses were required but here only one appeared to be in the right, at best. The jury found him not guilty.[35]

This was another setback against Oates. Perhaps because of this acquittal, Oates' usefulness was being seen as being in decline, for on 30 June his weekly allowance of £12 was reduced to £3 a week, which would have cut what he could spend significantly, but was still twice what a skilled worker would earn in a week. The other informers also saw their allowances cut as well at this time. However, by the end of November, in the run up to another trial, it was restored to £10 together with an allowance for food. In May he had also received two one-off payments, of £10 and of £30, the first for the discovery of Catholics and the other for unspecified services.[36]

Oates had other concerns. On 10 August, Simpson Tonge told the Privy Council that the Popish plot was a forgery concocted by Oates and his late father (he had died earlier in 1680, having done little more to actively further the investigation against the alleged plot).[37] Despite Tonge's associations with Oates in 1677-1678, Burnet wrote 'They had quarrelled afterwards; and Tonge came to have a very bad opinion of Oates upon what reason I know not. He knew of no subornation in that matter and that he was guilty of none himself'.[38] Five days later, he brought one Cooper, a former servant to Dr Tonge, to the Privy Council. This was so Cooper could swear that Captain Samuel Ely of the Guards could have bribed or corrupted Tonge's son into saying that the plot was an invention of Oates and Bedloe. Mrs Fitzgerald was also brought over with him to say that Ely had bribed her.[39]

A rumour was repeated in a newsletter in August that Oates had married the niece of Lord Shaftesbury.[40] This was a yet another pointer to his close association with the opposition peer. It was untrue.

Oates was also busy outside the court rooms. On 17 September it was noted that fourteen Irish priests and others were in London and Oates was entertaining them, even to the extent of providing them with shoes. He introduced them to Shaftesbury as they could be potential witnesses for an alleged plot in Ireland. Yet at least one observer noted 'I cannot hear that any of them is of any credit'.[41] Oates also had concerns about the number of Irish priests, claiming 800 were in London and they would 'give great apprehensions to Parliament when they meet'. According to Oates, 'walks in St. James' Park are so full of them that Mr Oates thought himself in another country, but durst not walk there, being in danger of his life'. At this time he also gave evidence against Captain Ely and one Choqueux, the King's firework maker, though a Catholic, but there is no evidence that either man was brought to trial.[42]

The privy council meeting was on 24 September to discuss Oates' complaint against Simpson Tonge. The latter was described by witnesses as 'a rude fellow and a common thief, abandoned by his father for his debauchery and that he would have reconciled himself to the Clerk of the Records to get a subsistence'. At the said meeting it was stated that the young Tonge was not even in England during the genesis of the plot so could know nothing. He wanted hundreds of pounds for his discovery, but 'he was found in many lies maybe denied what he himself declared'. He said that Lane and his wife had encouraged him.[43]

Another critic of Oates at this time was one Captain Thomas Bickley, who at a public meeting in Chichester, apparently said that 'Dr Oates was a very bad man, and it had been better he had never been'. When this came to Oates' ears, action was taken and a month later Bickley was hauled before the Lords to explain himself. However, as there was only one witness and they not certain, no action could be taken against him. In the circumstances, Oates had no choice but to forgive Bickley, who was then discharged.[44]

The second exclusion parliament finally met on 21 October 1680, to much support from many of the people of London. They were no more favourable to the King than the Parliament of the previous year and again called for James to be excluded from the line of succession, bringing in a second exclusion Bill in November. It was defeated in the Lords on 15 November. The political crisis was ongoing and was yet to be resolved as neither side was willing to step down from the confrontation.

As ever, it was not all plain sailing for Oates as not everyone agreed with him. Alexander Pare, a Westminster bricklayer, 'with the intention of bringing the same Titus Oates and William Bedloe to odium and infamy…spoke these scandalous and malicious words…"Mr Oates and Mr Bedloe are as great rogues as ever rob'd on the highway"'.[45]

Money was always one of Oates' concerns. On 9 November 1680 he wanted the House of Lords to petition the King that he had a larger allowance as at the moment he had but £12 per week to cover all his expenses.[46] He also tried to claim reward money for discovering the plot as did others, as well as for having found illicit Catholic correspondence and papers.[47]

On 27 November, William Russell/Napper, a priest, was before the magistrates on Oates' evidence and that of Miles Prance, for being a priest in England. He was later tried by a jury and found guilty and was sentenced to death.[48]

The most socially illustrious defendant to be put on trial was Viscount Stafford, which occurred in December 1680. Stafford was one of the five Catholic lords who had been named by Oates in 1678 as leading members of the plot and who had been incarcerated in the Tower of London since then. On 30 November, the 66-year-old William Howard, first Viscount Stafford, was brought to Westminster Hall for the first day of his trial before his peers. The charge was one of high treason, that he had been 'agitated by a Restless zeal, to promote what you call the Catholick Cause'. Due to the peer's age he was allowed to sit, and he did.[49] This was also the only trial in this series to last for more than one day; it was heard over several days.

The details of the plot were then relayed; about the plan to kill the King and to reintroduce Catholicism in England by force. Stafford's answer was 'he is not guilty of all or any of the offences charged against him'.[50]

Serjeant Maynard led the case for the prosecution and made reference to Oates' part in it. 'When that Oats first made a Discovery, it seems it had not that weight, that we think now it will with your lordships'.[51] He talked of a great many other matters, ranging from those in the reign of Elizabeth I to the gunpowder plot. There was even reference to the Knox and Lane case against Oates to try and discredit him as a worthy witness. He said that there was much evidence that Stafford had been seen with the other Jesuits in discussing how to kill Charles II.[52]

Oates was called as a witness and he gave an account of his entry into the Catholic Church in 1677, meeting Coleman, his discovery of 'the plot' and his journeying to France.[53] The evidence he initially gave did not directly concern Stafford, but was there to prove that there had been a plot. It was on the second day that he was called as a witness again, where he was asked to be more specific. 'Pray speak your knowledge of my Lord Stafford's involvement being engaged in the design' and this time he spoke about what he claimed he knew about Stafford. It was when he was in Spain in 1677 that he came across several letters written by Stafford in which the peer 'did assure the Jesuits in Spain that were of the Irish Nation, how zealous he should appear in promoting the Catholic design' and that he was working towards reconciling the different Catholic factions in England.[54]

Oates then said that in 1678 he found additional correspondence where Stafford was critical of Coleman's openness. Furthermore, another letter told that Stafford 'received a commission from him [Coleman] to pay for an army that would be raised to promote the Catholic interest'. Then Stafford told Fenwick that he was going to go to Staffordshire, Shropshire and Lancashire to see how much Catholic support there would be there for an insurrection. Stafford would be the army's paymaster (this had been stated in Oates' statements in 1678). He also talked to the Duke of Norfolk and Lord Arundel about the plot and that Lord Peterborough was also involved. When at Fenwick's, Stafford was known as Howard of Effingham.[55] There were then supplementary questions to Oates:

> 'Were you at Fenwick's when Lord Stafford came to his chamber?'
> 'Yes my lords'.
> 'Look upon Lord Stafford. Is he the same person?'
> 'It is the same gentlemen that came there under the name Howard of Effingham'.
> 'And he took the commission?'
> 'Yes he did so'.
> 'And he promised to effect it?'
> 'Yes. And he then said he was going down to the countrey, and he did not doubt that at his return, Grove should do the business'.

It was Stafford who said all this, and he also wrote a letter to St. Omers. Oates also saw Stafford in June to July 1678, talking about advancing the Catholic cause and also speaking disrespectfully about the King, uttering 'He has deceived us a great while and shall do so no longer'. After confirming that it was Stafford who spoke these words and at Fenwick's, Oates then said that he could not remember anything else at present. He was asked about the content of the letters that Stafford wrote. Oates thought it was about money and on private business.[56]

It was now time for Stafford to put some questions to Oates. He asked where Fenwick lived at the time Oates saw him there; at his lodgings in Drury Lane, Oates said. Stafford then said

> 'I will submit to anything, if I ever saw this man [Fenwick] or heard of him till the Discovery of the Plot'

Oates replied

'He came to him by the name of Thompson'.

Stafford said that the only man of that name that he knew was an English merchant in Brussels and he was not a Jesuit. Oates said that this was untrue but Stafford said it was true. Stafford also said that previously Oates claimed never to have seen him previously, compared to now when he said he had seen him receive the commission from Fenwick.

'I never said any such thing', Oates now said.
'I will willingly dye if I ever saw this doctor before in my life'.
'I excuse my lord for that, for I was in another habit and went by another name'.
'I never saw his face, nor knew him, nor Fenwick, nor Thompson'.[57]

Oates also claimed Stafford went to France in 1676 or 1677 about reconciling differences between Catholics, but Stafford said he had never written to any Jesuits.[58]

Next day was 2 December and Oates was called by Stafford to be cross examined by him and was asked when he first saw him; Oates replied that it was at Fenwick's, on Drury Lane in June 1678 when he saw Stafford being given the commission as paymaster general, to Howard of Effingham, as Oates had read it. Stafford replied:

'I declare to your Lordships in the presence of God, I never saw this man in my life. I never went by any other name…I never heard of Mr Fenwick the Jesuit…this is as true as I am alive'.[59]

The details of Stafford's arrest were read out and Oates was asked about his examination about Stafford in the past and he recalled these papers. Oates swore that the contents of what he had said was true. He read it out, about the revelation of the plot and Stafford's role in it which has already been recounted.[60]

Stafford discussed Oates accusing the Queen of being involved in the plot, and said of Oates:

'he is clearly perjured and so not to be believed…I do challenge Dr Oats at the Day of Judgement to say if he ever saw me in my life'.[61]

Next day Oates was called again by Stafford to answer his questions;

'He did say, he being a minister of the Church of England, did seemingly go over to the Church of Rome… I desire he might answer that first'.
'Yes, I did say, I did but seemingly go over'.
'I desire to know whether he was really a papist or did but pretend'.
'I did only pretend, I was not really one, I declare it'.

Above: The font at All Saints' church, Hastings, 2023. (Author's photograph)

Below: All Saints' church, Hastings, 2023. (Author's photograph)

ALL SAINTS · HASTINGS

1250	RALPH
1284	JOHN LE PETIT
1315	REGINALD
1338	RICHARD DE HATHELSEYE
1339	THOMAS PARL
1340	ROBERT BROK
1344	JOHN DE LEVERYNGTON
1348	JOHN DE TEMESFORD
1349	JOHN DE WYNDHULL
1349/50	WALTER DE GROBY
1360	WILLIAM DALBY
1370/1	ROBERT MAYN
1373	JOHN SOMER
1375	JOHN HERYNG
1396/7	JOHN IKLYNGTON
1396/7	JOHN HYNE
1397	THOMAS DEAKENE
1403	WILLIAM LOCHARD
1403	ROBERT RAVENSDALE
1544	WILLIAM LONGFORD
1585	HENRY ELKS
1587	RICHARD ROBINSON
1588	HUMPHRY MORGAN
1589	JOHN PRYCE
1592	RICHARD ROBINSON
1596/7	WILLIAM PARKER
1619	ALEXANDER CHADERTON
1636	CHRISTOPHER DOWE
1660	SAMUEL OTES
1681	JOSEPH TURTON
1683	WILLIAM SIMONDS
1690	JAMES CRANSTON
1722	RICHARD THORNTON
1726	RICHARD NAIRNE
1729	THOMAS BROADWAY
1740	THOMAS JENKIN
1763	WILLIAM WHITEAR
1779	THOMAS FULLER
1796	WILLIAM COPPARD
1803	WEBSTER WHISTLER
1832	JOHN G. FOYSTER
1849	HENRY S. FOYSTER
1862	GEORGE A. FOYSTER
1904	PHILIP J.T. BLAKEWAY
1907	CHARLES J. TERRY
1909	ALFRED H. BARROW
1916	EDWARD A. PENSON
1938	LESLIE HOOK
1951	JOHN R. SANKEY
1953	THOMAS G. SAVINS
1958	C. CHAMPNEYS BURNHAM
1966/9	FRANK R. LONG (PRIEST I/C)
1970/8	THOMAS G. SAVINS
	ST CLEMENTS WITH ALL SAINTS
1979/81	THOMAS G. SAVINS
1981/86	FRANCIS CUMBERLEGE

Left: Oates' father's name on list of Hastings vicars, 2023. (Author's photograph)

Below: Caius College, Cambridge. (Author's postcard)

St. John's College, Cambridge. (Author's postcard)

St. Bartholomew's church, Bobbing. (Author's postcard)

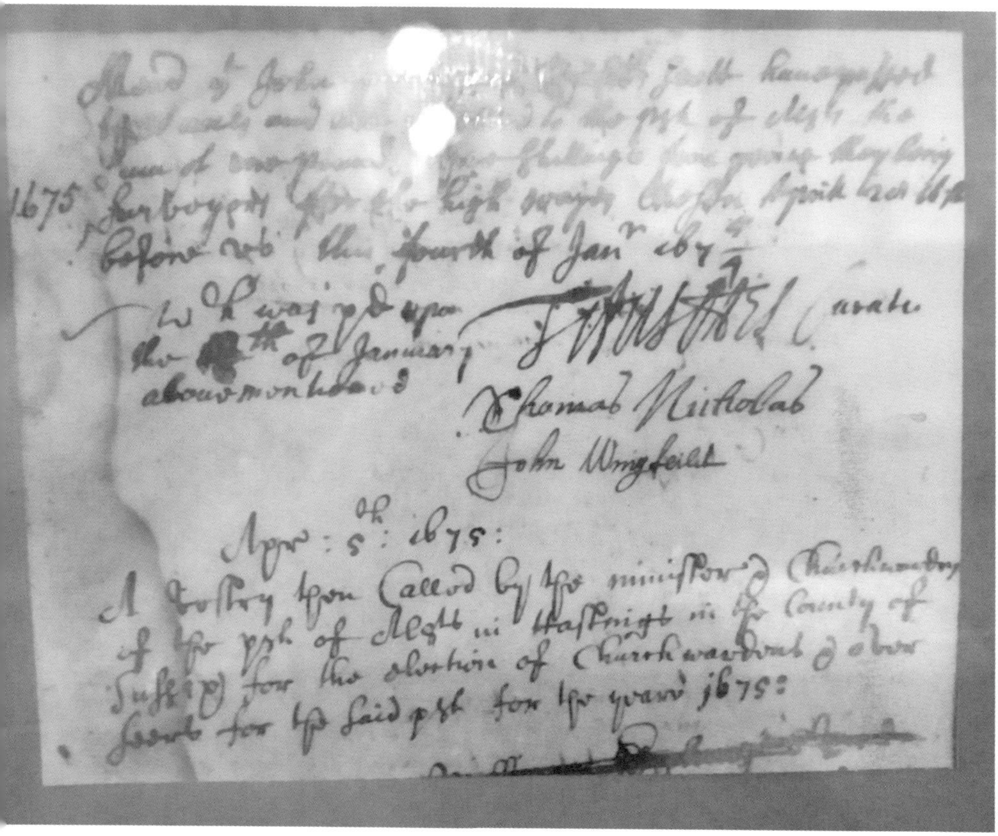
1675
before us this fourth of Jan^r 167[4/5]
Wch was pd upon the [illegible] of January above mentioned
[illegible] Curate
Thomas Nicholas
John Wingfeild
Apr: 5th: 1675:
A vestry then called by the minister & Churchwardens of the psh of [illegible] in the County of Sussex for the election of Churchwardens & overseers for the said psh for the yeare 1675:

Above: Oates' signature.
(Author's photograph)

Right: Titus Oates.
(Author's print)

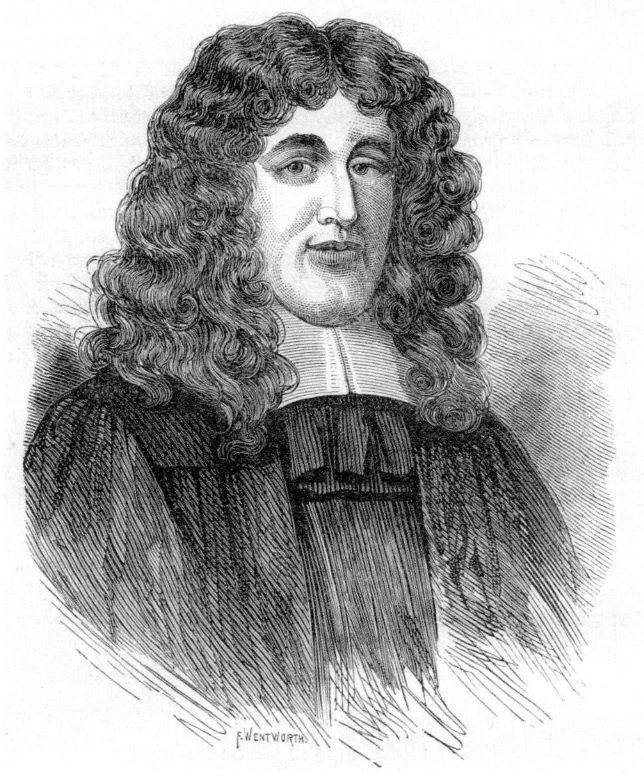

Charles II. (Author's postcard)

Prince Rupert. (John Coulter's collection)

Dr Gilbert Burnet.
(Author's postcard)

John Evelyn.
(Author's postcard)

Lord Justice Scroggs. (Wikicommons)

Queen Catherine of Braganza. (John Coulter's collection)

The Duke of Monmouth. (John Coulter's collection)

The Earl of Shaftesbury. (John Coulter's collection)

The Earl of Rochester. (John Coulter's collection)

Bibliotheca Curiosa.

AN EXACT DISCOVERY

OF THE

Mystery of Iniquity

AS IT IS NOW PRACTISED AMONG THE JESUITS.

BY

TITUS OATES, D.D.

1679.

Edited by

EDMUND GOLDSMID, F.R.H.S.

F.S.A. (Scot.)

PRIVATELY PRINTED, EDINBURGH.

1886.

Reproduction of one of Oates' pamphlets. (Author's collection)

Viscount Strafford. (Author's postcard)

Rye House, Hoddesdon. (Author's print)

Left: Judge Jeffreys. (Wikicommons)

Below: Titus Oates in the pillory. (Author's print)

William of Orange.
(John Coulter's
collection)

Titus Oates.
(Wikicommons)

Above: St. Margaret's church, Westminster, 2023. (Author's photograph)

Below: St. Margaret's churchyard, Westminster, 2023. (Author's photograph)

> Stafford asked him how long he had been in Spain and whether he was really a doctor.'
> 'I will answer to it, but I hope your lordships will not call me to account for all the Actions of my life'.

Stafford wanted to know whether Oates would take it on his oath that he was a doctor of Salamanca University. He was evasive.

> 'I am not ashamed of anything I have said or done'.[62]

Stafford also probed him about his testimony before the council about the description of Don John of Austria. Oates did not answer, but suggested referral back to the book of record. Eventually it was produced and Oates admitted that he had described the man in question. He added, 'I think there is no crime in it…I mistook his person'. It was shown that Oates had been in error. Stafford asked another question:

> 'I desire him to shew me the commission I received…I do not believe he can shew me my commission because there was none.'
> 'I could not keep any letters sent to the Fathers. I had a sight of them, but none to any particular use'

Stafford asked if Oates knew his hand and he said he had.

> 'So many commissions, and so many letters, as are spoken of, and not one to be found or produced'.

This lack of actual evidence was brushed aside by Oates. Oates said he saw Stafford at Dr Perrotts, with his son, but Stafford said he had never been there. Perrott was the father confessor to the Spanish ambassador. There was more discussion about identity and Stafford was adamant he had never seen Oates and the latter was equally adamant against this. He thought that he might have given Oates some money.[63]

Stafford then said what was in the letters that Oates referred to. Oates said he did not have any notes or kept any papers. To have done so would have endangered his life. Stafford replied 'that he is no competent witness' because he had switched denomination. He appealed to the lords, 'whether such a fellow, that will abhor his religion…be a man to be credited…is not a perjured fellow and no compleat witness? No Christian, but a Devil, and a witness for the Devil'.[64]

On day five, Stafford attacked all the evidence given by the witnesses against him. In Oates' case:

> 'whether he be a doctor or no, I know not, he would not own it here…Mr Oats all along before swore only I was in the Plot, now he swears I was in

it…And he saw letters subscribed by my name, but that my lords, I conceive is no evidence at all for he never saw me write nor knows my hand nor does he pretend to know me…his evidence now does not agree with his former… So his memory increases now he hath time to invent…he cannot be thought to be a Christian nor believe in God…'

This was because he had pretended to be a Catholic and said so in a derisive manner.[65]

Later the prosecution attempted to preserve the integrity of Oates, by stating that 'in the material part of his evidence is supported by other evidence'. There was evidence that he had been in Spain and had conferred with Jesuits in London. Because he had said so much already it was quite possible that he had not given all he knew immediately and so it was not unreasonable that his testimonies altered. His switching religious denominations was noted as not being unique and this should not damage his testimony.[66]

Sir William Jones, who led the prosecution's case, in summing up the evidence, paid heed to what the various witnesses had said. He gave credence to what Oates had said, noting 'his lordship was not pleased to call one witness materially to falsify Dr Oates' testimony, and I must likewise observe, that Dr Oates is, in the material part of his evidence, supported by other evidence'. He added that a Catholic witness said that Oates had had dealings with Jesuits and had been in Spain. Another Catholic said that Oates did know some of the Jesuits he had later accused of being in the plot, 'so 'I take these two witnesses to be a great support to Dr Oates as to the general matters which he evidenced of the plot'.[67] None of this explicitly supports the guilt of Lord Stafford, it should be noted.

It was also noted by Jones that it was objected that Oates had changed his religious denomination and so this should be held against the validity of his testimony. Jones countered this, observing that men did sometimes turn to another religion. Jones declared 'without that we would not have the first knowledge of the plot' and unless Oates could be accused of a crime or immorality his words should not be legitimately challenged. If Oates was a liar, 'if his Narrative be not true, he must be endued with more subtlety and wickedness than upon trial we can find him'.[68] Again, the unintentional irony will be noted by the reader here and it is noteworthy that Oates was still being believed by some over two years after he burst onto the national scene.

Serjeant Maynard also boosted Oates' evidence stating that he was a tool of the Almighty, 'the discovery of this plot is rather the work of God than man. It was first his act, in prevailing on Oates, to make this discovery, and when he stood single almost, what came to support his credit, but the letters of Coleman?' What Oates said was confirmed by the letters.[69]

Evelyn attended and later wrote his impression of Oates, that he was:

'a Person, who, during his depositions, should so vauntingly as he did, brag that though he went over to the Church of Rome, yet he was never

> a Papist, nor of their Religion, all the time that he seem'd to *Apostatize* from the Protestant: but onely as a spie; Though he confess'd he tooke their Sacraments, Worship'd Images, went through all the Oathes & discipline of their Proselytes, swearing seacrecy, & to be faithfull, but with intention to come over againe & betray them: That such an Hypocrite, that had so deeply prevaricated, as to turne even Idolator, (for so we of the *Church of England* esteem'd it) attesting God so solemnly, that he was intirely theirs, & devoted to their interests, & consequently (as he pretended) trusted; I say that the Witnesses of such a profligate wretch should be admitted, against the Life of a Pere'.[70]

Such a man who could claim to turn from Anglicanism to Catholicism and back again could not be trusted. He added:
'Such a mans Testimonie should not be taken against the Life of a Dog…From this moment foreward, I had quite lost my opinion of Mr Oates'.[71] Ailesbury referred to 'Oats and others their testimony. I regarded them no more than the barking of a dog. I as to Oates particularly, I have had it from sundry gentlemen educated at St. Omers, and who were on their oath at Oates' convention…that the miserable wretch…swore he had been in England'.[72]

However, another witness thought 'he spoke positively as to my Lord Stafford having Colonel Edward Cooke receiv'd his commission, and his owning and encouraging the killing of the King, with many shrewd circumstances, nor could any cross questions discompose him'.[73] This was the last trial at which Oates would give evidence as a witness against a Catholic defendant.

Nevertheless, Stafford was found guilty by a vote of those assembled in the House of Lords; 31 found him not guilty and 55 found him to be guilty. He was thus sentenced to death by beheading. Sentence was carried out on Tower Hill late on the morning of 29 December. On the scaffold he 'spoke with all scorn and contempt possible of Mr Oates and his evidence' and that he had never hitherto spoken to Oates or knowingly even seen him.[74]

This probably had no impact on Oates personally. He was still on an all time high. On 26 December 1680, Oates was dining with Dr Gunning, Bishop of Ely and Sir John Reresby, a Yorkshire MP and strong supporter of the King, at the bishop's table, which in itself showed how highly esteemed Oates still was. Reresby provided an insight into Oates' character at this time:

> 'the doctor, blown up with the hopes of running down the Duke [of York], spoke of him and his family after a manner which showed himself both fool and a knave. He reflected not only on him personally, but upon the Queen his mother and her present Majesty, till nobody daring to contradict him, for fear of being made a party to the plot, I at last did undertake to do it, and in such a manner that he left the room in some heat. The bishop told me that

> this was his usual discourse, and that he had checking him formerly for taking so indecent a liberty, but he found it was to no purpose'.[75]

Yet Oates' days in the favoured limelight were numbered. As 1681 progressed the wheel had turned and it was now the turn of the Whigs to be put on trial. Parliament was dissolved in January 1681 and new elections were once again held. Charles II next met Parliament at Oxford in March 1681 and dissolved it again and never recalled it again, thus cutting off a major forum of opposition against him, but also acknowledging that Crown and Parliament could not work together. He had no need to call it for revenue (as long as he did not wish to fight a war) as he had acquired a secret subsidy from France and his own income from customs and excise had improved due to greater administrative efficiency and a boom in trade. He could now afford to deal with his enemies; and not only high profile ones such as Shaftesbury. He was arrested in July and tried in November but a sympathetic London jury found him not guilty. Accused again in the next year he fled the country and died in exile in 1683. Elsewhere the King's supporters were increasingly in control, taking over the City of London, once an opposition stronghold. It was also safe for James to return from temporary exile.

Oates' politics were noted as being openly different. Smith recalled:

> 'Dr Oates hath in my hearing, I believe, a hundred times, affirmed very peremptorily that the supream power was in the people, that the King was but the people's servant and steward; that the people had power to Depose him; and set up another when they pleased; That the King was as deep in the plot and was as arrant a papist as his brother. Many times Oates has said to me, his [the King's] finger itches to bring in Popery, and French government. But it will not do. Let him remember his father; he must expect the same sauce if he goes'.[76]

This was not original; some thought that Charles II was sympathetic towards Catholics; vide his Declaration of Indulgence in 1672 granting freedom of Christian worship, having a Catholic wife and some Catholic mistresses and briefly siding with France against the Dutch in 1672-1674. Had the secret clauses of the Treaty of Dover of 1670, between Charles and Louis been generally known, then the anti-royalist cause would have been confirmed.

Oates reflected on the King's time in Oxford. He 'used to say that the King was as deep in the plot as the Duke, and as arrant a papist as his Brother, and that he had suborned witnesses to stifle the plot, and to throw it upon the Protestants'. Oates said that the young Tonge had been bribed by the King to speak against him.[77] He spoke in favour of the illegitimate Monmouth as being the heir to the throne (as had others earlier) and seemed to advocate armed rebellion, about how some would be prepared to 'loose their lives before they would part with their Arms, and if the King should come to demand them, they would fire upon him'.[78]

Oates was still in a furious state about the plot. On 13 April he spoke with Warcup in Richard's coffee house on Fleet Street, about a man in York who was to be tried there by a Yorkshire jury. Warcup wrote 'Oates told me twas a trayterous position and must answer it'. Presumably he thought the trial should occur in London and he be involved in it. Robert Bolron was a Yorkshire informant about alleged Catholic plotters in his county and had provided Warcup with a paper about Oates, to which Warcup told him about but wrote 'Oates [was] angry because I would not name the party'.[79]

According to Constant Oates of St. Olaves', Southwark, his brother, Titus Oates was meeting the leading opposition figure, the Earl of Shaftesbury, in January 1681 at Oates' house in Aldersgate. Apparently they were plotting together against the King to indict his brother James, Duke of York, for his Catholicism, but 'should doe nothing until they were sure of him'. Shaftesbury was seen by Samuel Oates to have 'incouraged him when he had told him about his railing against the government'. Thomas Merry and Colonel Roderick Mansell, two of Shaftesbury's supporters, together with Oates, were concerned about a further Exclusion Parliament.[80] Samuel also recalled that he and his brother met one Colonel Henry Danvers (c.1622-1687) in Newington in January 1681.[81] Danvers was a Baptist, had fought for Parliament in the civil wars, was a republican and a Fifth Monarchy supporter. A radical to his fingertips Danvers was involved in numerous plots and conspiracies in the Restoration era and eventually fled abroad.[82]

Samuel provided testimony to the effect that his brother Titus was influenced by others. The sheriff of London, Slingsby Bethell (1617-1697), a republican sympathiser, had persuaded Oates to go to Oxford for the Parliament 'against his owne inclination, for he refused but two hours before and said that he nor any that belonged to him should goe down'. However, 'it was the people of the Citty Clubs that never left till they had persuaded him out of favour with the court and by that means got him among themselves, wch I wish he could have been wiser for the time he was at court some men seemed to be doubtful of his standing for them'. Oates was apparently led astray by 'Shaftesbury and the Citty Clubs did withdraw his brother from his allegiance to the King'.[83] Certainly in 1682 Oates acted as a witness for Shaftesbury against Warcup.[84]

Oates was suspected of other matters. On 27 May 1681 Oates made a great harangue about someone visiting Danby about the Godfrey murder.[85] A week later, two Irishmen informed Lewis that Oates had been at a consult where a resolution had been taken to kill the Queen and James. Furthermore, at a meeting at Bowling Green Newington, Oates spoke 'very scandalously of the court of aldermen'. There was information against him of blasphemy provided by several witnesses. He was summoned before the court but the results are not known.[86]

The last man to be executed as part of the plot was Archbishop Dr Oliver Plunket of Dublin, Primate of Ireland; who was tried at King's Bench on 3 May 1681 and hanged, drawn and quartered on 1 July 1681. Oates took no part in the trial and the witnesses all came from Ireland. There were other trials; George Busby was tried at Derby assizes as a Jesuit priest and was found guilty and sentenced but none of these men were executed.

Yet belief in the plot was not wholly undimmed. Oates still had supporters. The electors of Northampton asserted in March 'That there may be a more full and perfect Discovery of that most hellish Popish Plot'. Similarly at the same time, those of Taunton called for 'That further search be made into this horrid Popish Plot, and the plotters and Abettors thereof brought to condign Punishment'.[87]

Oates' significance was certainly in the wane in this year. As in the previous year, his weekly allowance, which had been £10 for the first few months of the year, was cut to 40s, this on 15 April; Dugdale and Fitzgerald had their income likewise slashed.[88] His last payment of any kind was made to cover the time up to 2 September 1681. From then on until 1689 Oates was to receive nothing from the public purse.[89]

The year was not wholly bad for Oates; at some point the city of Exeter claimed that Oates had been right about Jesuits being disguised as preachers to presbyterian conventicles in Scotland.[90]

Constant Oates brought information about his father's and his younger brother's actions. He reported, on 25 May, that his father had been asking him to carry heavy batches of papers from a house in Southwark to his own. Apparently the papers concerned important figures in the state and seditious activity. Constant was willing to serve the King against his enemies. This involved providing information about him, 'my brother is and will continue fruitful'. One Bouthe, a glazier of St. Martin's, said that Constant told him 'his brother, Titus, was a base, unworthy, ungrateful rogue and was grown a most villainous and dangerous Whig'.[91]

Scroggs also found himself on trial, for having failed to successfully prosecute some of the men accused of the plot and for browbeating Oates and Bedloe at the Wakeman trial. He was accused of abusing them so much that they were never believed as credible witnesses thereafter. At the case of Oates versus Knox and Lane Scroggs' behaviour against Oates was attacked. Scroggs replied that he acted within the law and was acquitted.[92]

A new wave of trials began to occur now the 'Popish Plot' had been exploded. Edward Fitzharris was the first man to be charged with treason against the King. Oates, titled Dr Oates, was Fitzharris' first witness for the defence, on 9 June at the court of King's Bench. This was the first time he had been in such a position. He reported that he knew that Sir William Waller and Edmund Everard, an informer, had discussed the matter in question and asked the latter about it. Everard, Oates said, 'He told me he wrote the libel, and when I would not believe it, the man was a little angry that I would not believe it'. Oates thought he spoke badly but Everard said he would put it in writing and it would be printed. Oates said that the King had paid Fitzharris for his involvement in it, as part of a plot to discredit the opposition lords.[93]

Later that day, Oates asked that he might be excused from attendance at the trial, 'the crowd is so great, I cannot stand, the prisoner has nothing to say to me'. The Attorney General mused that there might be an attempt to kill Oates and so 'if you have any questions to speak to me, I will speak truth'. There were none, so he departed.[94] Fitzharris was found guilty on 15 June and executed at Tyburn on 1 July. Oates' intervention had little or no effect in the saving of his life. Later Oates fell out with one of the witnesses at the trial, Everard 'calling traitor, rascall, &c. for giving evidence against Fitzharris' and later threatened him.[95]

Another trial was that of Stephen College, tried for treason in Oxford on 17 August 1681; apparently having prepared to rise in armed rebellion against the King at Oxford. Oates was called as a witness for the defendant. He confirmed that there had been a petition from Edward Turberville and Macnammara to Mr Willmore. Oates had met Turberville who told him he would be a witness against College because 'the Protestant citizens have deserted us, and by God damn him we would not starve'. Turberville said the first part was true but the second was not. Oates reattested what he had said, 'Upon the word of a priest, what I say is true. My lord, I do say, as I am a minister, I speak it sincerely in the presence of God'. Clearly Oates believed that he was being universally viewed as truthful. He was fearful of Turberville and thought that any man who used such heinous language was not one to associate with.[96] Oates was asked for any other pertinent information. Nothing more, he said, but that he was under great temptation to change sides. When the Attorney General said Turberville had not done so, Oates remarked that 'I am a witness for the truth against falsehood and subornation' and felt that Protestantism was under attack. He said that Smith had used threatening words against College in Richard's coffee house. Smith was supposed to be a clergyman yet he damned the Gospel, Oates said. Oates then spoke of Dugdale, as he had lent him £50 so he could attend a trial.[97] Samuel Oates was also a witness for College, for he had met Smith on a social evening. He confirmed that there was no treasonable talk between College and Smith. There was only 'matters of common discourse, of eating and drinking'. Nothing of a philosophical nor religious nature was discussed.[98] College was found guilty and executed outside Oxford castle on 31 August 1681.

The Attorney General was later reported as having addressed Oates in no uncertain terms:

> 'Your bread you have from the King, your lodging in the King's Palace, you are obliged to the King for your life, and what esteem you have amongst men is on the King's account, and now will you behave so wickedly ungrateful for all his favours and mercies towards you, as I stand here in court in the

> justification of so notorious a traitor, contrary to your former allegiance to the King'.[99]

According to Smith, when Oates returned to London after the College trial, Oates said that 'Oh, there is a great man fallen this day in Israel. I wish I may lay down my life in so just a cause. He is his countries martyr…Our master is resolved to bring in Popery'.[100]

By the month's end, Oates was removed from his apartments in Whitehall and was forbidden the court. It was said 'Dr Oates, now degraded by the newsmongers to Mr Oates'.[101] Apparently the King told Oates personally:

> 'Mr Oates, I am assured that you have so far forgot your duty to me as to be guilty since your pardon of several high crimes and misdemeanours against me, I will not say of treason, though I believe as much, and I have good reason for my belief, however, I forgive you again; and leave you above board, but if you are any more faulty, I shall spare you no more than any of the rest of my subjects'.[102]

A near contemporary noted:

> 'The carriage of Mr Oates has been such, especially at the trial of College, where he was a witness against the King, in things therein he was notoriously disproved, that His Majesty thought fit to take him from him his pension he gave him, as also his lodgings he had from him, which was intimated to him with a command to leave the court'.[103]

Oates moved from Whitehall to the City and there was speculation that this was for health reasons or to be nearer Shaftesbury.[104] By September 1681 he was living in rooms in Broad Street.[105]

Apparently he arrived at his new lodgings with an armed escort. The landlady had been told that a clergyman was to be her new lodger. When she found it was Oates she cried 'I am undone! Undone! Undone! They are all French merchants, strangers, papists that lodge in my house. For the Lord's sake, persuade the gentleman to take other lodgings or else all my lodgers will be gone immediately'. Oates, for once, was apologetic and found other lodgings. This was in the house of an 'honest quaker' at George Yard near Lombard Street. His friends visited him daily and he talked about going to Amsterdam and taking up an archbishopric there as he did not like those in England.[106]

In September there is a reference to a committee to be formed to examine Tonge and Oates, but there is no further evidence as to whether this produced anything positive. It probably did not but it does show, once again, that, in contrast to 1678-1680, by now Oates was persona non grata at court.[107] This should be no surprise;

he had accused the King's wife of being in a plot to poison him and had accused those near the King's brother of treason, quite apart from being part of the process where over 20 men had been hanged. The wheel of fortune had turned once more and now it was against Oates. In July, the King had asked Warcup to find witnesses in order to try Oates for blasphemy, but, although in this they were unsuccessful, this points to another step in Oates' fall from grace.[108] One wonders why charges of sodomy were not pursued, given the allegations made in court against him in 1679.

There were reports made to Sir Leoline Jenkins that Oates was politically disreputable in his behaviour in the past three years. In July he was seen to frequent Mr Key's house in Angel Court, Throgmorton Street. Keys was a notorious presbyterian and apparently at his house were stored drums, trumpets and flags, the paraphernalia of an army, perhaps.[109] On 15 December, Owen Murphy reported to Jenkins that in September 1680 William Hetherington, who had spent time at Oates' house, asked Murphy to assist them. Apparently Oates said 'should you do what Hetherington and I will have you do, you will be as happy a man as ever came of your name'. They were to write him a statement about a plot that was purportedly written by him and then deliver it to the Lord Mayor, assuring Murphy of a reward of £100. Eight days later, Hetherington and Oates wrote down 'a whole sheet of paper'. This alleged that Charles II was a Catholic and he had been seen at mass, that the Queen, James, Ormonde and other lords were all part of a popish Plot to bring in a French army and reintroduce Catholicism in England. Murphy concluded, 'The whole design of Oates...was to take away the king's life'. He alleged that Oates was part of a plot himself to seize the Tower of London, and following Plunket's execution, there had been meetings to pursue this endeavour. Swiftly on the heels of this was an anonymous allegation that 'Dr Oates himself were tampered with' in order to prolong the plot.[110]

Oates and Shaftesbury remained close. Indeed, Shaftesbury was dining in Oates' lodgings when he was arrested for high treason.[111] Oates was to appear in a very minor role as a witness at the trial of Shaftesbury for high treason at the Old Bailey on 24 November 1681. One John Smith was a witness against the peer and he claimed that Oates' servant encouraged others to attack him. Oates said 'I know nothing of it, my lord'. He then admitted to having six servants but was resolute in his statement, 'it is a mistake, I know nothing of it; we went thither to refresh ourselves'.[112] Shaftesbury was acquitted. That evening there was anti-court demonstration which involved Prance and Oates, the latter shouting 'Ignoramus'.[113]

Another sign that matters were not going well for Oates was that on 21 January 1682 he was arrested for speaking scandalous words against Elliott: 'That Elliott was a great Rogue and a priest of the Church of Rome...turned Mahometan' and was fined £500, but obtained bail. In the press there was a reference to the 'lying testimony' of 'Dr Oates' in conjunction with this and when the case came to court, after the jury discussed the case for an hour, Oates had to pay Elliott £20 and pay legal costs. This minimal cost was 'in tenderness to the Dr's low condition'. With the ending of his pension, his financial standing was reduced. Later that year one of the men imprisoned after being accused by Oates as being in the plot, one Kearney, was discharged due to lack of witnesses.[114]

Oates was having little luck in trying to obtain money by being instrumental in making enquiries into lands held by Catholics. In August of this year, one William Fanshawe claimed that Oates had been obstructing his investigations into Catholic landowners and so summoned him to appear before him to justify his claim, but Oates did not appear. On 25 October, the king backed Fanshawe's claim to the reward paid for these discoveries.[115] A similar case came before the privy council on 12 January 1683. Here Thomas Hughes and William Smith asserted that they had found estates in Leicestershire owned by the Catholic Thomas Ireland. Yet on 19 December in the previous year, Oates had, they said, 'pretended to be the sole discoverer thereof'. Oates had given evidence against Ireland at his trial in 1679 but had done no more, so Smith and Hughes claimed 'those who made the Discovery, should be deemed the discoverers'. The case was resolved in their favour in May 1683.[116]

John Dryden (1631-1700), England's first Poet laureate, wrote some stinging lines about Oates in his poem of 1681, *Absalom and Achtophel*:

'Sunk were his eyes; his voice was harsh and loud:
Sure signe she neither choleric was, nor proud;
His long chin proved his wit; his saint like grace
A church vermilion, and a Moses' face;
His memory, miraculously great,
Could plots exceeding man's belief repeat,
Which therefore cannot be accounted lies,
For human wit could never such devise.
Some future truths are mingled in his book,
But where the witnesses failed, the prophet spoke:
Some things like visionary flights appear;
The spirit gave him o, the Lord knows where,
And gave him his rabbinical degree
Unknown to foreign university.
His judgement yet his memory did excel,
Which pierced his wondrous evidence so well
And suited the temper of the times,
The groaning under Jebusitic crimes.
Let Israel's foes suspect his heav'nly call
And rashly judge his writ apocrpyphal,
Our laws for such affronts have forfeits made;
He takes his life who takes away his trade.
Were I myself in witness Corah's place,

The wretch who did me such a dire disgrace
Should whet my memory, though once forgot,
To make him an appendix of my plot.
His zeal to heav'n made him his prince despise
And load his person with indignities[117]

There was evidence in 1683 that Oates was involved in the Whig plots against the King, known as the Rye House Plot. The dissolution of Parliament and the flight of Shaftesbury had made some of the opposition desperate. Denied legitimate means to attack the King they resolved on more desperate and violent measures. The more extreme Whigs, 'Phanaticks' to their enemies, planned direct violent action against the King's person and his brother on their way back from Newmarket to London in 1683 and this was to occur near to the Rye House, in Hoddesdon, Hertfordshire, a house owned by Richard Rumbald. The plot was foiled by the royal party changing the date of their journey back to London due to a fire in Newmarket. The leading conspirators were betrayed in June and were arrested; Lords Russell and Sidney were beheaded in 1683 and another lord, Essex, committed suicide in the Tower.

Samuel, on 18 January, said that he could persuade his brother to give information about the plotters.[118] At the end of the year, Oates was reported as being seen drinking with Major John Wildman (1621-1693), a former Parliamentary army soldier, lawyer and propagandist, and Charlton, at Wildman's club.[119] Wildman was an extreme Whig and in 1685 would be part of the attempt by Monmouth to bring down James II.

A contemporary biography of Oates noted that at this time:

'he went and herded himself among the factious part of the City, where he caballed, but was never trusted in the Grand Design, because as Colonel Rumsey said, he was too great a Rogue, however they maintained him very well, but his credit sunk lower and lower every day and was quite ruined upon the Discovery of the Phanatick Plot'.[120]

Smith agreed that this is what Oates was doing, consorting with the likes of Major Wildman and Mr Charleton providing him with sums of money, on one occasion £40. Elias Best, a hops merchant of Thames Street, also helped him. In Oates' rooms he met with Henry Starkey, Aaron Smith, a lawyer and Rye House plotter, Mr Hart and Colonel Mansell and they talked of rebellion, that they did 'Affirm and Discourse thus, We have 20,000 Horse and Foot, ready armed upon occasion. We value not the King's Guards and Forts…They would loose their lives before they would part with their Arms, and if the King should come to demand them, they would fire upon him'.[121] Others he associated with were Robert Ferguson (1637-1714), a supporter of the Rye House Plot and Monmouth, West, Goodenough and Richard Rumbald, a former Parliamentary soldier.[122] These men were leading radical Whigs and up to their necks in conspiracy against the Stuart monarchy. Ferguson was involved in the Rye House plot and the Monmouth rebellion. Rumbald had been one of the guards during Charles I's execution, was a leading Rye House conspirator and in 1685 was executed for his part in the Scottish rebellion under the Duke of Argyll against James II.

In 1685 Lord Grey, commander of Monmouth's cavalry, revealed what he knew of the Rye House Plot in return for his life. Nowhere does he mention Oates, though he does make frequent reference to Wildman, Ferguson and Colonel John Rumsey as being involved with Shaftesbury and Monmouth in plotting against the King and his brother. Oates mixed with these men and frequented a coffee house that the plotters used, but was not privy to the details of the actual plot.[123]

A hostile source made fun of Oates' apparent lack of knowledge about the plot:

> 'Mr Oates himself was enquiring after it t'other day at the Amsterdam [coffee house]. And it's a wonderful thing that he should know nothing of this plot; that every body talks of, and yet gave so exact an account of divers particulars of the popish plot that no body ever took notice of but himself.
> 'If this were a real plot, that man should be found able to give a rather better account of it, than ever he did of the popish one, for he has been hand in glove with the Chief conspirators…and a person as well known among the wayfarers'.[124]

In relation to this, on 24 June, Robert Spencer (1641-1702), the second Earl of Sunderland, secretary of state for the south, noted that the discovery of the plotters had frightened Oates, leading credence to the fact that he had associated with some of these men on some level. Oates allegedly intended to flee, as others had done, and Sunderland wondered if Oates should be stopped. No action was taken and there is no evidence that Oates left the country.[125] Warcup had written at the end of the previous year, 'Oates knew, I believe, all things, associations &c.' which is also suggestive.[126] Oates' active involvement in this conspiracy can be doubted, therefore, though he clearly consorted with some on the fringes of the plotting and doubtless sympathised with the plotters' aims. Now an outcast, he had no love for his former paymasters of 1678-1681. On 12 July John Gelson told Pepys that the reason for the attempt to kill the King was to 'make the Papists more odious that they might better serve their ends by them'.[127]

Meanwhile, Oates' father was resident at Half Moon, King Street, 'living there several years under vehement suspicion of Adultery'. He died there, described as 'a preaching weaver' on about 6 February 1683.[128] Oates' response to his father's death is unknown. Matters were not going well for Samuel Oates the younger, either. In December he petitioned for employment in the Royal Navy. He stressed his previous service in action against the Dutch and the Turks. He produced evidence from his family and the mariners of both Yarmouth and Hastings.[129]

Other bad news for Oates was in relation to his alleged personal failings. There was another attempt in January 1683 to charge him with sodomy. It is unknown whether this was due to past allegations going back to 1679 or further, or to new ones. The Recorder was approached but upon examination, the evidence provided seemed improbable and was dismissed as being both false and malicious. It was a difficult crime to prove and very few hearings about it appeared before the courts for these reasons.[130]

There was also a pamphlet purportedly by Oates published by the end of the year. It referred back to 'a huge and horrible popish plot' of 1673 and then in 1678 'she made foul faces and lookt very black in the fundament and fell into labour with this plot'. The pamphlet also referred to Oates' indebtedness, owing £20 for his linen bills and being seized because of it and being arrested for debt three or four times a week. It would seem that this was an attack on Oates, focussing on his financial embarrassments, in order to further discredit him.[131]

Oates was as obnoxious as ever. On sitting in the Amsterdam coffee house, apparently awaiting a nobleman, he got into an argument with one Mr Kidd. They were talking about the appalling state of the dirt on the streets. Oates argued 'At which word Mr Oates up with his cane, laid him over the pate' with 20 strokes.[132]

Chapter Seven

Decline and Fall, 1684-1688

With the Popish plot now at an end, the exclusion crisis over and the Rye House plot defeated, Charles ruled without Parliament. Enjoying external peace and a secure income he could afford to do so. It was now time to consolidate his position and he and his supporters began to move against the political enemies who had harried them in the previous years and these were principally the proponents of exclusion. The King's allies moved into those positions of authority in state at central and local levels. James was now to automatically succeed his brother Charles on the latter's death and now there was no more talk about Monmouth being legitimised nor James ruling with limitations. The Whigs' desperate assassination plot of 1683 had failed and the conspirators were dead or exiled (Shaftesbury died in Holland in 1683). The remaining Catholic peers in prison because of the plot were finally released in February 1684, as was Danby, and James was restored to some of his offices.

Oates was naturally unhappy about the course of events and without powerful supporters he was now an easy target for his enemies as he had fallen from grace. He complained, on 28 February 1684, about the writings published against him and singled out Sir Roger L'Estrange, a leading publicist for the court. Wanting to make his case to the privy council as in 1678, Oates was told he would have to contact a JP instead. His public worth had fallen so low. Sir Roger was his target specifically because he had 'vilified and Ridiculed the evidence of the popish plot', meaning Oates' word had been doubted and in print. Oates stated that he had had the King's backing, 'His Majesty was so sensible of the danger he was in'. Oates wanted financial recompense and for L'Estrange to be silenced as he had not only accused the witnesses of lying but he had by extension, abused the government as well. Nothing came of this.[1]

Oates complained that he no longer had access to the King, 'but for what cause of this I know not by reason of that forbidden the King's person and his court which I have obeyed and have not been at Whitehall these three years…I have business of importance with the King and council but I am unwilling to come lest I should offend him'.[2] He also complained in the next month to Dr Henry Compton, the bishop of London from 1675-1713, reminding him that 'when this popish plot was first discovered your lordship was very zealous in prosecuting popery'. He stated that L'Estrange had written 'that vile pamphlet of his called the Observator' and that was a 'vile libel' against him.[3] Oates had clearly little grip on reality; the tide had turned decisively against him and his former allies either would not or could not assist him.

Oates undertook the dangerous indulgence of ranting in public against James, now uncontested heir to the throne and it will be recalled that in 1678 he went out of his way to exonerate James from all involvement in the plot, even though he was to accuse the Queen of such. Now he had changed tack and did so in a most open manner, showing that his grasp on current reality was limited in claiming that:

> 'The Duke of York's a Traytor. A Rascal, a Papist, and a Traytor. A Traytor and in the Plot. He shall be hang'd. I shall live to see him hang'd. And hang'd. We'll have no more regard for him, than if he were a Scavenger of Kent Street. I hope to see him at the barr of the House of Commons, where there are many better men than he. If the Devil has a place in Hell hotter than the other, I hope he will bestow it upon him'.[4]

The vindictive side of Oates' character, never far away, came out when he talked to his one time confidante, Warcup, about James. Warcup had been praising the King's brother, but Oates insisted, 'he is a traitor and in the plot as you are a Yorkist, & Ill remember you for it'.[5]

This provocation was the action of an angry and disappointed man but was to have consequences for the isolated Oates. In 1684 James decided to take proceedings against Oates and an action of *Scandalum Magnatum* (defamatory speech or writing against a great officer of state) was brought, stating that Oates had referred to the Duke of York as a traitor. Witnesses were examined.[6]

Oates had been arrested on 10 May 1684 at the Amsterdam coffee house and was then detained in the Marshalsea prison. He was charged a month later that on 4 December 1683, he, in company had uttered these words, 'This letter cost me nine pence and I might have bought it for a penny. I know nobody is the better for it, but that traitor, James, Duke of York'. Several others were proceeded against in a like manner for the same offence. Oates' counsel told him that if he failed to enter a plea, judgement would be entered against him by default:

> 'He replied, according to his insolent manner, That as he never loved the Duke, so he did not fear him, and that he would answer the declaration when he thought fit; and that for the entering of judgement by default, he could not, for he would stay in prison, till there was a Parliament, and then he should come out, and others would be in his place'.[7]

Oates was unable to find bail so was in prison throughout. A Writ of Enquiry was held on 18 June. It does not seem that Oates was actually in court at all on this occasion. James Smith was brought forward as a witness and said that he heard Oates say these words in a coffee house in Westminster. Mr Whaley was next and recalled discussing the trial in 1680 of the Catholic Sir Thomas Gascoigne (he was acquitted) at the bishop of Ely's table with Oates. The latter said that James 'was a traitor' and later repeated the statement in the course of an argument with Whaley. Edward Johnson then said that on 23 August 1680 in talking to Oates, on the subject of calling another Parliament, the latter said 'No, not till York is either banished or hanged, but of the two, hanging is fittest for him'. Johnson told him not to talk like that but Oates replied 'I speak nothing but what is true'.[8]

The next witness was Randall Bowring and in October 1679 he was at a dinner where Oates was present, and there was general discussion about exclusion. Oates remarked 'I would not have you trouble yourself about that, for he shall be hanged before that time'. Oates was also heard to ask, after he gave a sermon at St. Vedast's Church, Foster Lane, in the City of London, over a glass of wine with the churchwardens in the vestry, whether 'any of them had dined with James, Duke of York, at any of the feasts of city, where the Duke used to come sometime?' No one answered. 'He would not dine with any man that had eat with the devil' Oates then commented. Mr Fairfax then recounted that in August 1679 he and Oates were travelling down to a by election in East Grinstead in a coach. 'We will have no more regard for him than if he had been a scavenger in Kent Street'.[9]

William Ashlock was another witness and he began by referring to Oates as Dr Oates but was reprimanded, 'Mr Oates, you mean' and Ashlock then began, 'Mr Oates' and recalled a gentleman from Sussex, name unknown, came to visit Oates in Easter 1682 and Oates said to the man that the Great Fire of London was began on James' orders, with the help of Sir Thomas Bludworth, then Lord Mayor. Troops then assembled on Blackheath were to have plundered the City and to have killed all the Protestant Dissenters. On another occasion, Oates allegedly said 'The Duke of York is the son of a whore and he should live to see him hanged; and if they could get a Parliament to their mind, they would soon send the Duke and all his gang out of England' for he must never expect to succeed the crown.[10]

Captain Richard Cressett, of Talbot's dragoons, was next to give evidence. In October 1680 Oates was lurking near the lodgings of the Duke and Duchess of York and Cressett saw him near the guardroom. Cressett said that Oates told him 'He is a Rascal, a Papist and a traitor and I hope to see hanged'. The soldier advised Oates to be more discreet in his talk. Oates was in Oxford in March 1681 and was in a pub when Sir William Jennings and one Mr Cranfield were about to toast the health of James. Oates told them 'Do not you drink York's health…Why he has ruined our nation; and if the Devil has a place in Hell more hot then I hope he will bestow it on him'. Justice Warcupp also witnessed his saying this. Finally, Charles Chapman said that when Mr Swift, James' attorney, confronted Oates more recently, Oates said 'I do not value the Duke or his attorney neither, I will plead as I see cause according to law; I declare I neither love the Duke nor fear him'.[11]

That was the last of the numerous witnesses who spoke at the trial against Oates. The judge then asked, 'Is there anyone here for Mr Oates, to offer any thing to lessen the damage?' No one spoke. The judge then went over all the witness statements already heard. There could be no doubt that Oates was going to be found guilty, and indeed he was.[12] The sum of £100,000 was demanded from Oates.[13] He could not pay the fine as demanded and therefore was consigned to prison until he could; virtually a life sentence in other words.

This was not all. Imprisoned priests were being released and pardoned.[14] Further proceedings were being taken against Oates. On 2 November 1684, the Earl of Sunderland instructed L'Estrange to take on oath all the statements of those who could testify that Oates was at St. Omers on or around 24 April 1678.[15] Clearly there was going to be another trial in which Oates was to be the defendant.

Oates was next present at the Old Bailey on 10 December 1684. He faced a bill of indictment from the Grand Jury of the City of London. He was accused of committing perjury when he had sworn in the trials of Ireland, Pickering and Grove, that he had witnessed that they had come to a resolution at the White Horse tavern to kill the King. He pleaded not guilty to the indictment and that his friends had the right to have access to him whilst he was imprisoned. This latter was agreed to and so he was remanded to the King's Bench prison.[16]

Worse was to come. Oates knew it and wrote on 30 January 1685 to Sir George Treby (1643-1700), JP and MP for Plympton, thus, 'I must pray you to consider of what letters you have of Mr Coleman's to the end that I may make use of them at my tryall'. He asked Treby to show 'what favour you can. It is my right to be preserved by all and every of those whom I have faithfully served'.[17]

The death of Charles II on 6 February 1685 and the peaceful accession of the Duke of York, now James II, was further bad news for Oates as it elevated his foremost foe to the top, though even had Charles not died at this juncture it is probable that he would have been acted against; the King's death merely delayed the hearing. The wheels of justice were already in motion against him and Charles was no friend of his. Yet Oates was seen as a man who still had some vestiges of support. On 27 March 1685 it was feared that there was a plan to arm the militia and that the latter were 'very ill affected towards the government'. It was then ordered that the militia had to return their weapons. A month later there were other concerns that 'several suspicious persons repair to the King's Bench Prison under colour of visiting other prisoners but go privately to Oates'. There was concern about a possible scheme to rescue Oates.[18] Neither fear was realised. However, this was a time of heightened tensions with rumours of possible attempts to oust James from the throne by armed force.

At nine o'clock on the morning of Friday 8 May 1685, Oates was tried for perjury at the court of the King's Bench at Westminster before judge Sir George Jeffreys (1645-1689). The indictment was read in Latin and English. The substance of the accusation was that Oates had 'sworn and had caused to be put to death Ireland, Pickering and Grove'. This was a gross simplification; there had been other witnesses against them and a biased judge in court. Yet Bedloe, Dugdale and Scroggs were dead and Oates had been the prime instigator of the conspiracy.

Jeffreys was almost a direct contemporary of Oates, having been born in 1645 and attended Cambridge; also leaving without a degree. He had embarked on a legal career in 1668, was knighted in 1677 and created a baronet in 1681. In 1683 he was made Lord Justice of the King's Bench, replacing Scroggs. He had presided over the high profile treason trials in 1683 of the Whig lords. Reresby wrote of him in 1684, that his progress had been 'for his quick parts and bouldness and zeale for the King's service, more than any perfect knowledge of the law had been soe obnoxious to all the late Parliaments' which had wanted him removed from his judicial appointments but the King would not hear of that.[19]

For some Oates was clearly yesterday's man. Evelyn, in his diary, had to reiterate Oates' former significance thus, 'who had made such a stirr in the whole Kingdome, (upon his revealing a plot of the Papists) as alarm'd several Parliaments, & had occasion'd the executions of divers persons, priests, noble men &c.'[20]

'I am to manage my own defence' said Oates and told the court that he had 'a great many papers and things' which would enable him to do so efficiently. Jeffreys allowed him to sit so his papers would be conveniently with his reach. Sir William Dodson was one of the jurors. To this Oates objected and he was challenged by both the Attorney General and Jeffreys. Oates told them that he believed the accused could object to any juror without giving cause providing the jury had its full complement of members. Jeffreys told him that he was mistaken in this. Oates replied, 'My Lord, I am advised so. I do not understand the law myself'. Both lawyers assured him that he was wrong as Dodson was sworn as a member of the jury.[21]

This was Oates' most prominent appearance in a court of law. Previously he had featured as one of several witnesses for the prosecution, and occasionally for the defence, in court. This time, however, he had the most prominent role as the sole defendant.

The other jurors were then sworn in. When the third next juror, Benjamin Scott came up to swear on the Bible, Oates piped up. He did so because Scott had been on the Grand Jury that had found the bill against him. The lawyers discussed it but Jeffreys let Scott swear. Oates then objected to the next juror, Thomas Fewliss, a goldsmith on Fleet Street. He objected against another juror, but as he had already sworn, the lawyers ignored Oates' plea.[22]

Oates then demanded that he had three very 'material witnesses', but they were all prisoners in King's Bench prison. Jeffreys said that this was not allowed. Oates said:

> 'My Lord, I shall want their testimony'.
> 'Truely, we cannot help it, the law does not allow it and you must be satisfied with it'.

The indictment against Oates was then read out. It was that on 16 December 1678 at Hick's Hall, the following – Thomas Whitbread, William Ireland, John Fenwick, Thomas Pickering and John Grove - were accused of plotting to kill Charles II; and that on 24 April 1678 the same had been observed by Oates at the White Horse tavern on The Strand.

> 'so as aforesaid had by his proper act and consent of his most wicked mind falsely voluntarily and corruptly in manner and form aforesaid did commit wilful and corrupt perjury and this is laid to the dishonour of God, in contempt of the Law, to the evil example of others in the like case of offending against the King's Crown, peace and Dignity; to this he has pleaded Not Guilty and that is the issue we are to try, if we prove him guilty we question not but we will find him so'.[23]

Robert Sawyer (1633-1692), the Attorney General from 1681-1687, gave the Crown case that Oates was in France from December 1677 to the end of June 1678. He said that Oates averred that he had not left St. Omers for more than a day in that period and that was to go to Wotton, two miles away from the Catholic college in question. Mr Hilsley, who was at St. Omers, would be brought to state that Oates was there when he left on that day to come to London.[24]

Phipps stated that Oates was a witness at the trials of the five men accused of conspiracy but added that in reality he was not there. Mr Hilsley would provide testimony against Oates, as said, and then Mr Burnaby would say he talked to Oates at St. Omers every day from 21-24 April and after. Mr Pool was another witness who would state that Oates was at St. Omers in April 1678. He concluded:

> 'My Lord we shall have many other circumstances, that will unanswerably strengthen this evidence, and show that our witnesses testifie nothing but the truth: one particularly is this, this Gentleman being a novice of the House, was the Reader in the Sodality as they call it, we shall prove that on every Sunday and Holy day throughout all April and May he did officiate in that place and did read to the Society there as the custom there is'.

First of all, witnesses at the first trial would state what Oates swore at the trial in 1678 and then witnesses would state that he could not have been present when he claimed to have been.

'I do not doubt that the Court and Jury will conclude he hath wilfully and corruptly foreswore himself; the said effects of which we are all witnesses of, it was to take away the lives of his fellow subjects wrongfully and it will appear to the world that he has been one of the greatest impostors that ever did appear upon the stage. Either in this kingdom or in any other Nation'.[25]

Mr Swift had been present at Ireland's trial. He was shown a record of it and agreed that it was true. The Attorney General asked whether Oates wanted it to be read so it could be seen that it was indeed authentic. 'I desire it may all be read' said Oates. The Attorney General then said that it was lengthy and he wanted to save the court's time if at all possible, but Oates persisted in his wish that it be all read out. The record was in Latin and it was queried whether the jury would be able to comprehend it all; Oates was not certain if it would be. Jeffreys decided it was not, only that the jury realised that Ireland was tried for high treason on 17 December.[26]

It was now time for the witnesses to step forward to swear that Oates testified at the said trial. Mr Foster was the first. He agreed that he was unhappy enough to have been on the jury at that trial. He was asked to speak up but said he could not do so because of a recent illness. Jeffreys then asked him to stand right in from of the jury so they could hear him. He told how Oates had sworn that on 24 April at the White Horse tavern in the Strand that Ireland, Fenwick and Whitebread were to pay Pickering and Grove £1,500 and say 30, 000 masses after they had killed the King. Edward Mico, a Catholic, had then drawn up a resolution to be signed, which occurred in Whitebread's chambers.[27]

Foster knew this to be fact because he had taken notes of the evidence he had heard in his role as juryman. When a published account was produced he bought it and compared it with his notes and found that they tallied. Oates asked if he could question the witness and when told he could, asked whether he (Oates) called the meeting he had witnessed was it a Consult or a traitorous consult? Foster thought that Oates had used both terms but that he would check his notes. The latter appears to have been the case.[28]

Oates then asked that Foster say whether he said that the three men were there together. Foster was unsure if Oates claimed that the three men came to the tavern separately or not but he maintained that they did meet and then signed the resolution in Whitebread's chambers. Oates asked the judge if he could ask Foster another question. Ask away said Jeffreys, as many as he wanted. This was whether the resolution to kill the King was made at the tavern or later. Foster said that the verbal resolution was made in the tavern and the written one was made later.[29]

The next question from the defendant was whether he had carried the resolution to be signed or whether he had just seen it being signed. Foster said that Oates swore that the latter was true and then Oates asked him again whether he was sure of it. Foster said he was. Oates concluded, 'He does say so indeed, but whether it is or no is a doubt'. Oates then asked whether he said whether the meeting took place in one room or in several? In more than one replied Foster.[30]

Oates asked about how accurate Foster's recollections were and after all, it was four years ago. He was told that Foster had checked his notes to be certain as to what Oates had said. Jeffreys asked Foster whether he had believed Oates in 1678 and he replied that he had no reason not to, so was then asked if he believed him now. 'We know how juries have gone alate' stated Oates, to which Jeffreys agreed, 'Ay, very strangely indeed, Mr Oates, and I hope we will never see them go again'.[31]

There was some question as to Foster's integrity, which the judge vouched for, before Oates asked him a final question: why did he say that he was unhappy to be on the jury in the court in 1678. Foster replied that this was because the jury were to try a man on a capital offence. The Attorney General then stated a summary of the case for the prosecution:

> 'My Lord, we prove that Mr Oates swore at the Tryal, which Mr Oates will not deny, for the fact, Mr Oates has printed it in his narrative, as we have now proved it'.[32]

Oates announced that he intended to question four of the jurors. This was seen as impertinence by Jeffreys. The Attorney General began to call his witnesses to swear that Oates was at St. Omers in 1678. Martin Hilsley was the first and he said 'I came from St Omers the 24th of April new stile where I left the prisoner Mr Oates.' In what year was this asked the judge.

'In the year 78. That is the fourteenth of April here and the three and twentieth new stile. I saw the prisoner at St Omers and went to school with him and on the four and twentieth and came from St Omers, and went to Callis, and from thence to England, but he was never in my company all the while I was coming for England, though he swore he came over with me'.[33]

Hilsley was asked if he knew Oates well; yes he did, and whether they were scholars there together, and again he agreed. He testified that he had not seen Oates on his voyage nor on the ship from Calais to Dover. He had arrived at Calais on 24 April and took ship on the next day, arriving at Dover at 10pm on 25 April.[34]

Oates asked when did Hilsley arrive in England and he was told the answer. In dialogue between Hilsley and the Attorney General it was said that Hilsley arrived at Bockton Street on 26 April and had stayed there for four or five days, before going to Gitterbourn and from there by sea to London. He met one Mr Burnaby at a relative's house. This was perhaps 21 April old style.[35]

Oates had questions to ask. The first was what religion he was and then where did he live. These were asked for him and Hilsley stated that he was a Roman Catholic, lived in the Inner Temple and had been studying at St Omers since 1672. 'Pray ask him what he did there, what was his business?'[36]

Jeffreys said that Oates must not ask him such questions because they could result in Hilsley being accused of crimes. Oates said it was relevant to his defence to know what Hilsley did. So Oates asked Hilsley when did he (Oates) arrive at St. Omers. Hilsey thought it was in November or December 1677. Oates wanted to know from Hilsley whether there were priests and Jesuits at the college but Jeffreys said that these were irrelevant questions. Oates insisted otherwise, 'Give me leave to make my defence, I beseech you'. Only proper questions were to be asked, warned Jeffreys. 'My Lord, I look upon myself as being hardly used in this case'.[37]

Oates asked whether he had been a witness at the five Jesuits' trial or that of Langhorn. This was deemed a fair question so it was allowed to proceed. Hilsley answered in the affirmative. Was he a creditable witness then, Oates asked. Jeffreys saw this as being unfair, and Oates then asked why Hilsley was present at the current trial. Hilsley replied that he was compelled by law to be there. Oates also asked him whether he was paid to provide evidence and Hilsley replied that he was not. Oates asked if Hilsley had ever heard of a Consult and the latter replied that there were meetings of Catholics called Consults and then was asked how often he had seen Oates at St Omers and told that he had seen him regularly there.[38]

John Dorrel, a former student at St. Omers, was the next witness. He stated that on 15 or 16 April 1678 he travelled from Brussels to England. He was not there when Oates was there. Oates asked him what his religion was and he replied that he was a Catholic. Oates stated, 'I desire my Lord that the court would be pleased to take notice of it, he owns he was reconciled to the Church of Rome'. Mr Osbourn was the next witness and he stated that he and Hilsley had discussed Oates' arrival at St Omers in 1677, under the name of Sampson Lucy and that he did not believe he would be admitted to the order. Again Oates confirmed that Osbourn was Catholic.[39]

Mr Burnaby then stated that he had met Hilsley on 18 April NS and then they went to St Omers the next day. He was at St Omers again from 2 May to 20 June 1678. There he saw his fellow scholar Oates on a daily basis. Burnaby admitted he was a Catholic and Oates demanded to know whether he was a Jesuit but Jeffreys told him once more that such questions were not allowed of the witnesses, which Oates complained was very hard on him. Again he asked if he had been at the trial of the five Jesuits and whether he was paid to be a witness and Burnaby said no to both. He also denied he knew of any Consult in London in April 1678 once Oates asked him about it.[40]

Another witness was one Mr Pool who recalled Oates arriving at St Omers in November 1677 and then seeing him there frequently. Henry Thornton testified that Oates was there from November 1677 to June 1678. He recalled seeing him often, especially in April and May 1678.[41]

Pool was not certain if Oates was at St Omers on 23 April, the day of a play he was putting on. Thornton was sure that Oates read from a devotional book every day in April and May. This was The Contempt of the Clergy. Oates tried to create the impression that Thornton could not be so exact in specifying that he was at the college when he claimed he was.[42]

Oates agreed that he was at St Omers until June 1678 but that he had been in England for a time beforehand. Thornton denied that he was ever absent save for a day at Wotton. William Conway also attested to Oates' attendance at the college from December 1677 to 20 June 1678. There was the following exchange between the solicitor general and Conway:

'Was he all the time you speak of in the Colledge?'
'He lay out one night'.
'What time was that?'
'In January to the best time of my remembrance'.

'Could he be out of the college any time and not be misst?'
'No my lord, he could not'.
'Did you miss him at any time?'
'No my lord'.
'Was he there in April 1678?'
'Yes my lord'.[43]

Conway recounted that as Oates was older than the other students he sat by himself on a table during meals and so he was very noticeable. Oates asked him the usual questions. Mr Haggerstone spoke next and recalled being in the same bench as Oates in rhetoric classes and having spoken to Oates on 25 April NS. He also recollected other days on which he spoke to Oates in April and May 1678.

For his defence, Oates called a number of witnesses, all of whom claimed to have seen him in London towards the end of April 1678, thus allegedly refuting the evidence already given by those former scholars at St. Omers college. The first to be called was Mrs Cicilia Mayo. She told the court that 'I saw him at the latter end of April'. This was at Richard Barker's house. Barker was ill and was convalescing in the country when Oates arrived there. He was in 'the strangest disguise that ever was' and it was wondered whether he had become a Quaker. Mrs Mayo said 'I never saw his face that time before that I know of'.[44]

In that case, Jeffreys reasonably asked, 'How do you know that to be Mr Oates, then?' She told that the household recognised him and that she spoke nothing but the truth. She added that Oates came to the house twice, the second time after three or four days interval. There was a young man with him and told her 'That Parson Oates had turned Jesuit'. She also saw him there at the end of May and the young man again pointed him out to her. Unfortunately the young man, known only to her as Benjamin, could not give evidence himself as he was now deceased.[45]

Other witnesses were also scarce. Barker had not been present and his two nephews who were, were now both dead, too. Dr Cocker was there, but he was now in Wales. Jeffreys commented, 'Tis a great misfortune to have so many dead, or so far remote [sic]' and Oates replied, 'My Lord, six years makes a great alteration in a family'. Other family members were in Lincolnshire.[46]

Mrs Mayo was asked about the times when she had seen Oates. She said it was within May but Jeffreys observed that she had begun by saying she first saw him in April. It was the beginning of May she now thought. He was there for a couple of months and she only knew it was him because she had been told so by others who did know him.[47]

John Butler was Oates' next witness. He had given evidence at previous trials but did not have any notes with him with which to refresh his memory and the judge said that it was right that he had not. Butler had known Oates before he went to sea and so was being reacquainted with him in May 1678. He said:

> 'I was a servant to Richard Barker and Mr Oates I had been acquainted with before he went to sea, he used to come to my master's house frequently and at divers times he din'd at the table and I waited upon my master there'. This was thought to have been in about May 1676.[48]

Two years later Butler claimed he saw Oates again at the house. He said

> 'I saw him disguis'd coming to my master's house…His hair was cut off, close cropt to his ears, and an old white hat over his head and a short grey coat over like a horse man's coat'.

Jeffreys questioned him as to the accuracy of his memory. Butler claimed that he could remember Oates arriving in May 1678 because his mistress Elizabeth Barker was buried in the February of the same year. He then provided additional details of Oates coming to the house that month, 'he comes into the yard where I was cleaning my Coach…He asked me what alteration there was in the family. I told him my lady was dead and the Estrucheon [sic] was over the door for her. He asked for Doctor Tonge when he first came into the house'. Apparently Tonge lodged there, but when he could not be found to be within, Oates left and apparently that was when Mrs Mayo saw him.[49]

Jeffreys tried to pin down why the witness thought that Oates had been there in May 1678 and he said it was because his master was absent being unwell following his wife's death. Jeffreys claimed that Oates might have arrived in June or July when others said he was in London, rather than an earlier month as attested by Butler. Dialogue was entered into with Oates as well, and Jeffreys began to question him, as to where he was lodging in London at that time as the witnesses had only stated that he visited the house only. Oates answered that he was unable to provide evidence for his whereabouts at that time but had good reasons for such because, 'can your Lordship or the Jury expect that I being then engag'd among & for the Papists & afterwards an Evidence against them to discover their Treasons can bring any of them to testifie against me now? No, they will certainly foreswear themselves, as these young fellows have all done'.[50]

Could Oates then identify any of the Catholic houses that he had stayed in at this time? He said that was not the point at stake, but Jeffreys thought that it was. Oates was adamant that he had provided good evidence for himself, 'I have taken the most effectual course that I could to provide for evidence to make my defence, and I think, by your Lordship's good leave, those that I have produc'd, do prove me here in Town in April and May 78'. He then produced another witness.[51]

This was Philip Page, but before he could testify Butler was re-examined and remind that he was under oath. Oates said that his witness was now being threatened. Butler insisted that he saw Oates in early May and that Mrs Mayo was there but that the other witness, Benjamin Turbet, was dead. He was questioned as to how did he know Oates if he was in the disguise he said he was. 'I did not know him when he first came in, till he spoke to me, and asked me how do you do John, and I recollected who he was, and it was Mr Oates'.[52]

The next time Oates arrived, he was wearing a different costume, 'a cinnamon coloured suit and a long black periwig that was curl'd down thus far, and a black hat with a green Ribband and green cuff strings about his wrists'. He dined there several times in the presence of the household and the Thurrells. Mrs Mayo was recalled and told that Butler and Turbet told her that the visitor was Oates, for she had never seen him previously. She claimed he only dined at the house once but Butler claimed it was several times, perhaps as many as seven. She also contradicted Butler as to what Oates was wearing; firstly a grey hat and a grey coat, wearing a brown wig, and later a black coat and a long brown periwig. Jeffreys observed, 'Here I know not how many contradictions in these witnesses' testimonies'.[53]

Oates accused Jeffreys of being far more searching with his witnesses than those of the prosecution's. Jeffreys said he must do so. Oates recalled Mrs Mayo and asked her a direct question about when she saw him. She replied that she had seen him but could not be sure who the others were around the table. Philip Page was eventually called. Oates asked him 'whether I was here in April or May, and in what year it was that you did see me in your master's house?. Page was uncertain, 'Truly I cannot be positive as to the year, but to the best of my rembrance it was 78'.[54]

Page recalled Oates coming in disguise to Barker's home, enquiring for Dr Tonge. He thought that Oates had close cropped hair, and was wearing a light coloured coat, with a broad brimmed hat and was carrying a stick. Oates asked him, finding Tonge was not there, the whereabouts of Barker and Page told him that he was at Putney. He could not recall the season nor the month of the visit, but that Oates then left. He could not recall Oates at the house at any other time, but when pressed as to when this was, all he could say was that 'to the best of my knowledge and remembrance it was in the beginning of May'. Oates made the point, 'the St. Omers men do swear through stich but my honest witnesses are cautious, it being so long ago'. [55]

William Walker was Oates' next witness and he stated:

> 'I do confess that I did see the man, and met him between St. Martin's Lane and Leicester Fields, and truly my Lord, I feel I may say it was my unhappiness to meet him, for I have had a great deal of trouble since…I am even weary of it, since I am an old man, but I do say that I did meet him at that end of town, between St. Martin's Lane and Leicester Fields, in a strange disguise, he was just like a Vagrant, a very Rascal'.[56]

Jeffreys then asked the crucial question; at what time did he see Oates? At this point Walker was vague and could only think that it was when the hazel trees were first in bud. What was the year, Jeffreys then asked. Walker said 'I cannot very well tell what year it was'. It was either 1677 or 1678. Jeffreys asked what was to be made of this evidence and Oates said it must have been a year and a half before Walker was witness at a trial in 1679. Walker recalled being at the trial but concluded on 'I could not speak positively'.[57]

There was then discussion between Oates and Jeffreys about whether the fact that he had made statements in late 1678 in the Commons about being an eye witness to the Catholic plotters in April of that year was evidence. Jeffreys said there was no point in examining the Commons journal or people who were there. Oates called Lord Devonshire who asserted that Oates had made those statements in the Commons in 1678. 'The votes of the House of Common are no Evidence at all' said Jeffreys to which Oates replied, 'They show what opinion Parliament was of'.[58]

Oates called other MPs and peers who had been present at his examination before them in 1678, but some were not to be found and others could not recall what had happened seven years ago. Mr Williams remarked 'My memory was never very good'. They agreed that the House had given him a good reception then because they believed then what he said was the truth. Oates complained, 'It is a great while ago and therefore it is a hard measure that I be brought to tryal so long after'. Jeffreys was unsympathetic, replying 'If it be a long time ago, we cannot help it; we cannot force people to prosecute sooner than they do'.[59]

Other peers and MPs had little sympathy for him and claimed they had not given him any credit in 1678 either. Oates said, 'My Lord, I am not at all concern'd at this; I value myself more upon my own Innocency and Integrity than any man's good or bad opinion whatsoever'. 'Ay, your innocence is very great' replied Jeffreys. Oates then said, 'Then my Lord, I will conclude my evidence'.[60]

Oates then went to try and call a number of peers and MPs. Most were not to be found. The bishop of London was, but pleaded a bad memory and when George Treby was called, he said that he had nothing material to say and when Oates asked about the Coleman correspondence, Jeffreys told him that this was not relevant evidence. He said he would call no one at present. It was now the turn of the Attorney General to continue the case for the prosecution.[61]

Oates was shown up as having been a perjurer on other occasions and where he had not been believed in court. On one instance Sir George Wakeman and Lord Castlemaine were both found not guilty in face of Oates' allegations. The false accusation of buggery at Hastings was also referred to. He went on to refer to Oates threatening witnesses to testify for him. One such was Clay, an imprisoned Catholic priest, who was told that he would be hanged if he did not state that Oates was in London in April 1678. Mr Smith, an Islington schoolmaster, had also been threatened by Oates.[62]

Wakeman and Lord Castlemaine then gave evidence that Oates had told lies against them in court. The former said that Oates claimed that he was to be paid £15,000 to poison the King. Castlemaine told how Oates accused him of talking treason. Oates tried to discredit Castlemaine as he had tried to do so with his old college scholars, by asking what his religion was. As with most of them, Castlemaine was a Catholic and said so. Oates was impudent enough, stating 'I am neither a shame to myself or mankind; what I have sworn is the truth and I will stand by it to my last breath, and seal it if occasion be by my blood'.[63]

The Commons Journals for 30-31 October 1678 were read, though Jeffreys could not see the relevance of them to the trial and said so. Oates then asked whether a Catholic could be a good witness. Jeffreys brushed this and a like question from Oates aside as being trivial and irrelevant. Lord Bridgewater had helped compose the Journals and he attested they were a correct record. Jeffreys said, 'But what is all this to our purpose now? What does this prove to the matter in hand?' He addressed the Attorney General, not Lord Bridgewater here.[64]

Eventually an extract was read, when on 31 October Oates swore that a group of men were plotting treason. Eventually another witness was summoned, one Lawrence Davenport, and he had been gaoler at the Gate House, Westminster. He stated that Oates had indeed threatened one Clay with death if he did not swear against the five Jesuits at their forthcoming trial. Oates said that this was not evidence but Jeffreys claimed it was evidence of his character. Mr Howard testified that he, Clay and Oates had had dinner in May 1678, but soon changed the month to July.[65]

An earlier statement of Oates from 1678 was produced in which Oates claimed that the Jesuit conspiracy in London was witnessed by him in May 1678 whereas earlier he had said it was on 24 April. Oates had no more witnesses to call, but insisted that an entry from 25 March 1679 be read out, which stated that the Commons had entire faith in Oates' narrative of the plot. It was now time for the summing up and Oates began.[66]

He did so by sticking to his original story by stating that it was claimed that he witnessed a murderous conspiracy at the White Horse tavern on 24 April 1678 and he insisted that this was the truth. He then said the St. Omers witnesses were all bogus who should not have been allowed to have given evidence, and gave them five reasons what this was so. Firstly he queried whether Catholics could be good evidences. The lawyers were critical of this attitude. Oates argued the point at length and would not budge from this opinion, 'a Papist is not a good witness in a cause of Religion'. Jeffreys harangued him for his impudence and threatened to remove him from court.[67]

Oates then objected to the witnesses' education as it had been in a Catholic seminary. Seminaries were illegal and those attending them ought to be punished, he said. Oates then cited anti-Catholic legislation to bolster his point. As previously, Jeffreys claimed this was all irrelevant and refused to let him proceed with quoting law from 1628. Oates then cited the evidence in his favour given by Mrs Mayo and Mr Butler. He went in to say that he had been believed in previous trials on the same evidence. He was critical of the evidence against him given by the seminary 'youths' and known Catholics such as Wakeman and Castlemaine. He also complained that he had been put in irons for 23 weeks and was told this was so that he could not escape.[68] Jeffreys stated that 'a papist is a good witness' in contrast to what Scroggs had often pronounced. Oates naturally countered by referring back to a great early seventeenth century lawyer, 'My Lord Coke would not admit a papist to be a good witness in any cause'.[69]

The Solicitor General then began his case, stating that Oates claimed to have been at the alleged meeting on 24 April but that there were witnesses who swore that he was not, starting with Mr Hilsley. He then summarised all the evidence given by the former scholars at St Omers to state that Oates was at the college from the winter of 1677 to the June of 1678 and added that it was difficult for any inmate to depart from the college without being missed. He stressed the importance of this evidence. He then turned to that of Oates' witnesses and cast doubt of their veracity, for they contradicted one another in their descriptions of Oates' appearance. He also thought it odd that Oates was seen by no one else at this time, when he knew many in London.[70]

Jeffreys praised the solicitor general's summing up against Oates. His opinion against Oates was hostile and he stated that he had had:

> 'greater respect shewn to him than branches of the Royal Family. Nay it was come to that degree of Folly, to give it no worse name, that in publick societies, to the reproach and Infamy of them, be it spoken, this profligate Villain was caressed, was drunk to, was saluted, by the name of Saviour of the Nation. O prodigious madness! That such a title as that should ever be given to such a Prostitute Monster of Impiety'.[71]

There were also a number of exchanges between the two men. Oates pleaded his case:

> 'Was there any man dealt with as I am, on hard such evidence offered to be given against him? Here they offer to blacken me with the imputation of that foul infamous crime of perjury'.

He added:

> 'It is not me they indict, but the whole Protestant interest is aimed at in this prosecution…for my own part, I care not what becomes of me, the truth will one time or another appear'.

Came Jeffrey's response:

> 'I hope to God it will'.
> 'I do not question it my lord'.
> 'And I hope we are finding it out today'.
> 'I appeal to the great God of Heaven and Earth, the Judge of all…I vow my evidence of the Popish Plot, all and every part of it, to be nothing but true

> and will expect from the Almighty God the vindication of my integrity and innocence'.[72]

Before the jury went out to discuss their verdict, Jeffreys asked if they would like something to drink; it had been a very long trial, but they told him they cared not for drink. They took a mere quarter of an hour before returning to court with the verdict of guilty. Sentencing, though, would be deferred to the end of the second trial. In the meantime, Jeffreys delivered his crushing but not unfair verdict on Oates, 'there does not remain the least doubt, but that Oates is the blackest and most perjured villain that ever appeared upon the face of the Earth'.[73]

The next trial took place on the next day, Saturday 9 May and here Oates was tried for perjury. The issue was whether Oates had seen Ireland in August and September of 1678 as he has said he had under oath in court in 1679. The prosecution could bring 41 witnesses against him. They began with Thomas Harriot, who had been the foreman of the jury at the trial of the five Jesuits in 1679. He attested that on that occasion, Oates had sworn that he had seen Ireland in the priest's lodgings on Russell Street on 8-12 August. Rainford Waterhouse had been another juror at that trial and he concurred with Harriot, stating to Oates, 'You swore that Ireland took leave of you'.[74]

Oates asked them if they were sure of what they had seen and they both said yes. Oates told them that he was being truthful, 'What I swore was the truth'. Another former juror on the trial was John Byfield and he gave similar evidence to the others; that Oates had claimed he had seen Ireland in those months of 1678. The prosecution had thus established what Oates had said on that occasion.[75]

However, the bulk of the witnesses were people who recalled being in the company of or otherwise seeing Ireland during those two months, when the priest had claimed to be in Staffordshire. They began with Mrs Anne Ireland, the priest's sister, who stated that she had seen her brother leave London at the beginning of August 1678. Oates denounced her as a liar, but the judge took the witness' side and rebuked him. Lord Aston was next and he stated that Ireland had left London with him to initially stay at Standon, his Hertfordshire seat. They had then travelled up to another of his homes, in Tixhill, Staffordshire. Oates queried this evidence and reminded the court that the peer was Catholic and so unreliable. Sir Edward Southcoat was another witness to agree with Lord Aston.[76]

There were then numerous other witnesses, including family servants who supported the main case. Some of them had travelled with Ireland, some had seen him at Standon and Tixhill. Oates constantly asked them if they were Catholics and so prone to lie. There was the following exchange between Oates and Jeffreys.

> 'I have so much charity for you, as my fellow creature, as to be concerned for you' said Jeffreys.
> 'It is not two straws matter whether you be or no; I know my own innocency'.
> 'You are the most obstinately hardened wretch that ever I saw'.

Soon afterwards Oates said

'My lord, I must speak the truth and I would speak the truth'.
'I think there is scarce a word of truth come out of your mouth'.
'These popish traitors, I am sure, will swear anything'.[77]

Not all the witnesses were Catholic; Richard Ingletrap, a servant, was not. The witnesses kept making their testimonies and Oates kept on trying to lessen the impact of what they said. Apart from asking them their creed, he also asked if they had been at the trial of the five Jesuits. William Rushton said 'I am a Roman Catholic and a loyal subject'. As the day wore on and the witnesses had all spoken, the Solicitor General announced, 'We have proved where he [Ireland] was every day in that time'. Oates boasted, 'I do not know where any witnesses you can bring against my credit'.[78]

Oates then began a speech in his own defence. He referred to his 'pretended perjury' and asked why, after six years, he was being put on trial and his word doubted. He concluded 'only that the hardship might be greater upon me'. He said that he had been unable to find the evidences he needed to support his case 'if not impossible for me to maintain the evidence I then gave'. This was because most of his witnesses were either dead, had gone abroad or had forgotten what they had seen. He added 'If such a practice as this be admitted no witness is safe in giving his evidence'. He told the court that the Popish plot was true and that he was being accused of treason not whether or not Ireland had been in London in August or September 1678.[79]

He then reminded the court that Ireland had been found guilty of treason. He said that the former judge, Scroggs, had believed the evidence of himself and Bedloe. He even cited Scroggs' speech at the five Jesuits' trial of 1679 about the impossibility of believing Catholic witnesses. Oates then referred to previous trials and how Warccup had taken his evidence against Ireland. However, his other witnesses were unable to appear and one who did, a woman from Uxbridge, had nothing relevant to say. He stated that Bedloe's evidence was true. He swore that he had seen Ireland in London on 8-12 August and at the beginning of September and that this was 'true, as I shall answer it before God'.[80]

Finally, he asserted that the Popish Plot was true. This was not the first time that there had been a Catholic conspiracy in England with the aim of overthrowing the Protestant status quo. Such had occurred in the reigns of Elizabeth I, then the Gunpowder Plot of 1605, the plotting against Charles I and Charles II. The revelations in Coleman's letters with La Chaise proved that what he was saying was true. He concluded 'no man must doubt but that must be a plain proof of the plot and enough to vindicate me'.[81]

Oates then asked for legal counsel, and was given a week to find a lawyer to prepare a defence for him, 'which is more than ordinary'. Meanwhile, the Solicitor

General went over all the evidence that had been given and the judge summed up, adding 'this case has taken up a great deal of time'. The jury took half an hour before coming to the decision that Oates was guilty on this charge. Yet a week later, on 16 May, a Mr Wallop of the Middle Temple appeared in court for Oates. Oates said he wanted more time in order for his counsel to peruse more records. At least a day or two, he pleaded. The court refused to grant him an extension. Wallop had nothing to say at present. Oates argued that Crown witnesses, as he had been, cannot be prosecuted and that Ireland's trial was legitimate. The Attorney General said that Oates was wrong on these points of law.[82]

Evelyn made reference to the trial thus:

> 'it being exceedingly tedious, I did not much endeavour to see the issue of it, considering that it would certainely be publish'd: Aboundance of R:Cath: were now in the Hall, in expectation of the most gratefull conviction & ruine of a person who had ben so obnoxious to them; & as I verily believe had don much mischief & greate injurie to several by his violent & ill grounded proceedings. Whilst he was at first so unreasonably blowne-up, & encourag'd, that his insolence was no longer sufferable'.[83]

Ailesbury wrote that, concerning Jeffreys, 'knowing well the Justice Jeffries' unlimited passions, I expected he would show himself in his true colours, but I was greatly surprised at his good temper, and the more because such impudent and reviling experiences never came from the mouth of a man as Oats uttered'. He added that 'the prisoner had the most just and fair trial that has ever been in any court of justice. His impudent deportment was without example, and on my conscience, no such scandalous perjury was ever so clearly detected'. He also thought that the laws were too lenient towards him.[84]

On 16 May Evelyn merely recorded, 'Was sentenc'd Oates to be whip'd & pilloried with uttmost severity: &c:'.[85]

The sentence was actually rather lengthier than this. Firstly, he was to be fined 1,000 marks. Secondly, he was to be stripped of all his clerical robes. Third, he was to stand on the pillory at Westminster Hall from 10-12 on Monday next and with a notice attached to his head declaring his crime. On Tuesday he was to do likewise but at the Royal Exchange. On Wednesday he was to be whipped from Aldgate to Newgate. On Friday he was to be whipped from Newgate to Tyburn by the common hangman. Furthermore on 24 April, each year for the remainder of his life, he would stand at the pillory of Tyburn, opposite the gallows from 10-12. Likewise, every year, he would stand on 9 August at the pillory near Westminster Hall and on the following day at Charing Cross, on the next day at Temple Gate and finally on 2 September, at the Royal Exchange.[86] It was considerably harsher than the previous sentence as it included the strong possibility that Oates might die whilst being pelted in the pillory on top of being imprisoned.

Jeffreys added the following remarks:

> 'This I pronounce to be the judgement of the court upon you for your offences. And I must tell you plainly, if it had been in my power, to have carry'd it further, I should not have been unwilling to have given judgement of death upon you. For, I am sure, you deserve it'.

He added, 'Mr Attorney, we will take care that the clerk will distinguish the judgements in the entries'. Oates was then removed from the court.[87] Apparently 'He boor this with ane impudent courage, and mocked the court, and boldly told, he was suffering all this for the truth, owing all he said was true'.[88]

Godfrey Harcourt, commenting on the trial thought that, of Oates, 'he carry'd himself with much impudence in most tryals'. He also commented on Jeffreys' verdict, 'he believed all he swore was false and that innocent men lost their lives by it & that he thinks him to be ye Greatest Villain that lives'.[89]

Reresby met the King on the day of the judgement and the latter told him that there had been a meeting of Jesuits on 24 April 1678 at St. James's. Had Oates known of this, then it would have been more difficult for James. Furthermore, 'The King said upon it that now Oats was thus convicted the Popish Plott was dead. I answered it was long since dead, and now it would be buried; which he approoved soe well of'.[90]

It could have been even worse, as a contemporary publication noted, 'Perjury, by bearing false witness upon oath, is punishable with the pillory…burnt in the forehead with a P…and his goods confiscated'. It is probable that Oates had little or no goods, but at least he avoided a branding marking him out forever as a perjuror.[91]

Oates' first public punishment was noted by Evelyn on 22 May:

> 'Oates, who had but two days before ben pilloried at severall places, & whip't at the Carts taile from New-gate to Algate; was this day placed in a sledge (being not able to go by reason of his so late scourging) & dragd from prison to Tyburn, & whip'd againe all the way, which some thought to be very severe & extraordinary; but in case he were gilty of the perjuries, & so of the death of many innocents, as I feare he was; his punishment was but what he well deserv'd: I chanc'd to passe in my Coach, just as Execution was doing on him: *A strange revolution*'.[92]

Burnet also commented on the punishment:

> 'which was executed with so much rigour, that his back seemed to be all over flead [flayed]. This was thought so little if he was guilty and too much if he were innocent, and was illegal in all the parts of it: for as the secular court

> could not order the ecclesiastical habit to be taken from him, so to condemn a man to a perpetual imprisonment was not in the power of the court: and the extream rigour of such whipping was without a precedent. Yet he, who was an original in all things, bore this with a constancy that amazed all those who saw it. So that this treatment did rather raise his reputation, than sink it'.[93]

Samuel Jeakes the younger of Rye, who had just described his travel to London to his wife on 21 May 1685 only had this to write about what he had seen. 'Yesterday Oates was whipped at the carts taile from Aldgate to Newgate'.[94] It was reported that Oates was ill of the fever following his beating.[95]

There were mixed responses among the crowd, as one might expect from those who had been involved in the anti-Catholic displays of the late 1670s and those who had supported the King, though in 1685 the latter were in the ascendancy as James II had acceded to the throne amidst general rejoicing:

> 'the common people were furiously inraged against him, calling him 100 bloody rogues and villain, which, if reall, is a true character of that beast, the populace, for within these few years they were crying him Hosannas as the great saviour and preserver of the nation; now the mobile cryes Crucify &c.'

On the other hand:

> 'However, it appears all the vulgar did not take pleasure in his suffering for some of them brook the pillorie wheir he had stood, for which several of them were apprehended and punished'.

Furthermore, his sister asked that his second whipping be cancelled, but she was rebuffed, being told 'he deserved to be hanged'.[96]

On 18 May it was noted that Oates had been divested of his canonicial habit and there was an inscription on his hat, 'He stood in a flaxen periwig and a morning gown over his clothes'. Apparently about 10,000 people gathered to hear the judgement. He was pelted with eggs. An unsympathetic pamphlet noted:

> 'Battered so with Rotten Eggs
> Both on the Face, the Body and the Legs
> And begs as beggars do for Bread and cheese…
> Was he not once Saviour of the Nation?
> The just reward of bloudy perjury'.

James was told what had happened and was displeased about those who favoured Oates. Thus on 19 May, 'The King being informed of some disorder that happened the day in the city at the time that Oates stood in the pillory', he instructed the London sheriffs to ensure that the like did not recur.[97]

John Wright noted in a letter to Robert More of Loselely on 21 May, 'Oates was pilloried on Thursday and Tuesday, was severely whipt yesterday & will serve thus the same fate tomorrow'.[98]

Others were sympathetic, with Dr Edmund Calamy, a nonconformist minister, later noting:

> 'In this year (1685) saw Dr Oates whipped at the cart's tail, the second time, while his back, miserably swelled from his first whipping, looked as if it had been flayed. I also saw Alderman Cornish, executed, and was much affected with both. Dr Oates was a man of invincible courage and resolution, and endured what would have killed great many others. He occasioned a strange turn in the nation, a general lethargy that had been of some years continuance. By awakening us out of sleep, he was an instrument in the hand of God for our preservation. Yet, after all, he was but a sorry foul mouthed wretch, as I can testify, from what I once heard from him in company'.[99] Similarly, on 23 May 1685, in Leicester, 'This day the Rabble was very disorderly upon the pillorying of Oates'.[100]

Another account by spectators shows there were other sympathisers there (according to a story which surfaced in January 1689), for Oates wore a fresh gown and a fur cap and when one man threw a rotten egg at him, the thrower:

> 'was apprehended by the company and haled through the dust to the pillory, and there forced to kneele down in the dirt, and aske the Doctor pardon which he frankly gave him'.[101]

Some did not think that Oates' punishment was strong enough. A pamphlet to argue such was produced in 1685, based on the mischiefs he had created in the country and to the Church of England. The pamphlet stressed the importance of the third commandment. There was much then about the importance of witnesses. It later stated, 'what has a pillory formidable in it?...enduring a little pelting with rotten eggs and Turnips'. The 'loss of one or both ears' might be a juster punishment.[102] 'Can a pillory be sufficient to punish a contempt of God?, the violation of the Religion of an oath, the perverting Justice, and disappointing the excellent design of wholesome laws?'[103] Another pamphlet noted, 'His sentence, though it may seem severe, is much less than he deserves, our English law makers as never imagining the possibility of so unexampled an offender, having provided no punishment equal to the demerits of such unprecedented villainy'.[104] Another referred to Oates in most derogatory terms: as an 'Insect of Hell, a foresworn murderer', 'Infamous and Base, 'this Imp of Hell' and 'Quondam Saint, this idol thing'.[105] L'Estrange published his *Brief*

History which was highly critical of Oates, Bedloe, Tonge and others and their role in the plot. Of Oates, he wrote of that 'malicious humour that he brought into the world with him, and an Habitual Course of wickedness'. He stated that the letters to Bedingfield were forged and that Oates and his ilk were liars.[106]

Matters elsewhere looked briefly favourable for Oates. In Scotland the Duke of Argyll landed in Scotland in May 1685 to ferment rebellion against the new King. A month later, the exiled Monmouth arrived in Dorset to claim the throne he believed was his by right of birth, alleging he was not only the first of Charles II's sons, but was also legitimate. In a declaration made on his behalf in the June of that year, it was stated 'witnesses prove Oates yt was ye saviour of ye Nation and has been ye first sufferer' from James II.[107] Among Monmouth's supporters were some of the men that Oates had consorted with earlier in the decade, republicans and radicals. However, Argyll's revolt crumbled and he was beheaded. At Sedgemoor on 6 July, after a night time battle of several hours, Monmouth's forces were routed (in the penultimate battle on English soil) and the man himself captured and soon beheaded; many of his followers were hanged or transported when faced with Oates' nemesis, Judge Jeffreys in what has been called the Bloody Assizes.

After these episodes, James' future must have seen assured. Parliament was loyalist and voted the King the revenues he needed and he began to establish an army whose size and efficiency had not been seen in Britain since the days of Cromwell. There was economic prosperity and no sign of any possibility of James being removed. Oates' fate was apparently sealed and the possibility of death in captivity must have seemed probable.

Oates' low reputation was being reinforced elsewhere in London. On the King's birthday on 21 October 1685, an effigy of the pilloried Oates, bearing the words perjury and forgery, was burnt at a bonfire in Drury Lane. The like occurred in 1686 at Lincoln's Inn Fields.[108]

Whilst he was in King's Bench Prison, there was a rumour that a woman employed in the prison as a bed woman (ie cleaner) bore Oates a child. Anthony Wood of Oxford added 'So the common report in London', though it is not reported by anyone else. Petrie relays this as an undoubted fact, however, doubtless to further blacken Oates' name, whereas as Wood reports it there is certainly room for doubt here. If this was true, then it is Oates' first known sexual relationship with a woman, but there is no knowledge as to what occurred to mother and child, let alone their identity.[109] His time in the King's Bench prison was not a happy one as he was loaded in irons and complained in February 1688 that he was almost crippled because they were on him for so long. The Lord Chief Justice's answer to this was that they were there so he could not escape.[110]

In a pamphlet published in 1696 Oates elaborated on this theme that he had:

> 'suffered some thousands of stripes, whereby he was put to unspeakable tortures, and lay 10 weeks under the Chiurgen's hands…weak in bed, and

> attempted to pull off the plaisters applied to his Back and threatened to destroy him…loaded with irons of excessive weight for one whole year without any intermission even when his legs were swollen with Gout and to be shut up in the hole or Dungeon whereby he became impaired of his limbs and contracted convulsion fits to the hazard of his life'.

However, sympathisers among the nobles and gentry provided him with £400 per year.[111] On 28 July 1685 one John Atterbury wrote, of Mrs Lee, 'she is acquainted with Otes, and us'd to visit him, and that she has furnish him with a sum of money, since he was whipt'. Apparently she had also aided other radicals with money: one Chadwick, an open supporter of Monmouth and one Braddon, a supporter of the Rye House Plot. Atterbury thought she was 'as pernitious a woman as any in the three kingdoms'.[112]

Although Oates was under lock and key, concerns about him were not over. On 16 September 1686, there was an order to search his lodgings, because there might be 'certain dangerous seditious papers tending to the disturbance of His majesty's government and the general peace'. It is not known what, if anything was found there and this may have been a symptom of anxiety of the King and government as to possible disaffection, despite the crushing of two rebellions in the previous year.[113] There was also the news that in prison Oates had been talking treason as overheard by a witness and thus the possibility that he might be hauled before the King's Bench again. Possibly because of this Oates was banned from speaking to anyone, yet he wrote a letter, on 19 November, where 'he desired so soone as it might be that he whom he writ to would come speak to him for it might do him a kindnesse'.[114]

Meanwhile, Oates' regular punishments in public persisted. On 10 August 1686 he was to be seen in the pillory outside Westminster Hall; two days later he was exhibited at Temple Gate.[115] The like occurred in the next year but what was then noteworthy was the response of the crowds towards him, as Ellis wrote on 13 August, 'the mob was not at all uncivil to him'.[116]

Oates was still attacked in print. Although old news he was not allowed to be wholly forgotten. One pamphlet had in its title 'a Monster called by the name of Titus upon Oates'. It reminded the reader of some of Oates' falsehoods. One was his apparent ability to be in two places (London and Valladolid) in April 1678. Secondly was his false claim to have been bestowed a doctorate from a place (Salamanca) he had never been to. Finally there was the fact that initially he had told the Privy Council that he had no more revelations to provide and later did just that.[117]

L'Estrange, one of Oates' doughtiest foes throughout the decade, wrote a full length book in which he had much to say about Oates, none of it good. He began by observing 'The Devil is never so Dangerous, when he presents himself in the Shape as an Angel of Light'. He goes on to state that Oates amongst others 'made the Plot'.[118] Later he refers to Oates as 'That Inexhaustible Fountain of Invention and

Slander' and as 'Damnable Otes'. [119] There is much more in this vein as L'Estrange carries on to cast doubt on Oates' tales, concluding 'That this Plot was a Cheat no one can doubt'.[120]

On 11 August 1688, Oates was pilloried at Charing Cross as per usual.[121] Next day, doubtless as a result of this, Oates petitioned his greatest enemy whom he had much abused, namely James II. He began his petition with self pity, stating 'I have no friend that can attend your Majesty with my Petition'. However, 'Necessity drives me to it'. He said that 'I am miserably oppressed by Mr Ellis the marshal of your prison of the King's Bench'. Ellis was a Catholic, needless to say. Ellis had taken liberties to oppress him and had denied Oates access to his servant. Oates claimed he was lame and unable to help himself due to his lengthy imprisonment. Ellis was described as 'rather a Turk than a Christian'. He finally stated 'I am under great Apprehensions of being murdered by him, which you may prevent'.[122] The petition was ignored. Later in the month he was pilloried at the Royal Exchange.[123]

Such was the case in 1688, as Abraham de la Pryme (1671-1704) noted after conversation with a friend who had been in London. By this time, James had lost some of the esteem that he had enjoyed in 1685 as the political pendulum was swinging against him:

> 'I heard him say he saw Oats that discovered the popeish plot whipt according to his condemnation, most miserably; and as he was haild up the streets the multitude would much pitty him, and would cry to the hangman or he whose office it was to whipp him, "Enough! Strike easily! Enough etc." To whom Mr Oats replyed, turning his [head] cheerfully behind him, "Not enough, good people, for the truth, not enough!"[124]

By this time external matters were looking more optimistic for Oates. By the autumn of 1688, James had managed to alienate his natural supporters, the Anglican Tories, who had stood by his late brother in the crises of 1679-1681, whilst doing nothing to improve his position among their enemies. His attempts to better the lot of the Catholics by extra-Parliamentary methods had been the cause of this. The final straw was the birth of a legitimate son on 10 June 1688 and the prospect of a line of Catholic monarchs succeeding the elderly King. Seven magnates had invited William of Orange, his son in law, to come to Britain. William assembled an army and a fleet and awaited a favourable wind. In face of this emergency, James granted a general pardon to many in October 1688, but some were excepted from this; Oates was amongst them, as were radical associates of his such as Wildman, Rumsey and Ferguson; Burnet was also excepted, men accused of high treason and 'some other notorious crimes'. Many of these men were exiles.[125]

Yet there was a rumour, 'a hot report came into the City' on 28 November that Oates had died by poison whilst in prison, but when a man checked he found that this was untrue. It did, however, reveal the level of support for Oates, for otherwise 'there had been a formidable insurrection in the City that would by force have inquired into and revenged his death'.[126] Next month Oates claimed that a priest told him who the real killers of Godfrey were, but this secret he never divulged and why a priest should reveal this to this arch anti-Catholic is another question.[127]

Chapter Eight

A Revival in fortunes, 1689-1705

Following the birth of an heir to James II and an invitation by seven leading Englishmen, William of Orange, married to James' eldest daughter, Mary, arrived in the West Country on 5 November 1688 with a substantial army. James II led his numerically superior forces westwards to meet him and encamped around Salisbury. Given some desertions, the incumbent monarch did not feel able to countenance military action, abandoned his troops (not for the last time) and attempted to flee the country. He failed and when returned to London he met his Dutch son-in-law, who allowed him to leave the country, which he managed on the second attempt, arriving in France on Christmas day. For some weeks Britain was without a monarch until the Parliaments of England and Scotland offered the crown to William and Mary, who were crowned joint monarchs (as William III and Mary II) in February 1689. This offered Oates the chance to revive his fortunes now the monarch who had instigated proceedings against him as Duke of York in 1684 and as King in 1685 was no longer a power to be reckoned with.

It was reported on 13 December that 'Dr Oates, I am told, drest in all his Dr robes againe, and expects liberty quickly'.[1] It is presumed that Oates was out of prison in January 1689 as then one Henry Muddiman saw him walking through St. James' Park 'very fat and trimme' to meet William of Orange.[2] He eventually won an audience with William after having to wait for two or three days. The latter 'received him very kindly, and spoak very comfortably to him & when the Doctor returned back a gentleman of quality mett him who did not himself look very cheerfully, and said to the Doctor You look well. The Doctor replied It is time for honest men to looke well'.[3] It was not only with Britain's new ruler that Oates found popularity. In the same month, he and Captain Wilkinson went to Kidd's coffee house in Bartholomew Lane and '*A great croud followed the Doctor with great acclamations*'.[4]

To an extent he was now in a strong position. James II's efforts in 1685-1688 to lighten the burden of Catholics in Britain and allow Catholics to take positions of power in the armed forces, the universities and elsewhere could be seen as being part of an actual Catholic conspiracy to reintroduce Catholicism. Therefore, Oates' warnings of a Catholic plot in 1678 (apart from the main thread of an assassination conspiracy) could be seen to have some validity. Additional 'proof' of Oates' 1678 statements was that in 1689 there were to be military challenges in both Scotland and Ireland (the latter aided by France) in favour of James II. And now that James II, the Catholic monarch, was in exile, his supporters were far too cautious to publicly attack their enemies such as Oates.

Oates wrote a pamphlet to flatter William. He wrote of 'The Joy which your Presence has universally inspir'd into the Hearts of the people of England, has even, in my Dark Abode, reach'd me also'. As soon as Oates, so he said, heard the news of William's arrival, 'I, with the Rest, though in a greater measure, rejoyc'd at the Apprehension of my long dispair'd of liberty'. He referred to the revolution as 'the most Glorious Action of the World'. He made reference to 'the late Popish Conspiracy' that he was involved against and that now all must be convinced of the truth of his narrative of it. He now wrote that William was the 'skilful and charitable Physician' to have saved Britain from the new Catholic plot and so 'May your Highness ever be the Guardian angel of these Kingdoms'.[5]

Apart from his writings, now that he was once more a free man, it was not enough that Oates should allow himself to sink back into that obscurity that he had emerged from in 1678. He needed it stated in public that he had not been in the wrong in 1684 and 1685. He needed a return to the limelight where he and his reputation could be vindicated.

Oates made his case to the Houses of Parliament in early 1689, 'representing his great sufferings' and was given leave to bring in a writ of error.[6] He began by stating what he had done a little over a decade ago, 'discovered a horrid Popish Conspiracy, for the Destruction of the late King Charles II, his Present Majesty... and the Protestant Religion...and proved it so fully that several Parliaments and Courts of justice, before whom he gave his Testimony, declared their belief of it'. He continued that the House of Lords 'being sensible of the great Service of Oates, gave him their thanks'. His information had then led to the conviction of a number of Catholic 'conspirators' in court.[7]

His document then came to the objections that were made against his testimony. These were that he was not present at the Jesuit meeting on 24 April 1678 at the inn on the Strand, and that some of those men he said were there were apparently not even in London. He reiterated that they were there and that he had produced witnesses who claimed he was in London at the said time. He claimed that the witnesses from St. Omers had been all bribed to testify against him, 'with places and offices in the Army, and had sums of Mony given to them'. He said that his revelations had been fully justified by later events, 'The Papists themselves having justified Oates in his testimony, by their open and avowed violations of our Laws, Liberties and Religion and executing such things in the Reign of the late King'.[8]

Some still opposed Oates. Ailesbury 'moved the petition be given him back as Charles II had referred to him as Titus Oates, clerk' (and in this the late King was being generous, given that Oates was improperly in holy orders). Oates refused to alter his petition. 'He lived scorned and hated by all men' claimed Ailesbury, though this is an exaggeration based on Ailesbury's own views of the man.[9]

On 20 March 1689, Oates, Tonge and Bedloe were ordered to come before parliament to tell what they knew of the Popish Plot and the death of Sir Edmund Berry Godfrey. The latter two were dead (Tonge having fallen out with Oates as the former's role in the exposure of the plot was totally outshadowed by Oates), however. Given the events of 1685-1688 the Catholic 'menace' seemed only too real and now with war against Catholic France, Oates' old stories gained a new lease of life and there was renewed sympathy in them. On 4 April he brought in three writs of error against the judgements of 1684-1685. The House of Lords agreed to hear judges give their opinion. This occurred on 17 May and they gave their opinion for the judgements made against Oates.[10] He also petitioned the Commons on 23 May, stating his discovery of the plot and then his incarceration with the wish to them giving him a royal bounty.[11]

On 25 May Oates claimed that Danby, now Lord President of the Council, had blocked investigation into the plot in 1678. Danby, Oates' old enemy, now reinstated in the lords said that Oates might be returned to the pillory. All the bishops except Burnet (now bishop of Salisbury) were opposed to him and he was sent to Marshalsea prison for a breach of parliamentary privilege. Three days later he pleaded for mercy and claimed that his latest crime 'proceeds from Ignorance or Inadvertency and humbly begs your lordships' pardon'.[12] On 30 May Oates was told that 'There were exceptions taken at his stiling himself DD in his petition'. He replied 'That he is Doctor of Divinity and had his degree at the University of Salamanca'. He was told to strike it out but replied 'He could not do it, out of conscience'. Next day the Lords heard the judges' opinion about Oates' previous punishments whether they should be reversed or that they were indeed cruel and unjust.[13]

On 1 June the Lords decided to reverse the judgement on Oates from 1684. They then made an address to the King and queen to pardon Oates from all his punishments as previously decreed. On 7 June the King issued a pardon for Oates.[14] The Commons also decided on 11 June that a Bill be brought in to reverse such judgements because they had been an attempt to stifle the investigation of the Popish Plot and so were corrupt.[15] Charles Hatton noted on 11 July, 'The friends of T.O. will have ye judgement to be erroneous'.[16]

Eventually the judges unanimously agreed that the judgement on him had been 'erroneous, vicious, illegal, inhumane and cruell' and that the annual whippings had been illegal. On 23 July that year Oates was pardoned for the 1684 conviction.[17] However, the perjury convictions for 1685 were upheld by 35 to 23 and so he was incapable hence of giving any testimony in a court of law.[18] There were further debates, with the Bill of reversal going back and forth between Lords and Commons in the next month and the matter was not finally resolved until 13 August. Yet he remained in prison until 20 August.[19]

Oates wanted more than a pardon; he wanted money. On 25 July he asked the Commons for such. He reminded them as discoverer of the plot he had been awarded

£624 per annum, £60 for lodgings and a further £240 for the actual discovery. He had had no public income for eight years, had been pilloried, imprisoned and had endured great sufferings. He was now poor and in debt and so asked that his pension be restored.[20]

On 19 September, Oates was granted an income of £10 per week, easily enough for a single man to live comfortably on and far more than most men.[21]

After his release, it was noted that he put 'on habit again, with his Doctor's scarf as having passed his degrees at Salamanca'. He styled himself 'Titus Oates, DD'. Furthermore, 'He had the impudence to go to Lambeth, to see the Archbishop of Canterbury, John Tillotson (1630-1694), and that prelate was so weak, as to admit him to his table, and the King and Queen's health going about, he impudently cried "My Lord, I will see first what King William and Queen Mary will do for me before I drink their health"'.[22]

A pamphlet was written by Oates and allegedly aimed squarely at the Catholics, who began by describing them as a 'residue of poor, seduced and deluded Papists, who obstinately shut both eyes and ears against the clearest light of the Gospel of Christ'. He went on to admit of himself, that 'there be none in this Nation…oweth less kindness to your tribe' but 'upon account of Brotherly Love and Charity' he would give them advice for the salvation of their eternal souls. He confessed that 'Indeed, I myself was lulled asleep, by the allurements of the Popish Syracuse'. He added, 'I persuade all men to renounce the Doctrines of Devils and embrace the Christian faith'.[23]

He then began to attack Catholicism, beginning with the doctrine of papal infallibility, and after listing misdeeds of popes in the past, added 'These are demonstrations of the Pope's fallibility and the fruits of his manifest wickedness… wicked works of the Romish man of sin'. Latin was criticised as being part of the Catholics' 'walk in darkness'. The alleged baptisms of bells and communion cups was attacked, as was the adoration of images, the celibacy of the priesthood and the former sale of indulgences. He concluded that 'all people be terrified at the name of Popery'.[24]

He also wrote much more. He helped John Tutchin to write a book about the Bloody Assizes, thus casting his enemies, James II and Judge Jeffreys, as villains (Jeffreys died in the Tower of London on 18 April 1689, doubtless to Oates's glee). Then there was *A Display of Tyranny* about how, during 1678-1688, there had been a descent into tyranny by legal means. Oates used the book to assert the truth of the Popish Plot and to condemn his own trial and punishment.[25] The writing of these books and pamphlets was not just to further his political and religious views but just as importantly, to make money for the author, but there is no record of how much he made.

Another book was an attack on the agents of the former monarchs. He dedicated it to Sir John Barnardistan (possibly meant to be Sir Thomas, 1620-1707, who was heavily fined and gaoled by Jeffreys), whose ancestor (Sir Nathaniel Barnardistan, 1588-1653) had opposed the early Stuarts. The book mounted a defence of the Whig 'martyrs' such as Shaftesbury, Essex, Sidney and Russell. James and Jeffreys were major targets of the book, the former whose reign 'would have finished the Ruin of the nation, in the Dissolution of its ancient and well established government and the Blood of its best patriots'. The late judge had 'betrayed the Rights of the subject'. His own trials were discussed and here he attacked the witnesses, 'All imaginable art was employed by the Chief Justice and the King's Counsel to perplex and confound this'. He referred to 'the canting witnesses', 'another supposed perjury' and 'that man of Blood, Jeffreys'. He attacked those who attempted to 'stifle' the plot, as in the case of Nathaniel Read in 1679. There was also a defence of Shaftesbury at his trial and those of other Whigs.[26]

Oates was of an argumentative nature in public. Shortly after the defeat of James' French-Irish Jacobite army at the battle of the Boyne on 1 July 1690, Oates was in a coffee house and was exclaiming loudly about it. He referred to the former monarch as a 'Tyrant Rascal' and hoped that his premier general, Richard Talbot (c.1630-1691), first Earl of Tyrconnell, 'that Rogue' should be hanged. A gentleman who overheard these comments, asked Oates if he wanted James served as his father was, i.e., executed. 'Yes, says Titus, better he be hanged than three kingdoms endangered'. The man said that he hoped that Oates might have repented his views and that if William III knew of his strong views about his father-in-law, then he would not have pardoned him and added 'That King William was a base man for granting him his protection'. Oates would have denounced the man in public as a Jacobite (supporter of the exiled James II) but a magistrate of his acquaintance persuaded him against it. On another occasion, a man overheard Oates saying that the Stuart monarchs were 'Tyrants, Papists and murderers' and had tea thrown into his face.[27]

In some quarters Oates was lauded. John Phillips' published history of the last two reigns makes no doubt that Oates had been right in 1678, 'while the King and his Brother were thus riding Post to ruin the Laws and Religion of the Kingdom, the Discovery of the Popish Plot by Dr Oats, brought all their Measures for a time, by laying open the Secret Contrivances…for the introducing of Popery and Arbitrary Government'. Apparently 'Oats himself narrowly escaped Massacred' and 'finding himself thus betray'd and abandoned by the King'. At the privy council meeting, 'he managed himself with that Courage, that though he was Browbeaten and opposed most strenuously…he stood as firm as a Rock'.[28]

Oates' plight over the Knox and Lane case, as dealt with in Chapter Five, was sympathised with. Oates' handling at the hands of Jefferys and James in 1685 is also highlighted; 'the first Act of his Revenge in England, brake forth upon Dr Oates'. He writes, 'the Doctor was first of all Scourg'd by the Common Executioners beyond all Precedent, and then Condemn'd to perpetual Imprisonment. A Sentence so void of all Christian Compassion'. Phillips was enraged that Oates 'the Detector of a most Horrid Popish Plot' was condemned by the evidence of 'known Papists, and some of them nearly Related to the Executed Traytors'.[29] No mention is made, needless to say, about the lack of hard evidence nor the subsequent executions of Catholics.

Trouble and Oates were never far away. On 7 May 1692 he was examined by magistrates for suspicion of 'reflecting on the government and dispersing King James' letter about his queen being with child'. Oates's fellow radical and associate from the 1680s, Ferguson, was also in trouble with the government at this time, too.[30] Given that Oates had previously being antagonistic towards the former King and vice versa, this may seem like a volte face. Stating that the former Queen was pregnant would have given comfort to the exiled King's supporters, the Jacobites. By 1691 the Jacobites in Ireland and Scotland had capitulated.

Despite having only shown limited interest in the fairer sex hitherto (if the anecdote passed on by Wood in 1688 is to be disbelieved), Oates was married on 17 August 1693 at St. Mary Magdalene's church, Old Fish Street in the City of London. This was an Anglican church and a Wren church, and was then very modern; dating back to only 1687 (the former church being destroyed in the Great Fire of 1666). The marriage licence referred to him as 'Dr of Divinity', aged about 45. His bride was Rebecca Wild, who had been baptised at St. Botolph's church, Aldersgate, also in the City of London, on 11 October 1670 (one contemporary refers to her as Mrs Wild which has led some to think that she was a widow, but the parish registers clearly indicate not). Her parents were John and Rebecca Wild and they provided their daughter with a dowry of £2,000, which a cynic might well think was her principal attraction in Oates' eyes. A contemporary biographer thought so, claiming Oates enjoyed 'six bottles and six dishes a day' and so needed the money to maintain his lifestyle. Rebecca's parents may well have supported Oates' politics and religious denomination and so pushed her towards him in matrimony. The Muggletonian sect, which the Wilds belonged to, was a radical branch of Protestant nonconformity which emerged during the Commonwealth. The age disparity of the groom (45 years) and the bride (22 years) was not for the time particularly noteworthy. John Evelyn was 27 and his wife 12 when they wed (though they did not live together for another four years) and James II when Duke of York was 40 and his second wife 15 on marriage in 1673.[31] An early biography simply commented, 'he married a Young Wife, whose Youthful desires and Nocturnal expectations quite overpower'd the Doctors abilities, even to a surfit'.[32]

An early biographer commented about the prelude to the wedding:

> 'It is highly questionable, how he should manage an Address so successfully, who had never been over famous for an Amour, unless 'twere with those of his own sex, 'twas perhaps a Complication of the Lady's virtue and good humour that imply'd her Condescension, rather than the Doctor's merit should preside in an Affair of that niceness'.[33]

There is no detailed account of the wedding nor the ensuing marriage, except for a pamphlet which described this wedding. This was written by one Thomas Browne, titled Salamanca Wedding, 'which severely reflects on Dr Oates' marriage'. How much of this true is another matter, but it is certainly evidence for how Oates was then viewed by some. The author began it thus, mockingly, 'the famous never to be forgotten Dr Oates was married'. There is then a reference to his sexuality, 'for a person of his Constitution that always expressed and perhaps inherited an aversion to the Fair Sex and besides has found a back door to bestow his kindness and strength elsewhere to confine himself at last to the infinite Desire of matrimony, it is unnaturally unexpected a change as for an old miser to turn prodigal'.[34]

Apparently when this momentous news was announced in a London coffee house, all discussion of the ongoing war with France and the price of commodities ceased for two hours. Apparently 'Everybody stood amazed, and it was a considerable time before they could recover themselves out of the astonishment'. The author of the pamphlet continued, 'God forbid we should ever live to see a Brood of suckling antichrists come out of the Doctor's loyns'. He added that the Muggletonians pretended to possess the power of damnation for others and so 'We must now expect to see a motley race of half saviours and half Damners'.[35]

Browne suggested two reasons why Oates undertook the marriage. 'The Doctor had two reasons to incline him to marry in his old age'. One was that his old co-conspirators – Bedloe, Dangerfield and Dugdale were dead and so 'due care were not taken, the species [of informers and perjurers] would be intirely lost, resolved as far as was in him, to prevent its utter extinction and raise up seed to the popish plot itself'. Secondly, he 'made a vow to sow his wild oats, and not to hide his talent, which God had plentifully given him, on an Italian napkin'.[36]

Apparently a nonconformist minister advised him to propose to Mrs Margaret Wild, though 'A maid was by no means for his turn'. She was apparently the widow [actually a daughter] of a Muggletonian. The minister argued 'in her the Doctor might have open and free ingress and egress as oft as he pleased'. Apparently 'she was no charmer'. Yet at their first meeting, Oates 'was so extreamly smitten with the Gravity and Goodness of her person that he could neither eat nor drink (which was more) till the business was concluded'. However, two questions were asked by Oates over the marriage licence, 'Whether he would have a licence to marry a Boy or a girl' and 'whether he would have a licence for behind or Before'. Oates lost patience with the minister and raised his cane to the man 'and thundered out You Rascal, as thick as Hops'.[37]

Oates' marriage promises included the keeping of a male servant under 60 years of age, to hang up a picture of Sodom in the bedroom and to teach the children of the marriage to swear as soon as possible. Oates said he would now 'attack' his wife in bed or elsewhere and that she would make amends. Oates was 'very merry' at the marriage ceremony as he ate his beef. After dinner Fifth Monarchy men danced and performed a spiritual jig, while his new wife looked disconsolate. Why so, women present asked her, 'She very much doubted whether she should be able to bear the weight of the saviour of three nations'.[38]

Finally at 10 that night Oates went up to bed, his wife being there already. Then, 'The bed continued in a trembling fit most part of the night, which, I suppose occasioned the report of an earthquake…Tis not doubted but the Doctor behaved himself with great Gallantry'. An astrologer from Moorfields predicted a boy would be born.[39]

Ailesbury, another hostile critic of Oates later wrote that 'he married a lady Baltinglass, a heap of flesh and brandy'.[40]

After doubtless reading or being made aware of the contents of Browne's pamphlet, Oates prosecuted, as he had in 1679 over the Knox and Lane allegations. The lengthy tirade had made many references to his homosexuality and his alleged interest in children. Browne was taken into custody on 31 August whilst on Cheapside but bailed. In the next month the Grand Jury found a true bill against him so the case could proceed in law.[41] It was not reported as to what happened next, if anything and perhaps the case was dropped. However, Oates was still well thought of at court, as it was noted that his wife kissed Queen Mary's hand that September, an improvement from the position in the previous year.[42]

The married couple had at least two children, both baptised at St. Margaret's church, Westminster, which was the parish where the Oateses lived (they lived in a house in Axe Yard, where the Pepyses had resided in the later 1650s (both Pepys and Milton had been married there in the 1650s and one of Charles II's sons had been baptised there, too). Axe Yard was a small street leading west from the King Street connecting Westminster Abbey to Charing Cross and so was just to the south of Whitehall Palace. Their first known child was Rebecca Crisp Oates, baptised on 3 October 1700 and their second was Anna Sophia, baptised on 31 May 1702. Since there is a cross at each baptism entry it is possible that neither lived for long. Anna's burial was recorded on 13 April 1704. In both cases the father's name is noted as Dr Titus Oates; clearly Oates was once again asserting a title he had no right to.[43]

Money was a continual source of concern for Oates. Apart from his annual income granted in 1689, he often approached the government with a begging bowl. In 1694 he was given a royal bounty of £100.[44]

Oates continued to be a turbulent character. In December 1695 he was up before the ecclesiastical courts for having allegedly struck one Mr Green, chaplain to the Archbishop of Canterbury.[45]

Oates was in financial difficulty in 1696 and wrote a petition to Parliament for relief. He began by stating that in 1678 he had 'discovered a horrid Popish Conspiracy' when the 'Popish Party pursued your petitioner with an Implacable Malice', which included attempts to murder him. He recounted that he had been given a pension but then was gaoled and cruelly treated as recounted in the previous chapter. He had been given another pension in 1689-1692 but this had been discontinued and so he was in a piteous condition, 'your petitioner is ruined, he living in the time of his sufferings, and such an allowance of £40 per annum was taken away, contracted debts for which he hath been sued by his creditors'. He owed £500 and not only was he the sufferer but 'his poor wife and family must perish and your petitioner starve at last in prison'. What he was in need of was an allowance of £40 per month.[46]

He also took to writing for publication, as he had done several times since 1679. He wrote a biography of James II in about April 1696. The book was full of praise for William III 'may he long live, to assert and preserve laws'. He added 'This present conspiracy against your Majesty and Government [a Jacobite assassination plot against the King of 1696] hath not only provoked me to publish the Arts and Methods of the late King, used for the destruction of our laws, liberties and Religion, in conjunction with the Popish Party, but it hath encouraged me to dedicate the same to your Royal name and patronage…it will not only entirely justify the truth of the Popish Plot, for the discovery of which I have undergone a fierce firey tryal'.[47] Evelyn wrote, 'Oates dedicated a most villainous reviling book against K. James, which he presumed to present to K. William, who certainly could not but abhor its speaking so unfavourably & untruely of his late beloved Queen's owne father'.[48] As with his accusation against Catherine of Braganza, Charles II's wife, in 1678, Oates had scored an own goal if he desired to ingratiate himself with the King, as much as he hated the exiled monarch.

Edward Ellys wrote a pamphlet in opposition to the controversial sentiments expressed in the book. He was aggrieved that the book was 'a most execrable Attempt to vilify the memory of King Charles the First and all those worthy persons that adher'd to him'. He attacked the author's defence of the regicides and his aspersion on the King's supporters. The martyred Archbishop William Laud was attacked in the book as an 'Arch traytor' and Ellys was most unhappy about this. He described Oates as 'this monster of a man' and 'that indignation ye ought to conceive among the insolence of so prodigious a villain'.[49] Unlike the case with Thomas Browne over his pamphlet, Oates does not seem to have taken Ellys to court.

By June of this year, Oates was in debt to the tune of £500 40s to one Richard Malkin. Unable to pay, Malkin employed Richard Knippe, bailiff of Westminster dean and chapter. On 12 June Knippe took goods and chattels to pay Oates' debts. Later this year Oates, his father in law and one John Mather, proceeded against the said Knippe for having acting unlawfully in seizing Oates' possessions and put forward a Bill of trespass. On 19 November 1696 Knippe took the case to the court of Chancery. Unfortunately the result is unknown.[50]

On 27 October 1697 the penurious Oates asked for an advance of £20 and on 8 December he was granted £50. On 15 July 1698 the King gave him £500 to pay his debts and in August of that year he was awarded £500 from the royal bounty. He was then granted an annuity of £300 for him and his wife for life out of the post office revenue, starting from Lady Day.[51]

A neighbour of Oates in Axe Yard was William Fuller. They had seen each other often, Fuller recalling that Oates had 'been puffing about the court'. As neighbours, Oates invited Fuller to his house for dinner. John Tutchin was a regular guest there and they used to 'talk mightily against King James, and the best word they could afford that Prince was Rogue and scoundrel Rascal'. Fuller had never heard such bad language before. Reference was made to Oates' earlier life, 'it was a glorious thing to discover a plot and he that would serve a nation must do as the good Doctor had done; fear nobody and strike at all that stood in his way'.[52]

Oates and his friends were clearly extremist Whigs as they 'preached up Liberty and Property and spoke very despicably of all Kings not sparing him on the throne, they said he employed Rogues and Tories Men that would betray and ruin the Protestant Religion'. They also spoke strongly against the Finch family (the Finches included the 2nd Earl of Nottingham, a leading Tory MP) Oates asked Fuller to lodge in his house, which invitation he accepted. This was at the cost of 50s a week and soon Fuller owed Oates £9. He had to borrow money from Oates too. Apparently Oates 'pretended an unspeakable love for me'.[53]

Whilst there, Oates and Tutchin prevailed upon Fuller to see a copy of his information to the King. Oates was abusive to Fuller and referred to the Popish Plot. 'I could not bear his continual foul language' wrote Fuller and left the house to return to his old lodgings. Aron Smith saw Fuller and Oates together at a tavern in the City and Smith told Fuller, 'The Doctr is a good and honest man he saved his Country, and deserves well from all good men'. However, he warned him that Oates was unpopular and this would rub off onto Fuller; Tories and Jacobites would cast aspersions on him. Even after he left, Oates and his cronies would visit him 'until I began to be as great a Whig as the rest of them', being easily deceived by their specious pretences and professions of virtue, of which too late I find, they had not one Grain'.[54]

On 23 November 1697, Oates wrote to the Duke of Bolton thus: 'The Court Whigs have a mind to keep an army of 30,000 men, to enslave the nation, but I hope those two rogues Seymour and Musgrove, who never did a good thing, will oppose the notion and save the nation'.[55] It should be noted at this time that the Nine Years War in which Britain had taken part against France, had come to an end and so there was no obvious need for a large standing army in peacetime. As in the 1670s there was the suspicion that a standing army could lead to a ruler usurping civil power as had occurred in the 1650s and 1680s.

It was not always Oates who initiated controversy. As with the case six years before, he was the subject of attacks in writing. In September 1699 one Mr Edwards, a printer, was tried at the Old Bailey for printing a dialogue between Oates and one Colonel Porter, 'wherein are many atheistical expressions and ridiculing the late conspiracy'.[56] Unfortunately the surviving Old Bailey records of trials do not record this, so its outcome is unknown, but presumably Edwards was not found guilty; there was, after all, plenty of evidence that Oates indulged in atheism and that the 'Popish Plot' was untrue.

In 1699, Oates' religious life took a new turn, or perhaps it would be more accurate to state that he reverted to that of his father and his early years. He returned to the Baptist Church. He was only readmitted after a campaign of two years and after 'a full examination and true reformation' had taken place. He appeared genuine. 'The seeming sincerity of his religious protestations, not only continued in his many letters, but also in his daily converse with them, in the end gave them some hopes of his integrity and true reformation'. His letters were 'full of seeming sincerity and sanctity, and earnest and pressing desires' for admission, 'thro' the grace of God he desires admission into their communion, to be a comfort to him and the brethren... to know of our Holy God and the direction of his Church'. He had 'no other designs, than the true glory of His name and the credit of his everlasting Gospel...he might walk with them in truth to adorn the doctrine of God his Saviour'.[57] In a book, after the following statement, 'The supream Judge by which all controversies are to be determined...can be no other but the Holy Scripture, delivered by the Spirit'. To this conventional piece of Christian doctrine, Oates wrote 'Agreed Titus Oates'.[58]

Oates made his initial overtures to a young man who was rich, confessing that he had been a black sheep for 27 years but wished to regain the fold. He said that he refused a bishopric in the Church of England several times and likened the clergy of that Church to Belials and Devils, especially most of the bishops who sat in the House of Lords.[59]

Initially he did well. As has been noted he was a competent speaker and a persuasive man. As a newspaper reported, 'Dr Oates held forth in an anabaptist meeting in Wapping to the great satisfaction of his Auditors'.[60]

Yet, and it may not surprise the reader, 'he did not long continue before his conduct discovered his hypocrisy'. The cause of this was the death, on 6 October 1699, of Hester Moore, a wealthy female member of the congregation of the Baptist chapel in Wapping, in the East End of London. She was the widow of Thomas Moore and in 1691 had married one Anthony Parker, but had since separated from him because of his ill usage of her, but not before settling £800 on him in exchange for being allowed to dispose of her estate as she chose. Her estate consisted of £1,100-£1,200. The trustees of the estate decided to discuss its settlement with Oates, perhaps because they trusted his judgement. Oates' first step down the slippery path was to take it upon himself to enter the pulpit a half hour before the funeral service began in order to stop the expected sermon; yet another way of thrusting himself into the limelight. The congregation 'unwilling to make any disturbance, submitted to the rudeness and obstinacy of the doctor'. The funeral sermon was postponed until the following Sunday, which displeased Oates, who 'with much passion and unbecoming words, he told the officers of the church, that from that day forwards, he would never preach more amongst them.'[61]

This was not all that Oates gave offence in. Earlier he had given the church a pulpit cloth, a table cloth and cushion. After the fuss over the funeral sermon, he sent a servant for such to be given back to him and then, four months later, returned them with an apology and an excuse that his wife had wanted them back, not him. Oates had also worked as an auditor for the church and appeared to apologise for his earlier behaviour, 'seemingly to offer all reasonable satisfaction'. However, this was all subterfuge, 'He had a secret game to play' and that was to ruin the executors of the will of the said deceased lady. These were George Reynolds and Henry Burroughs, the men who had prevented him from preaching the funeral sermon and had advised his brethren that Oates should no longer preach at the church.[62]

Oates then worked against the administration of the will which was being decided by the consistory church court, a court which dealt with some wills in London. He claimed that the court was 'the vile remains of Popery'. He was also angry about the will's executors on a personal level, and 'zealously solicited the said case'. He lobbied the friends and relatives of the deceased to alter the court's decisions in a manner antipathetical to the executors. Then he made a volte face and claimed that the will was in fact valid and should be administered to the benefit of the deceased's husband. Pretending to be magnanimous, Oates arranged a gathering of interested parties but included the lawyers for Parker to the surprise of Reynolds and Burroughs and there was quarrelling 'abetted and encouraged by the said Doctor'. Oates claimed that the deceased had told him that the husband had already benefitted from her to the extent of over £2,000. Apparently, 'he cared not which of the parties got the case, as the respondent Burroughs was ruined' and that 'God had put a Rod into his hands, herewith he would scourge Burroughs' and lastly said 'I will swing him and when I have wore it to the strap I will lay it by'. However, others disputed what Oates had claimed and stated that in the past they had banned him from visiting her. Oates reiterated that he was angry that he and his wife had been barred from attending the funeral or him preaching the funeral sermon. He was angry that the church officials had preferred the services of a young preacher not him, who, he said, had been a doctor of divinity for 20 years. However, he denied he wanted revenge, but would leave that to God, whilst admitting that that would take time.[63]

The case, which had begun in 1699 was not settled until November 1702. It was decided at the Chancery Court. Oates underwent the embarrassment of being shamed as being noted as being a perjurer.

The Baptists were now very much against Oates, 'this infamous man…he is by way of odium on that profession denominated such'. They recognised him as an Anabaptist rather than a Baptist and had only been the latter truly 'under the tutelage of his father in his youth, and for a little time afterwards'. He had then been an Anglican, a Catholic and an Anglican again. They thought 'if he be not restored to the communion, with the Church of God, he shall always mourn like a turtle'. They tried to reason that their acceptance of him was because of 'his plausible character and behaviour'. He was furthermore excluded as 'a disorderly person and a hypocrite'.[64]

Oates was before the courts again in July 1702, as he apparently 'sometime beat Mrs [Eleanor] James in the court of requests, being tried at the Westminster sessions, pleaded guilty and was fined six marks'.[65] Apparently Mrs James was at the said court at the same time as Oates and she heard him 'speak very disrespectfully about K. Charles II and also of the word of God'. He was wearing clerical garments and she asked him why he wore such whilst professing to be an Anabaptist. 'In Answer to which he returned her (As a mark of his favour) a dreadful blow on the Head and had he not been prevented by a Gentleman (something civiler than himself) he would have repeated his strokes'.[66]

In court she asked that Oates be forced to cease wearing his robes, that his cane be burnt and that part of his annual pension be given instead to the widows of poor clergymen. This for the sake of religion as Oates was a scandal to it. She did give him some credit, 'Indeed he was made an instrument to discover the Popish Plot and had he kept to Truth, he might have done some good service'. She added, though, that Oates, 'whose actions are as black as Hell' and was 'more like a Devil than a Doctor' and that Oates was known as such.[67]

Oates' counsel argued that he had acted in self defence, that 'she made the first assault, by pulling him by the sleeve'. After some deliberation the court decided against this interpretation of events. It was stated that Oates had been involved in 'customary scandals that the Defendant had been guilty of, against the dead as the living...and of the evil consequences that had attended them'. The court decided that he must pay a considerable fine. Oates confessed his guilt and 'promising to refrain from such scandals in the future and withal alleging he was above a thousand pounds in debt and consequently incapable to pay a large Fine but must be obliged to lie in Prison all his life for its payment'. He promised never to molest Mrs James again, was given a token fine and dismissed from court, 'but not without a severe check for acting so irreverently and unbecoming for his profession'.[68]

One of Oates' enemies remarked that in both Charles II's reign and more so, in that of William III, Oates was of a vexatious nature:

> 'he never failed to give his Attendance in the Court of Requests and the lobbies, to solicite hard in odd points and Deliberation, that might terminate in the prejudice of the Church, Crown or of any gentleman of the loyal or Church of England Party.
> 'He was looked upon as a Screech Owl, ever boding Mischief...He was never seen to hold Dialogues, with any but the rankest Party men, unless it were to Rascal them over...all else avoided the Air of him, as of a stench of Hell'.[69]

He was also seen as a curiosity, as Thomas Brown noted in a survey of the sights of London at the turn of the eighteenth century, having found him in a coffee house that overlooked the Court of Requests:

> 'He is a most accomplish'd person in his way, that's certain. The turn of his face is extremely particular; he has the longest chin of any clergyman in Europe; by the same token they tell me a merry story how he cheated a two penny Barber by hiding it under his cloak. In short, his mouth stands exactly in the middle of his face, like the whole in the centre of a target'.[70]

An early biographer of Oates had this to say about his last years:

> 'he spent the remnant of his life in a kind of Hugger Mugger [confused or disorderly in nature] felicity, being even with the world in this point, that whereas scarce any Body but shunn'd and abus'd him, so that there was very few that the Doctor did not rail at: His company was never acceptable to any, both from his scandalous character and perverse blunt humours...the Doctor aim'd at, was to be taken for a plain, free spoken man, but his spirit was much too capricious and haughty to be trusted with that character, who turn'd it into downright railing and slander...as for his religion, no man cou'd ever tell what creed he possess'd, he had shifted through all without ever being devout in any'.[71]

It is often noted by historians that Oates died unremarked. Certainly the elderly Evelyn does not record it in his diary. The world had certainly moved on from the heady days of 1678-1681. Most of the main players in the drama had died (Shaftesbury, Charles II, his brother, Tonge, Bedloe, Dugdale), though Danby was still alive. Anne, William III's sister in law, had succeeded him on his death and had been Queen since 1702. Britain was involved in a major war, known as the war of Spanish Succession, in a coalition against France and her allies, and Britain's Duke of Marlborough was beginning to show his military genius with his victory at Blenheim in 1704.

However, of the few surviving newspapers for the year of his death, at least one covers the month in which he died, and it was reported there. Apparently, 'Dr Oates upon his deathbed declared yt in gen[era]ll what he swore about the popish plot was true'. This should come as no surprise, as he attested similarly in the 1690s; similarly Bedloe stated likewise just before he died in 1680.[72]

A contemporary history more or less agreed with Oates, stating 'That there was at that time a Popish plot and that there always has been one since the Reformation... scarce any body calls into question'. It was stated that the Coleman letters proved it. However, the exact nature of this plot was unclear, whether it was to restore Catholicism in Britain or not. Significantly Oates was not mentioned by name but it was claimed that witnesses to the plot 'might come to darken truth'.[73]

An early biography noted 'he Dyed of that Distemper on Thursday the 12th of July 1705, and was Buried some Days after in great State and Splendour'.[74] Thomas Hearne (1678-1735), librarian at the Bodleian Library, antiquarian and Jacobite, recorded on 16 July 1705, 'On Thursday last (July 12) died Titus Oates, the sham Salamanca Doctor'.[75] Luttrell also recorded the fact, writing 'Yesterday dyed Dr Titus Oates, famous for the discovery of the popish plot in 1678, for which he had a pension of £300 per annum from the government'.[76]

These two comments are contrasting assessments by contemporaries on Oates' life and achievements. Hearne, as a Jacobite and supporter of James II and his successors, is clearly opposed to the man who implicated the former King and his co-religionists in conspiracy and treason and so refers slightingly to Oates' mendacity about alleging to have a doctorate from Salamanca University, as previous critics of Oates noted in the previous century. Luttrell writes rather differently, making no reference to Oates as a perjurer and liar, but referring to him as a hero justly rewarded by the government for his endeavours.

Another near contemporary verdict came in an account of that year of Anne's reign. It noted 'About the middle of July died Dr Oates'. There was a summary of his life and career:

> 'He was the Discoverer of the Popish Plot in 1678, for which he was first mightily caressed – But maliciously interweaving Improbabilities and Falsities with Truths, in his Depositions; and the Popish Interest prevailing by Degrees, in that Reign, the Doctor was discountenanced and ridiculed… whipp'd after the most unmerciful manner imaginable…The Daringness and Courage of the Man was beyond Example he having been often heard to say, He did not question but he should live to another Turn, and triumph over his Enemies, which indeed, came to pass after the accession of King William. Many who would not allow him to be a good Evidence, were forc'd to own he prov'd a good prophet, by some things that afterward, came to pass, which concern'd very well with his Depositions. He was of a firey Temper, and violent Humour, variable in his Religion, and ran the whole circle of it in England, except that of Quakerism. He wrote his Narrative of the Popish Plot, a sermon or two, and gave years after the Revolution, there came out, under his name, three volumes full of scurrility and indecent language towards that unfortunate Prince'.[77]

This is a positive account of Oates, stating that there were truths in his accounts of what was basically true, and crediting his character with being daring and brave. Those hanged partly on his words were forgotten and all sympathy is to Oates, having been whipped to martyr status. He is deemed a prophet, yet the main thrust of his deposition, about a plot to murder Charles II and instal Catholicism by force, was untrue. Yet it does not idolise him, with reference to his temper and language and his inconstancy in denominations.

There was also a published elegy about Oates which was hostile to him. It began:

> 'Gone. And no comet to portend thy fall
> No storm to usher in thy funeral
> No Tempest tho' as violent as the last.
> Nor yet to spread the news one sullen Blast'.

The text refers to 'his crimes' and his impudence' before giving a mock epitaph:

'Here rests, since all must have a grave
A reverend doctor, and a reverent knave
A harden'd sinner in a saint's disgrace
He's dead, perhaps he's d- and here he lies'.[78]

There was also a biography of Oates published in the year of his death.

Another early biographer, writing in the year of Oates' death referred to Oates' life of 'scandal and infamy' and 'his own flagitous actions, so notoriously known in the ordinary counsel of his conversation and manners'. He was 'a son of Darkness', 'a subtle, designing knave'. Finally he concluded, 'He was an Honest Man among knaves, and a Knave amongst Honest Men'.[79]

It was not known by Oates' previous biographer where Oates was buried. It would have been customary to have been buried in the churchyard of the parish in which he lived; ie St. Margaret's Westminster. And indeed that was where he was buried, presumably in the churchyard to the west of the church on 14 July, referred to in the appropriate page covering burials in parish register as Dr Tybus Oates. What is not known is why and how he died. He was aged about 55 on death; a little older than Charles II and this not an unusual age of which for a man of the time to die. His will was proved on 16 August 1705 at the court of the royal peculiar of dean and chapter of Westminster. Perhaps needless to say, there is no memorial plaque to Oates at St. Margaret's.

His early biographer wrote these final words:

'For which and all other his habitual and voluntary crimes, he was call'd aside by Death and the Devil...to give an account, and if he be damned, which I'll not undertake to say, tis neither my Fault nor my concern…Here lies a Rogue by many thousand votes, And to convince the world, on't here lies Oates'.[80]

Meanwhile, his widow, who continued to receive the annual pension of £300, remarried on 31 January 1706 at St. James' church, Clerkenwell, to one George Chadwick, a gentleman. They had a son, George Chadwick, baptised on 23 April 1706, a daughter Charlotte, baptised on 22 March 1709, and another son, George James, baptised on 30 March 1710; all at St. Margaret's church, Westminster. Her husband died on 26 March 1712 and she lived until January 1746, then resident at 25 Baldwyns Gardens, Holborn.[81]

Chapter Nine

Later Reputations

As has been said in this book's introduction, few have much good to say about Oates, but within that spectrum, interpretations have varied. Although there has only been one previous biography, books about the Popish Plot and the killing of Justice Godfrey have discussed Oates and given a short biographical sketch of his life and career up to 1678, and on occasion, afterwards. Both the *Dictionary of National Biography* (1895) and the *Oxford Dictionary of National Biography* (2004) feature an article about him; the latter also has a smaller article about his father. Studies of Charles II and the seventeenth century give less coverage to him as an individual, but none can omit him and the so called Popish Plot.

Despite the continued popular anti-Catholicism and legal restrictions on Catholics in public life in the eighteenth century, historians in that century were hostile towards Oates. Roger North, in a book published in 1740, referred to him thus:

> 'He was a low man…He was a most consummate cheat, Blasphemer, vicious, perjured, impudent and sawcy, foul-mouth'd Wretch…He was never seen to hold Dialogues with any but the rankest Party Men…a literal Tool of Party, for indeed all else avoided the Air of him, as of a Stench from Hell'.[1]

John Oldmixion, another early eighteenth century historian, condemned Oates' character, 'I knew Oates, he was dull enough' but in the main supported his allegations:

> 'Oates was a passionate, rash, half-witted Fellow, and his want of Judgement might run him a little too far into Particulars: But that there was a treasonable Plot in general, &c., that the Persons he accus'd were particularly engag'd in it, there is no reason to question…'[2]

Thomas Smollett's multi-volume *History of England* was no less severe, writing that the era was 'engrossed by a very remarkable influence of villainy and imposture'. As to the man himself, 'He was an abandoned miscreant, obscure, illiterate and indigent'. Smollett noted that Oates was indicted for perjury, dismissed for unnatural practices from the ship he served on, he pretended to be a Catholic, and this was 'The fountain of all this intelligence' and the Popish Plot was caused by his wanting to be revenged on the Catholics and his seeking money.[3]

David Hume, writing at the same time, was similar, saying of 'Oates, the informer of this dreadful plot, was himself the most infamous of mankind'. He was the son of an anabaptist preacher and chaplain to Colonel Pride, as well as personally a perjurer and dismissed from the Navy for unnatural offences. As a Catholic convert he was 'This abandoned man'.[4]

Later in the eighteenth century, Oates fared no better at the hands of James MacPherson in his *History*. During his stay in London in 1676, apparently Oates 'abandoned himself to every vice'. Referring to Oates and Tonge, MacPherson observes that the latter was scarce less abandoned or less wicked than himself'. Oates was 'a bold and impudent man, a person who shrank from no undertaking, as he was possessed of no solid understanding'.[5]

The nineteenth century Lord Macaulay was not sympathetic to Oates' nemesis, James II, but nor was he favourable about Oates, writing, 'Titus Oates, a clergyman of the Church of England, had, by his disorderly life and heterodox doctrine, drawn on himself the censure of his spiritual superiors'. He was responsible for having 'constructed a hideous romance, resembling rather the dream of a sick man than any transaction which ever took place in the real world'.[6]

Not all authors were hostile to Oates. In an anti-Catholic book of Victoria's reign, the author depicts Oates as a heroic martyr against the evils of Catholicism. It noted that neither Oates nor Bedloe recanted their views on the reality of the Popish plot, 'to their eternal credit'. It stressed his trial of 1685 and the sufferings inflicted on him thereafter. The witnesses from St. Omers against him were described as perjurers. As to his character, 'His firmness and courage, even perhaps to a Fault, have been visible through those mentioned'. He was 'open and frank', generous, witty and humorous. He bore numerous whippings bravely.[7]

This latter book was very much an aberration. Thomas Seccombe wrote in a chapter in a book of biographical studies, published 1894, that he was 'the king of liars' and that he was 'a human being, who, it is believed, has hitherto successfully repelled the advances of the most intrepid of biographers'.[8] Seccombe later wrote the entry in the *Dictionary of National Biography* about Oates, describing him as 'perjurer' and claiming his father as a Cambridge graduate and then rector of Marsham in Essex.

Pollock concurred in part, writing less than a decade later, that Oates 'has justly been considered one of the world's great imposters'. Yet he did not wholly damn him, writing:

> 'But in the field of broad humour Oates bears the palm. There is, after all, something laughable about the rascal. His gross personality had in it a comic strain. He could not only invent, but, when unexpected events occurred, adapt them on the instant to his own end. His coarse tongue was not without a kind of wit. Whenever, he appears on the scene, as has been said of Jeffreys, we may be sure of good sport'.

Pollock's book has been described by a later historian, John Kenyon, as being anti-Catholic and indeed it was attacked by Jesuits of his own era. Yet this is not to say that Pollock merely treats Oates as a comic character:

> 'Yet to his victims he was an emblem of tragic injustice. Very serious were his lies to the fifteen men whom he brought to death. The world was greedy of horrors and Oates sounded the alarm at the crucial moment'.[9]

As the book progresses, Pollock makes another scathing attack on Oates:

> 'By nature he was a bully, brutal, sensual, avaricious, and gifted with a greed of adulation, which, in a man of less impudence, would have caused a speedy ruin, and shrewdness and promptitude were qualities not without a certain value. His vices had not yet grown to be notorious…In person, Oates was hideous…His voice rasped inharmoniously, and he could tune it at will to the true Puritan whine or scold on terms with such a master of abuse as Jeffreys'.[10]

The only biographer of Oates to date, wrote as Jane Lane (a woman who helped Charles II escape from England in 1651, from whom she was descended). Her real name was Ealine Kidner Dakers (1905-1978). From the 1930s to the 1970s she wrote predominantly historical fiction, set in the seventeenth and eighteenth centuries. She wrote from a Catholic and a Stuart perspective. Her approach is that of a defender of the Stuarts, and though there is an outburst against Charles II, he is usually depicted as thinking and acting rightly. Shaftesbury is castigated, as are the common people. There is an unremitting hostility to Oates, of whose attitudes, emotions and thoughts the author possesses an impossible knowledge. Her biography of Oates was one of the three works of non fiction she penned. She begins the biography in no uncertain manner:

> 'The England of sixteen hundred and forty nine suffered two national tragedies: the execution of King Charles the First, and the birth of Titus Oates. The first was the result of a violation of the Law and Constitution. The effect of the second was the writing of the darkest chapter in the history of English justice. The death upon the scaffold of the King, the supreme authority, followed upon a trial in which there was not one shred of legality; the birth of the obscure baby preceded a series of judicial murders without parallel in the story of these nations'.[11]

She concludes with a summary of his effect:

> 'This man had shaken a throne, he had threatened a nation with civil war, he had played not an inconsiderable part in bringing about the Glorious

> Revolution…He had been the companion of Kings, the protégé of dukes and earls…He had loosed on England to prey on society the worst criminals of the underworld…To great men like the Five Lords, as to humble men like Stratford and Medbourne, his bare word had brought death, imprisonment or ruin…His voice, that peculiar, affected voice, uplifted in accusation had instituted a period of terror unparalleled in the history of a great and ancient people'.[12]

The book was reviewed in the *Punch* magazine in September 1949 and the reviewer (known only as F.B.) referred to Oates as 'That outrageous and repulsive ruffian' and 'the monster of pathological malice' who did much to create 'that chaos of iniquity called the Popish Plot'.[13]

The blurb for Kenyon's book calls Oates 'a psychopath'.[14] A psychopath is one who has no concern for others in the pursuit of his own ends and lacks remorse. They are usually focussed on only short term goals.

Stephen Knight, writing about the murder of Sir Edmund Godfrey, has no doubt about Oates' evil, introducing him as a 'devil'. Throughout the book, Oates is continually denigrated, 'His hatred of Jesuits', 'his rancid imagination'.[15] He also suggests that Oates was insane: 'It could indeed be argued that Oates' evil was the product of mental illness and so perhaps more understandable'.[16]

Another writer about the Godfrey murder, Alan Marshall, concludes that Oates was a man who aimed at respectability and acceptance in society. He was a fantasist and invented evil where none existed. In his world he was the hero, the 'Saviour of the Nation' and he truly believed that this myth was true.[17]

On 12 May 2016, in a BBC Radio Four series titled 'In Our Time', presenter Melvyn Bragg discussed Titus Oates and the Popish Plot with three English academics: Claire Jackson, Mark Knights and Peter Hinds. It was almost an hour and gave a good and measured synopsis of the episode, though some key players, such as Shaftesbury and Bedloe, were never mentioned. Oates was described as 'somewhat of a rogue…with a history of disappointments and failures'. Curiously enough Bragg gave 1727 as the year of Oates's death, possibly confusing it with that of George I or Sir Isaac Newton. It perhaps overegged the pudding with reference to the executions of Archbishops and lords (note the plurals used).[18]

A couple of YouTube videos can be seen about Oates. One is a brief 10 minute sketch of his life and career, with a few errors in detail. The other was produced by the National Archives as part of their 2022 exhibition about plots and conspiracies.[19]

Local histories of Sussex and Hastings usually refer to Oates. One from the early twentieth century concluded after a brief account of his life and career, 'That Titus was the most famous inhabitant of Hastings should reconcile those who have made less mark in history to the blessings of comparative, or even positive obscurity'. Comparing Oates to Admiral Sir Cloudesley Shovell (1650-1707), the same author writes of Oates as 'a contemporary historical character who achieved even greater prominence'.[20]

Another local historian, in reference to Samuel Oates, mentions 'his notorious son' who in Hastings was 'apprehended for some offence and sent to Dover'.[21]

Oates has been referred to in the centuries after his death by others as well as historians. In the press Oates has been usually held up, accurately enough, as a perjurer as for comparative purposes with other figures who are similarly being attacked in print. The Rev. Guiness Rogers in 1889 in defending Liberal MP Charles Stuart Parnell, wrote that he had been the 'victim of an attempt at moral assassination without parallel since the date of Titus Oates'.[22] Not all references to Oates are accurate, as an Irish newspaper in discussion of Oliver Plunket noted that Plunket had been 'unjustly accused of conspiring with Titus Oates in the Popish plot'.[23]

References were made to Oates in the press in the last two centuries. This was especially the case in localities where Oates had resided. This was certainly so in Hastings. As might not be unexpected, he came in for much abuse, the 'infamous' Oates, 'classing Titus Oates with the world's worst men…it is doubtful whether the day will come when Hastings will pride itself in nurturing this most wonderful liar', 'one of history's most infamous perjurers'.[24] Oates frequently appeared in talks and booklets about Hastings history. On a historic walk in Hastings, when Oates was mentioned, a man in the crowd said, 'Yes, I remember at school I had to write an essay on Titus Oates. Didn't he invent the Popish Plot in the days of Charles II and cause a good many innocent men to be sent to the scaffold?'[25] Another newspaper compared Oates blaming the Catholics to Hitler blaming the Jews and McCarthy blaming the Communists.[26] There are some interesting parallels between Oates and McCarthy. Briefly, in 1950 Senator Joseph McCarthy claimed that within the American State Department were numerous Communists. This followed the conviction of one Alger Hiss for perjury and McCarthy's allegations were supported by other Republicans. There was, however, no proof for any of these fears, but since America was then involved in the Cold war with the Communist powers (and a real war in Korea), the global context made them seem very plausible. McCarthy went on to accuse others, including the Secretary of the Army and the President himself. As with Oates, he overreached himself. In 1954 McCarthy was condemned and then became increasingly discredited.[27]

Yet another writer in a Hastings newspaper had radically different views. 'Little are the good people of this country aware how much they owe to the efforts of Titus Oates; the self sacrifices, trials and tortures undergone by the great man in the cause of rectitude and probity'. This was after stating that he was 'a man whose infamy was of the highest value in the promulgation of goodness, whose genius for treachery and whose perfection in lying were the incentives and mainsprings of fidelity and veracity in countless human beings'.[28] After a largely critical article, one journalist ended on a note of some sympathy. 'Whatever drove this sad and lonely man to manipulating others and total immorality, we may never know'.[29]

Curiously there have been race horses and prize pedigree dogs named Titus Oates.[30] Likewise, pubs are often named after historic figures but usually ones with a claim to fame such as the Winston Churchill in Kensington. But some have been named after criminals such as Dick Turpin, Burke and Hare and (for 12 years) Jack the Ripper. No pub has ever been named after Oates but there was a delicatessen in Mill Lane, Oakham named after him in the 1990s.[31] Quite why this should be so is another matter, for though Oates was born in Oakham, his reputation was not, except to extreme anti-Catholic Protestants, a glorious one. Oddly enough, a letter published in an early nineteenth newspaper finished with the author stating 'my renowned ancestor, Titus Oates' and this individual lived in Cock Lane, London, though did not elaborate on why he thought Oates was illustrious.[32]

There have been many films and TV drama featuring Charles II as a major character; possibly more than any other British monarch but certainly up there with Henry VIII, Elizabeth I and Victoria; more than any other Stuart, certainly. However, there has never been a novel, film or television drama focussing on Oates' life and career. This is not surprising. Oates is hardly a fit choice as a hero as some criminals can be depicted. However, he has appeared in celluloid form in two BBC1 television drama series. One was *The First Churchills* (1969) and the second was *Charles II: The Power and the passion* (2003).

The First Churchills focussed on the lives of John and Sarah Churchill, later the Duke and Duchess of Marlborough. Episode three of twelve was titled 'Plot, Counter Plot'. Here Nicholas Smith played Oates. Churchill and his wife are discussing matters and the former tells of news of a Catholic plot being told to the council by a 'rogue' with a 'strange name', 'Titus Oates'. Sarah says that 'This young man who pretended to be a doctor of divinity was without doubt the greatest liar that has lived since Annanias, yet there was some fact mixed with his lies'. Oates is shown in clerical garb and is not the ugly fellow as reported by contemporaries, though no oil painting either.

Oates is shown before the privy council and presents a precis of his narrative. He is questioned about the assassination attempts (by knife, by pistol and by Wakeman poisoning him) on the King's life by the sceptical privy council, but provides detailed and ready answers. The King catches him out over Don John of Austria and this convinces him that Oates is 'The most lying impudent dog that was ever whelped'. Charles is persuaded to take the plot seriously and suggests a pardon and pension for Oates but wants him kept away from himself.

Oates states that he will accuse no man falsely. The crowd are seen to be supportive of Oates and hold up banners with his name on. Shaftesbury and his supporters aim to manipulate Oates to benefit their cause. We later see Oates in court accusing Coleman of high treason. He then accuses Ireland, Pickering and Grove of the same. Oates is not seen in the next episode, 'The Lion and the Unicorn' but he is referred to by Sarah who states that 'the nation was run stark mad', and that, with some exaggeration, 'Catholics were hanged everyday on the evidence of Titus Oates who made a good living thereby'. The narrative fast forwards to early 1681 with reference to acquittals and Stafford's execution. Godolphin relates that

'Shaftesbury and Oates still rule Parliament and the City'. The next we hear of Oates is through Shaftesbury's imminent trial and predicted acquittal. In Chapter Eight of the drama, set in 1692, 'Dr Oates' is referred to twice as an instigator of plots for money and in targeting the unpopular as well as one prominent individual. Here, Oates is essentially a minor character, a villain motivated by greed.

Charles II: The Power and the Passion was shown on BBC1 with Rufus Sewell as the King and Eddie Marsan played Oates; the only other major figure in the Oates tale, below the rank of the major politicians (such as Danby and Shaftesbury) to appear are Kirkby and Tonge (Godfrey appears in the drama in Chapter Two dealing with efforts to deal with the plague in London, but as above his murder goes unmentioned, presumably for reasons of time). In Chapter Four we are shown Kirkby (unnamed) telling Danby about the plot to kill the King. He is very vague and confused as to details and Danby is sceptical. Eventually he refers to notes given to him by Tonge and when Danby asks who wrote them, Kirkby says, 'One who knows the conspirators intimately. His name is Titus Oates'.

Oates is then shown watching an effigy of the pope being burnt and is telling Tonge about Jesuit priests, referring to them as being 'like ravening wolves' and about children being 'torn from their mother's arms'. He talks of 'screams of burning innocence' and is told 'Stop, Titus, I cannot listen' but he continues. He is being shown as an anti-Catholic fanatic, but then the more 'rational' motivation becomes clear when Tonge states 'Kirkby must have talked by now' and Oates replied 'If not, England is lost'.

A royal official arrives on the scene and calls for Oates. He pipes up, 'At your service, sir. Scholar, philosopher, loyal guardian of the flame of truth' he plumps up his own importance. Oates and Tonge come before Danby, with Charles eavesdropping on the conversation. Oates tells him what he knows, that '6,000 Catholics will rise as one and slaughter us all in our beds'. He mentions 'London streets running with honest Protestant blood'. When asked how he knows this he tells 'I overheard it in the Queen's household'. He goes on to say that Louis XIV 'that demon and the pope are the true authors of the plot', they are 'shoulder to shoulder in villainy' with the Queen and the Duke of York (as noted Oates initially exonerated James).

Danby is in disbelief and wants the three put in the stocks. Oates is defiant, 'If you condemn us, the King will die and you will be held accountable'. The King then reveals himself and asks for proof. Oates names the Queen, the Duke of York, the five Catholic lords and Coleman as the principal conspirators. He claims he has letters showing their guilt. He says that he has often warned ministers of the Catholic conspiracies in the past but has been ignored.

Charles then asks where in the palace did Oates overhear the plotting. Oates claims to know the place, but when he walks around the palace he cannot locate anywhere except a small room containing a privy. Charles is not convinced and tells Danby 'Nothing this scoundrel says can be believed. I'm off to Newmarket in the morning. I do not wish to be bothered by this scoundrel again'.

Oates is ingratiating to Danby: 'At your service, my lord'. He then appears before a group of ministers. He shows them the letters and claims to know the Catholic lords in question. When he is told that the handwriting does not match any of the alleged writers, Oates tells them that Jesuits are trained to write in disguised hands. He identifies the writers and says of Lord Stafford, 'of all these villains he is the worst'. Oates has another suggestion to make, 'Examine the Duke's household for all the evidence you need of them'; and urges 'Strike now my lords. Hesitate and all might be lost'.

Oates is then taken to a remote place in the palace by the Duke of Buckingham and is beaten up and threatened with being stabbed. He says that Christ came to him in a dream to tell hm about the plot and that he was to be the instrument to save the country. When in extremis, he says that he had a position in a Catholic boys' school and that 'the boys lay filthy charges against me. I lost my position and I determined to have my revenge on their whole stinking Catholic filth'. This is Oates' true motivation and is the only hint about his sexuality. Buckingham then decides to use Oates in order to attack the Duke of York and 'even your ridiculous lies will be believed'.

We later see Coleman questioned about the letters he has written, but he denies all involvement in a plot. He is later seen being hanged. Charles continues to disbelieve Oates, 'At least put the perjured villain in prison where he belongs', but is told that he is under Parliament's protection. Oates' words are shown as gaining credence: 'Oates said Coleman's letters would contain treason and they did' as a minister relates. Oates is shown telling an audience about tortures the Catholics wish to perpetrate and that the pope 'hates our liberty, works every day to destroy it' and that the people need Parliament to defend them. He is also shown in Parliament denouncing the Queen as an accessory to murder.

In private the King tells his wife that Oates is a fraud and 'Oates' lies condemn him', but we are also told 'Oates has the whole country terrified'. Stafford, in a prison cell, after being found guilty of treason, is then shown being visited by the King. He urges him to confess to save his life but the lord refuses and is subsequently beheaded.

In the 1969 drama, Oates is dressed formally as a clergyman and wearing a long wig. The 2003 drama shows him dressed more casually and with his own hair; it is only the scene in parliament where he dons a wig.

The 2003 drama features a commentary by some of those involved in it, though not the actor playing Oates. They decide that Oates first appears as a comic and then appears more horrible and dangerous when the consequences of his talk is shown. Oates is described as 'the most absurd bigoted liar'. The search for the room in the palace is shown as comedy. It is noted that the Buckingham and Oates scene is an invention to show that Oates, like 'all bullies and bigots', is 'a fearful coward'. Oates' role after the plot is not disclosed, though the fates of the main characters are.

As an anti-hero, Oates might well be a fit choice for a TV drama. Murderers have been depicted as the leading characters in drama; serial killers George Joseph

Smith and John George Haigh have had dramas focussing on their lives and crimes as the leading figures. Yet both came to fitting ends on the gallows and justice is done; whereas Oates died of natural causes. Both these said killers had looks and charm of a sort; Oates had none. Oates' apparent homosexuality might also prove problematic to any adaptor of his life. Code breaking genius Alan Turing can be (and has been) shown as a hero and martyr but Oates cannot, without considerable selectivity of the known facts.

There is also at least one novel in which Oates is a major character. This is in Kate Braithwaite's 2018 historical fiction first titled *The Road to Newgate* and then altered to *The Plot*. Here Nathaniel Thompson, a printer, publisher and Licenser, (based in part on Sir Roger L'Estrange, but a younger man) and his wife and their two friends (one William Smith, once Oates' schoolmaster) are in opposition to Oates in a story based in the London around 1678. Oates is, perhaps naturally, portrayed as a malevolent and dangerous villain.

For a historical novel, it is relatively accurate and where it is not, the author usually makes reference to it in her historical aftermath. Oates is first seen in the Commons, describing the plot and there is a summary of its articles. He is described as a monstrous figure, which is not unlike reality. Nat Thompson is against Oates from the start and it is not long before Anne, his wife, is also. They become personally involved when William Smith is thrown into Newgate due to Oates' lies and they begin printing material hostile to Oates, including *The Observator*.

There are a number of confrontations between Oates and his enemies; at the Fullers Rents inn, at a theatre, in the street and elsewhere. Oates usually has a number of sycophantic allies with him. He is shown as a truly repulsive figure, mentally and spiritually as well as physically. He is a vindictive and spiteful bully, with coarse and brutal manners and language, never afraid to lie when it helps his cause and creates a great deal of unpleasantness. His homosexuality is hinted at. He even has Miles Prance (Dugdale features not at all, Tonge is given one scene with Thompson, as is his son and Bedloe is only mentioned) swear that Thompson was seen celebrating mass and so has him torn from his wife just as she is giving birth and sent to Newgate; later their house is burnt down and Thompson is burnt in effigy. The trial of the three men accused of Godfrey's murder and the trial of three Jesuits features; that of Coleman is referred to. None of the other trials are shown, though Wakeman's is mentioned in retrospect.

Thompson has Oates' antecedents investigated and so the reader learns some of Oates' parents, childhood, schooldays, university career, his earlier perjuries and his brief clerical and naval careers. It is pretty accurate historically. Thompson later discovers the truth of Godfrey's death, which is the solution advocated by Alan Marshall in his book about Godfrey's demise (see Appendix three). However, this leads nowhere and the book's concluding chapters cover the trial of Oates for perjury as to the alleged Jesuit meeting on 24 April 1678. Jeffreys presides. It is a pretty accurate rendition of the trial, with Oates and Jeffreys exchanging insults, Oates' witnesses and the Crown witnesses from St. Omers and of course, Oates' being found guilty and sentenced to annual floggings and perpetual imprisonment.

The author notes that in reality the trial was in 1685 and not some years earlier as she has telescoped events somewhat. The book ends with some sympathy for Oates' plight and then on his leaving prison after James' exile, he is joined by his father and they walk away companionably. In reality, of course, Samuel Oates had died some years previously and Oates' obnoxious career was far from over in 1689.

It is also curious to note that Captain Lawrence Oates (1880-1912), who went on to die heroically in an act of self sacrifice in an attempt to save his comrades at the South Pole in 1912, was also known as Titus. This is a clear reference to the shared surname of these two very different men and the Christian name of the well known seventeenth century Oates was used for the early twentieth century one. Apparently his fellow officers called him by this nickname and sharing the same surname as Titus Oates, Titus perhaps rather obviously suggested itself.[33] This is a pointer to a greater historical knowledge (on some matters at least) possessed at that time compared to the later twentieth century. This author was never termed Titus until 2023 when talking to a former colleague at the British Library.

Ronald Fraser played a character called Titus Oates in 'Selected Target', the first episode in the third series of the great police drama series, *The Sweeney* (1976). Appropriately enough he is a criminal who helps mastermind a major (non-violent) bank robbery – and gets away with the takings. He is portrayed as a cunning and clever operator and indulges in philosophy. The viewer learns that during the Second World War he was a conscientious objector, thus disposing 1970s (and later) audiences not to like him. A book commenting on the series in detail makes no allusion to the identity of the character's namesake.

Physically there is very little to mark Oates. There is, perhaps naturally, no statue or plaque for him, or even a pub named after him. The houses in Axe Yard are no more and the church he was married in has been demolished. The church where he is buried does not commemorate him. All Saints church in Hastings, where he was baptised, has a small notice on a wall about him. There is much about him online, though of a rudimentary nature. Perhaps this is just as well.

Last Words

Oates' claim to infamy is of being the man who invented the 'Popish Plot' that never was and in doing so 28 men went to their deaths in 1678-1681; mostly priests, but including a nobleman and an archbishop. Yet it should be said of these trials which led to the defendants being executed, that he was a prominent witness for those dealing with eleven defendants 'only' and a minor witness at that for another three. It should also be remembered that he would have had no significance or weight had there not been a great history of anti-Catholicism and statutes against Catholics, especially priests. Similarly the unpopularity and suspicion of Catholic and French influence at the highest levels gave substance to such allegations. Neither of these were of Oates' doing. Nor should we forget that he was not the only instigator of the plot nor the only witness. Kirkby and Tonge played their parts in introducing it to the King. Bedloe, Dangerfield, Dugdale and Prance were also important in fanning the flames of the fire. The judiciary also played their role in influencing the jury to return verdicts of guilty in many of these trials.

On the other hand, while conceding that Oates, as with anyone else, did not operate alone in a vacuum, he did play a major role in the Plot. The gunpowder was there and it was he who, along with Tonge and Kirkby, struck the initial match and whereas they faded from the picture he maintained the tale throughout. Without him it is probable that Tonge would never have had any role in its inception. Oates was not the first to bring it to the attention of King and government, but in September 1678 it was he who laid all 81 articles before the Privy Council. Then there was the tragedy of Sir Edmund Berry Godfrey and the finding of suspicious papers in Coleman's possession. Thereafter, for a time, Oates was cossetted by government with what he desired; lodgings, protection, money and power, all of which he exploited to the full. From being an impoverished nobody he was now a affluent somebody.

Throughout the trials of 1678-1680, Oates was a prominent and deadly witness. He gave testimony against men he knew and those he knew of, without any real evidence at all. He was a skilled liar, imaginative and inventive, and was also blessed with good luck and sympathetic lawyers, at least at first. As a witness he was often put to hard questioning by the defendants and was often in difficulties in framing convincing answers; yet was, at least in some of the trials, helped by the lawyers in court.

But he was no friend to the monarchy of Charles II. Once he fell out of royal favour in 1681 he began to show other colours, that had been there previously and perhaps inherited from his father. He began to openly consort with radicals and republicans and showed his contempt for the monarchy and paid the penalty for such. After 1685 only the revolution of 1688 offered him the prospect of relief and this he seized. Monetary concerns were one of his major motivating factors throughout the life; perjury was a means to an end, whether it was taking money at school, clothes at university, hoping for a schoolmaster's place at Hastings, before taking the higher rewards and fame in 1678-1681. Out of pocket, his recently found position doubtless helped him find supporters among the King's enemies. From 1689 to his death he was in receipt of a public pension.

He was also a great troublemaker, sometimes for money but in part for its own sake. This obviously was directed to Catholics from 1678, but his venom extended towards others whom he encountered, both before 1678 and afterwards. The difficulties that the Wapping Baptists experienced from 1699 were not obviously motivated by money. Likewise he was a trouble to many others and was no slouch in taking his enemies to the law, though not always successfully. There was a vicious streak in him that could also take a physical form, if his victim was weaker than himself, whether forcing his attentions on a friend's sister at Cambridge or assaulting Mrs James in 1702.

His greatest claim to fame was his role in the 'Popish plot', which he more than any other single individual did so much to establish and to maintain. He never lost faith in his creation, at least not in public. Despite all that had happened in the 1680s, he maintained its existence well into the next decade. But he perhaps had no option for a man of his character. To admit that he had been wrong, to confess that it had been a work of fiction would have undermined his whole public image. He would have been a nobody, as he had been until 1678. Fame was something he wanted, perhaps it was a drug that once savoured he could not live without.

The investigation of the 'Popish Plot' coincided with the exclusion campaign of 1679-1681. Indeed the former predated the latter. The extent to which the latter grew out of Oates' allegations cannot be known. That it helped fuel it seems undeniable however. Both ended in ruin and failed in their aims, yet for two years they dominated national politics.

There is much that we can never know about Oates, largely because he never felt a need to explain himself to anyone. Although often surrounded by others, he seems to have lacked an ability or possibly a need, to form close human ties. Other people were there to be exploited, usually for material gain. The only family member who he seems to have been close to was his elder brother Samuel, and then not for long. Oates did not seem to care about the negative effect he had on the lives of others; perhaps he enjoyed it and so can be fairly described as a misanthrope.

Possibly Oates felt that he was one of society's outsiders and so thought that his attacks on it were justified. If he was homosexual that would be a further reason why he thought he was outside conventional society and perhaps felt that he was not bound by its laws and conventional Christian morality, though he was happy to use those laws when it was to his advantage.

Oates' public persona is well known; he helped make it so along with his detractors. Oates the private man is largely unexplored and unknowable. He was a son, a brother, a husband and a father. Quite what he was like to his family and friends is hard to know. He seems to have had no other interests save religion and politics and a liking for the good life.

Although unlikeable in himself, the causes that Oates espoused were usually popular ones. Anti-Catholicism was one which could not fail to gain an audience in the seventeenth and eighteenth centuries, both at popular and official levels. It could be a source of both adulation and reward. This was so in 1678-1681 and after 1688. James as Duke of York and later King was an easy target that Oates did not fail to attack. We should never forget that even at the nadir of his fortunes in 1685-1688 Oates enjoyed a degree of support, as he had from 1678 and was to do again in 1689. He was a populist and had many supporters; impressive for a man of relatively humble origins in the society in which he moved.

Although the main tenet of the Popish Plot – an attempt to kill Charles II – was untrue, some argued that the general idea of a Catholic onslaught on Protestant Britain held good. They would argue that the attempts made by James II to espouse the Catholic cause in his reign showed that Oates was not wholly wrong. But, though there was an imposing chasm between the two, the reactions to James' actions had assisted the cause of anti-Catholicism, and would be used by its adherents in the eighteenth century.

There can be little doubt that Oates was a scoundrel throughout his life. He achieved little that was positive and did much that was destructive. It was not only his role in initiating the 'Popish plot', which led to the deaths of innocent Catholics. His lesser actions outside this period could and often did, have very unfortunate results for others. Whether he was the century's worst Briton is surely open to dispute, however, and can only be decided by an assessment of other contenders. Some could suggest Cromwell as being more destructive, but Cromwell also has his supporters. Morally, perhaps Rochester could be condemned by others.

Oates' significance can only be explained by two factors. Firstly the explosive situation in which he operated, with rampant anti-Catholicism, distrust of court and government and a willingness among others to take him seriously. Secondly there is the fact that Oates was undeniably a skilled operator. Despite his looks and uncouth speech he had all the gifts of an unscrupulous salesman. He came across as knowledgeable and convincing to most and had no moral qualms. The combination of the two was deadly.

Appendix One

The Plot's Victims

L'Estrange wrote in 1687, 'I know not how many Priests, Jesuits and others have Dy'd for't as a Plot'.[1] Various numbers have been bandied about in print about the number of men hanged as victims of the 'Plot'; usually either 15 or 35 are stated, 'more than 30' albeit with no explanation as to how these figures have been calculated nor who they are. This is odd; the current zeitgeist is that emphasis is being put on murder victims and the innocents caught up in crimes and conspiracies. This author has ascertained, using primary sources, chiefly Luttrell's *Brief Relation*, the plot's 28 victims (those 11 for which Oates was one of the principal witnesses against have been *italicised*).

All executed at Tyburn, London, unless otherwise stated.

William Staley, tried at King's Bench, 20 November, hanged on 26 November 1678
Edward Coleman, tried at King's Bench, 27 November, hanged on 3 December 1678
William Ireland, tried at the Old Bailey on 17 December, hanged on 24 January 1679
John Grove, tried at the Old Bailey on 17 December, hanged on 24 January 1679
Thomas Pickering, tried at the Old Bailey on 17 December, hanged on 25 May 1679
Robert Green, tried at King's Bench, 5 February, hanged on 21 February 1679
Lawrence Hall, tried at King's Bench, 5 February, hanged on 21 February 1679
Henry Berry, tried at King's Bench, 5 February, hanged on 28 February 1679
David Lewis, tried at Monmouth, 28 March 1679, hanged at Usk, 27 August 1679.
Thomas Whitebread, tried at the Old Bailey on 13 June 1679, hanged on 20 June 1679
William Harcourt, tried at the Old Bailey on 13 June 1679, hanged on 20 June 1679
John Fenwick, tried at the Old Bailey on 13 June 1679, hanged on 20 June 1679
John Gavan, tried at the Old Bailey on 13 June 1679, hanged on 20 June 1679
Anthony Turner, tried at the Old Bailey on 13 June 1679, hanged on 20 June 1679
Richard Langhorn, tried at the Old Bailey on 14 June 1679, hanged on 14 July 1679
John Plessington, tried and hanged at Chester, 19 July 1679
Andrew Bromwitch, tried and hanged at Stafford, 1679
William Atkins, tried and hanged at Stafford, 1679

Philip Evans, hanged at Cardiff, July 1679
John Lloyd, hanged at Cardiff, July 1679
Charles Mahoney hanged at Ruthin, 12 August 1679
Francis Johnson, tried and hanged at Worcester, 22 August 1679
Nicholas Postgate, hanged at York on 17 August 1679.
John Kemble, hanged at Hereford, 22 August 1679.
John Wall, hanged in August 1679.
Thomas Thwing, hanged at York on 23 October 1680.
Earl of Stafford, tried at the House of Lords, on 29 November – 6 December, beheaded on Tower Hill, 29 December 1680.
Archbishop Oliver Plunket, tried on 8 June 1681, hanged, drawn and quartered on 1 July 1681

In addition several Catholics died in prison, 1678-1684, their exact number unknown. They include Lord Petre, Thomas Bedingfield, Matthew Medbourne, Richard Gerard, Edward Mico, Francis Levison, Francis Nevill, Charles Lloyd, Anthony Hunter and David Kemish.

Appendix Two

Oates' Sexuality

We now come to the question of Oates' sexuality. Homosexual acts between men were then known by the law as the crime of buggery and sodomy and from 1533-1861 it was a capital crime. These were seen, legally, as unnatural offences and this condemnation was sanctioned by the Bible in many passages in both Testaments, which would be well known by most people. As a contemporary publication noted, 'The Sin of Buggery…is now rarely practised amongst the English', having been introduced by foreigners and practised mainly by such.[1] However, we must be careful about the use of language. The term homosexual was not employed until the 1890s. As Alan Bray has noted, 'To talk of an individual in this period as being or not being a homosexual is an anachronism and so misleading'. Buggery and sodomy were terms used for sex between men and between people of either sex and animals. The term debauchery included a host of sins: pride, excess, laziness and contempt for the poor as well as sexual misbehaviour.[2]

Sodomy was seen as the province of the abandoned rake/libertine who might also enjoy sex with women and was a republican in politics. It was 'not a coherent notion, but a cluster of associations' and was 'deployed rhetorically as a way of establishing the unacceptable otherness of a political opponent'. Sexual relations between men were termed sodomy but this condemnatory term of officialdom failed to encompass the whole range of sexual and emotional feelings. It was deemed a sin but not a sexual identity. It was only towards the end of the seventeenth and the beginning of the eighteenth century that a separate sub culture/identity emerged with the institution of molly houses where men could go to meet other men for sex.[3]

It is worth noting that to accuse an enemy of 'unnatural vice', whether incest, homosexuality, bestiality or paedophilia, was a common smear tactic in the seventeenth century. Accusing any man of these was a sure way to blacken his moral character and had the added attraction of not having to produce much in the way of solid proof. A loyalist tract of 1682 accused Scottish Covenanters of being 'Buggers, Bestiality, incest and adultery'. Major Weir, a Covenanter officer, was accused of indulging in all these and he was hanged in 1670 for them.[4] Jacobite enemies of William III accused him of unnatural vice with his confidante Hans Wilhelm Bentinck and critics of James I and the Duke of Buckingham had done likewise. These offences leave no physical evidence that could have been detected in the seventeenth century and are no easy matter to prove, save for contested witness testimony. Yet the mere suggestion of them would have caused the majority to be outraged and horrified. The allegations against Oates did not surface in public until 1679 when for some, he was a figure to be attacked for his actions since the previous year. It was an offence which was rarely prosecuted; at the Old Bailey from 1674-1704 only five such cases were heard; and in three the defendant was found guilty and so sentenced to death. Two of these three took place with animals.[5] It is worth noting that Oates was never tried for such offences, let alone convicted of them.

Oates' sexuality has been dealt with differently over the decades; sometimes not at all. Seccombe, in his article in the 1890s *Dictionary of National Biography* refers to the charge laid against Parker thus, 'a disgusting charge' and later to 'the superior villainy of his [Oates'] private life'.[6] Sir John Pollock, writing over a century ago was necessarily vague. Of the Hastings allegation against Parker, he wrote:

> 'he conspired with his father to bring an *odious* charge against the schoolmaster...Oates' *abominable* evidence was proved to be false'. Of his dismissal from the Navy, 'He was expelled upon the same grounds as he had formerly urged against the fortunate schoolmaster'.[7]

The reader who has not read any other work than this is perhaps left in somewhat of a quandary as to the exact nature of these offences. However, when the Knox and Lane affair is highlighted the astute reader will rumble what is being hinted at, 'Lane charged his master ...with the commission of an unnatural offence'.[8]

Jane Lane is a little more explicit, but is also circumspect. The offence which Oates accused young Parker of was described merely as being 'unnatural' and refers to sodomy in the next paragraph as being a capital offence.[9] Regarding his dismissal from the Navy, Lane states contemporary sources, which are explicit enough, before writing her own verdict:

> 'The subject is an unsavory one, but it is essential to an understanding of Titus' character. There can be little doubt that he was a pervert, though this is the only instance in which he was actually punished for that vice. More than one accusation of sodomy was to be brought against him in the future, but as these were made after the year 1678, when he became immune from justice, he always escaped. When he went to school again, as a grown man, his superiors deemed him dangerous to the society of boys; and in his latter years, when it was safe to criticize him, there was scarcely a squib or a broadsheet published concerning him which did not contain a mention of his unnatural vices'.[10]

The statement above says as much about the author and the time (1949 being the year of publication) in which she lived as it does Oates. It should be noted that although Oates sat apart from the boys in the dining hall at St. Omers, there is no explicit evidence that the reason for Oates' segregation was the concern that he might be what is now termed a paedophile as Lane hints. Only one of the former students who testified against him in 1685 hints at such intimacy. We should also note that there is no contemporary reference to any court martial or formal disciplinary action against Oates for his behaviour afloat, which one source states that he escaped to avoid. We should also note that not every pamphlet written against Oates from 1685 alludes to his sexuality.

On the subject of the pamphlet describing Oates' marriage, Lane is suitably coy, with reference to 'his astonishment, in the frankest possible terms, that a man of Titus' unnatural habits should enter into matrimony'. She adds 'After speculating (in unprintable fashion)…' and discusses the Browne pamphlet detailed in Chapter Eight.[11] Again, Lane is coy about the wording in the pamphlet. She is also brief when describing the Oates versus Knox and Lane court case of 1679.

The late twentieth century saw a greater degree of candour concerning sexual matters after relations between adult men ceased to be a criminal offence in 1967. John Kenyon, controversially by current standards, makes no bones about the subject:

> 'Oates was dismissed for homosexual practices, and he was lucky not to be tried for his life. The fact that Oates was an active and practising homosexual had always been known, but historians have evaded one obvious conclusion: that this explains the astonishing ease with which he was admitted to certain Catholic circles which one would have supposed barred to a disreputable Anglican clergyman with heterodox leanings'.[12]

Presumably Kenyon is suggesting that some Catholic priests were homosexual. Kenyon later states, after erring about Oates 'marrying a wealthy city widow', one of the myths of the story now enshrined as fact through repetition:

> 'He seems to have abandoned his homosexuality, or perhaps he had always been bi-sexual: there is a well attested story [not so, a rumour relayed by Anthony Wood of Oxford] that he fathered a bastard in the King's Bench prison in 1688'.[13]

Knight writes, 'Titus had to cope in adulthood with the added disadvantage of being homosexual when Homosexuality was considered an atrocious crime'. He later added that Oates alleged that Parker had buggered "a young and tender man-child"'. As to the navy, 'Despite the known prevalence of homosexuality aboard His Majesty's ships [not so according to premier historian of the Navy, N.A.M. Rodgers] in the solitary weeks and months at sea, Titus' behaviour aboard the Adventure made him notorious'. Once on shore, Knight recalls that a recent historian has suggested that Oates was the member of a homosexual group.[14] As has been noted, those writing in the 1990s onwards have made no bones about Oates' sexuality but did not proceed into any detail or analysis.

Marshall notes that homosexuals in the seventeenth century did not see themselves as such. He is adamant that Oates was both homosexual and a paedophile, writing 'There seems to be little doubt that Oates engaged in sodomy...evidence for Oates' sexuality goes beyond mere satire'. He goes on to state 'There seems little doubt that he was a paedophile...[and was]...positively dangerous to young boys'. Marshall's evidence stems from the pamphlet about Oates' marriage as cited at length in the previous chapter and from the fact that he falsely accused William Parker of indecent behaviour with a child.[15]

The author of the *Oxford Dictionary of National Biography* described Oates as an 'informer'. He concludes that he 'remains an unusual figure in British history'. He notes that there have been several explanations about his personality and career and notes that earlier authors were 'repelled' by his homosexuality. He claims that Oates was driven by 'a psychotic's revenge...a desire for acceptance and respectability...a fantasist: a man who saw himself as the of saviour of the nation...and the secret hero' whereas he was ultimately a failure.[16]

A more recent author, unlike earlier ones, ascribes one reason for Oates' leaving the parish of Bobbing to his homosexuality heading the list of offences. Parker is described as being guilty of pederasty, perhaps not the best known of words to many readers. As with Knight, Oates is described as being a practising homosexual when at sea. However there is nothing about a possible homosexual ring of which he was a later member.[17]

Jenni Uglow in *A Gambling Man* makes a casual reference to Oates being arrested in the 1680s whilst 'cruising for boys'. The BBC programme referred to Oates exiting the Navy (but nowhere else) due to being accused of sodomy.[18]

The most extensive discussion of Oates' sexuality or rather how it was portrayed in anti-Oates satires, comes from Paul Hammond in both a chapter in a collection of studies and in his own book. Hammond studies the language used in a number of contemporary satires about Oates. Of his sexual nature, Hammond is in no doubt, writing 'That Titus Oates was sexually interested in other men is as securely established as a biographical fact as one could expect for such a question in this period'. He adds that though the reasons for Oates leaving various schools and colleges are not clear, the reason for his departure from his naval career is, and his false accusations of paedophilia against Parker at Hastings are 'not difficult to speculate on the psychological motive for such an accusation' (the author did not know of Oates's similar accusation against another schoolmaster when at school a decade earlier). He argued that there was more gossip about Oates than was documented and the comments about him featured in political satires, often a page or two long at most, rather than in more lengthy and considered tracts.[19]

Hammond refers to a number of such pieces. In *Hue and Cry after Titus Oates* (1681), there is the line 'He seldom frequents the company of women, but keeps private communication with Four Bums…He is one that preached B-----y [Buggery or Blasphemy] before weavers'. This pamphlet describes Oates as a bestial figure, far less than a man. In another satire Oates is seen gazing on a bare bottomed boy and Cupid fires an arrow at him. It associates Oates with Turks and Cardinals, both viewed as those who indulged in sodomy. In *Auricular Confession* of 1683, Oates declares 'Of all the catalogue of crimes, I am of this only innocent, having the strongest aversion to the use of women the right way'. Another pamphlet published the next year has Oates saying, 'For my own spending I will keep/Of Boys three hundred more/They are at my appetite more sweet/Than Bawd or Backsore whore'. A Jacobite verse discusses William III and Oates as 'Sham doctor and sham King', though sodomites both.[20]

Hammond then discusses the impact of such texts. He suggests that 'co-opted here into a conservative political discourse, in order to suggest that he and his cause are a perverted parody of, and threat to, the body politic'. Here, 'sexuality is part of this political discourse'. Because Oates was shown as being physically deformed and sexually deviant he was far removed from the audiences of these tracts and so his credibility was under severe attack. 'Sodomy in these texts is an over determined trope' and reinforced the view of Puritans and Catholics as being unattractive alternatives to Anglicanism and social stability. They are the 'other'. They were evidence of the anxiety and fear of men who sought to make bonds of a non-sexual kind with other men and their view of masculinity was a form of safeguarding the social and political order. Oates' fantasy world 'threatened to make the public sphere incontinent and unintelligible'.[21]

A refreshingly neutral remark comes from the most recent historian of the murder of Godfrey, 'Whatever Oates' sexual orientation, he certainly had no qualms about using accusations of sodomy to advance his own interests'.[22]

There are, then, a number of points of discussion about Oates' sexuality. Firstly there is his behaviour at school; his alleged encounter with a fellow pupil and his subsequent accusation of this offence by the master. Then there is the question of his accusation of young Parker in 1675, his departure from the Navy in 1676, the accusations of Knox and Lane in 1679, an accusation in early 1683, the possible fathering of an illegitimate child in the same decade, his marriage in 1693, subsequent children, and the numerous publications which allude to his nature. We need to discuss these one by one.

It is worth noting that nothing is heard in public of Oates' sexuality until the Knox and Lane case of 1679. This is in part because Oates was not a nationally known figure until the autumn of 1678; whatever people thought or said about him hitherto is unknown. Oates' enemies, such as those he had wronged including Elliott and Smith, and those publicists for his enemies, such as North and L'Estrange began to make insinuations in print against his sexuality from then on. Naturally they would do so. Pamphleteers, whether the author of the letter from Amsterdam and the one about his marriage made reference to his homosexuality. Yet Burnet was not wholly opposed to Oates; certainly he was opposed to the Catholic cause and to James II and yet he was happy to give homosexuality as the reason for Oates' expulsion from the Navy. However, Ailesbury, another enemy of Oates, does not hint at his homosexuality and nor does Evelyn.

On the other hand he was not wholly unknown to woman. His first alleged encounter is with his friend's sister at Cambridge. Then there is a reference to him marrying one of Shaftesbury's family, perhaps to getting a woman pregnant whilst in prison and of course his marriage and children. Some of these have little foundation (he did not marry into the Cooper family), the third is rumour and the fourth is hardly cast iron evidence of his sexuality either way. There is the possibility that Oates was bisexual, as in the case with the better documented Earl of Rochester.

The Knox and Lane accusations of 1679 were an attempt to discredit Oates' standing as a witness against the Catholics he had accused of treason, and paid for by Danby. They could have been true, of course. It was certainly known about at a very public trial and the subsequent publications about it only served to give publicity to Oates' alleged homosexuality. Certainly others followed where Knox and Lane had led.

At this distance of time it is impossible to ascertain whether Oates was homosexual, bisexual or not. There is no doubt that some of his enemies decreed that this was so and attacked him using this medium. Yet they were hardly unbiased and so the question is whether their accusations should necessarily be taken at face value. Evidence that would be more conclusive, such as a court martial record or contemporary observation from Bobbing and Hastings would be valuable. They do not exist but though there is clear evidence that he and his father were reviled among the elite in Hastings, the admittedly scanty evidence from that time does not suggest that Oates was labelled as what would now be called a homosexual. There is, however, one witness account (of the many which exist from the 1685 trial) of him being rather too intimate with a lad at St Omers. Again this is a hostile witness for the prosecution at his trial for perjury. How much weight should be put upon it is a moot point. However, hostile contemporary references to his time at Bobbing do not include sexual misdemeanours; these have been tacked on by some modern historians. Apart from the Lane and Knox case there was no attempt by his many enemies to try and press charges of sodomy against him in a court of law. The verdict then, can only be an open one and readers must decide for themselves. To be accused of an offence by one's enemies is not in itself proof that these accusations were true, but equally it is not evidence of innocence. Perhaps the Scottish verdict of 'not proven' might be least unsafe as a verdict.

Appendix Three

The Killing of Justice Godfrey

The killing has never been solved. Ailesbury wrote that it was 'a subject the truth of which will never be known', though there have been various theories about it, ranging from this being a case of suicide, but made to look like murder, in order that the beneficiaries of his will (his brothers) gained from it, to this being death by either Catholic or Protestant conspirators or apolitical robbers. Kirkby has been accused, as has Oates. An early twentieth century historian, Pollock, argues that there was some substance to there being a Catholic conspiracy at this time. Later in the century Stephen Knight, a well known conspiracy theorist, alleged (though was not the first to do so) that a group of republican plotters killed him, with the murderous Earl of Pembroke as the murderer, but his evidence is very circumstantial with much use of the words 'doubtless' and 'without doubt' and some rhetorical questions.[1] Marshall gives the various suspects as being rogue Catholics, the Earl of Danby, the Earl of Pembroke, Shaftesbury, a republican gang, Oates, Bedloe, the Godfrey brothers or an unknown man or men.[2] Echoing Ailesbury, Mackenzie wrote that it was 'One of the most famous of all British unsolved mysteries'.[3] This is a dubious assertion; relatively few have heard of this compared to the better known mysteries concerning Stonehenge, the Princes in the Tower, Jack the Ripper, the Loch Ness Monster and the disappearance of Lord Lucan.

The limited facts seem to be as follows. Godfrey was noted as being in a depressed frame of mind in the days leading up to his death. On the other hand, as Burnet noted 'He believed he himself should be knockt on the head. Yet he took no care of himself'. He seems to have disappeared by the early afternoon on Saturday 12 October. He did not return home that night and on the next few days his brothers looked for him without success. Then on Thursday 17 October his dead body was found a mile to the north of London by Primrose Hill, Hampstead. He may have been attacked prior to death as there was evidence of bruising on his abdomen. He had also been strangled and then his sword had been driven through his body. His watch, cane and money had not been taken. He had not died where he was found, for his shoes were clean and there was white wax on his breeches of a kind used in candles by 'persons of quality or Papists'.[4] It was political dynamite and stoked belief in Oates' stories.

Oates himself has been accused of the murder, though not by contemporaries. Judge Sir James Stephens wrote two centuries later that 'I should think it not at all improbable that Oates himself was the murderer or the contriver of the murder'.[5]

Another Victorian author concurred, writing 'That Oates was capable of it or of any other atrocity is a matter of demonstrable fact'. This was because Oates clearly benefitted from the mysterious murder as the Catholics could be easily blamed and so credibility in his stories was reinforced.[6] Lord Birkenhead agreed with them to an extent: 'Oates and his colleagues, or unscrupulous men behind them, may perhaps have committed the murder in order to rouse popular feelings against the Catholics'.[7] Others disagreed. Novelist John Dickson Carr believed, 'Titus Ambrosius [Oates] was the right villain, but the wrong murderer. He is the right voice, but the wrong hand. He lacked the courage to stand up physically against physical opposition – steel, fists, firearms – in a physical contest'.[8] There is certainly no evidence that Oates was a man of personal violence except for his attack on Mrs James in 1702. Alan Marshall also points to the fact that at the time of Godfrey's murder Oates was lodged in Whitehall and had guards to protect him from any potential assassins and so Oates could not have been stalking the streets in pursuit of Godfrey. As with Carr and Knight, Marshall deemed Oates a physical coward and would never have risked injury or death by trying to kill a man known to be armed.[9]

Most recently of all, Andrea Mackenzie has suggested that the Duke of Buckingham might have been behind the killing. Godfrey might have had papers entrusted to him by his friend Coleman which implicated Buckingham in French schemes to bribe the opposition. He was a violent man (he had killed the Earl of Shrewsbury in a duel a decade previously) and might have employed Colonel John Scott, another man of violence. However, unlike many authors on this topic she is rightly not firm in this conclusion, attesting that all this is speculation and that we will never know what really happened.[10]

Knight, however, dismissed the possibility of Oates as murderer as a red herring, citing Carr as concluding that Oates was a physical coward and would not have had the nerve to commit murder personally.[11] Marshall, however, argues that there was no murderer – again an unoriginal hypothesis – and that he committed suicide, but that his brothers, who were the principal beneficiaries of his will and Godfrey was a rich man, made it appear as murder so as to avoid his estate passing to the Crown as befitted a suicide, as well as chiming in with their opposition politics.[12] After finding their brother hanged, they then ran a sword through him to give the impression of murder. More recently the idea that Godfrey was a homosexual who was being blackmailed by Oates has been raised by Andrea Mackenzie and dropped.[13]

Kenyon argues that 'some unknown criminal' might well have killed him because he was a magistrate and not because there was anything Plot related. It may have been that he did not take any possessions from the body because that would have made it obvious that the authorities would be looking for someone like them. He could have hidden the corpse for a time until he found transport to take it elsewhere. Kenyon concluded 'this the merest speculation, of course'.[14]

And that is where the matter must rest, as Ailesbury remarked at the time. That the death benefitted Oates and those opposed to the Catholics is undoubted but that does not mean that Oates was the killer. The killer's motivation (assuming he was killed) as is his identity and at this distance of time, barring fresh evidence, is unlikely to be definitively ascertained, as in the better known case of the man titled Jack the Ripper.

Perhaps the key questions to consider are not only who killed him and why, but where did the killing take place and why and where was it concealed for five days. What did the killer/s seek to achieve by a delay in the discovery? How many people were involved in the murder and the initial concealment? These questions are difficult to answer and so the conundrum remains.

Godfrey's death was not motivated by obvious gain, so a common footpad or gang can be safely ruled out. It seems probable that Godfrey was killed on the day of his disappearance and then concealed in a room in which there was candlelight. He was subsequently moved to where he was found five days later. The moving of the body was probably because it could not be found where it lay because that would implicate the killer/s, especially if it was somewhere they were associated with. It was probably not carefully planned because after his death it took some time to procure the necessary transport to remove the body to Primrose Hill. Anyone planning to kill Godfrey would have had all this in place already. In fact this is a pointer to the theory that this was a suicide made to look like murder and so that implicates his brothers who stood to gain financially and politically.

To strangle someone and then run them through with a sword twice is another pointer away from murder. Killers usually use one method of murder, though they may well use overkill, stabbing and shooting someone far more than is necessary. To strangle and then stab a victim is almost unknown. So, given Godfrey's known melancholia, added to the additional worries caused by Oates' revelations which he failed to report, perhaps because they implicated Coleman, a friend of his, suicide seems most likely as a solution. His body was found, by whom it is unknown, but clearly by someone who would benefit by it being thought that Godfrey was murdered. They then drove the sword twice through the corpse in order to make the suggestion of murder all the stronger. Whoever it was, was clearly unprepared for what they found and so concealed the corpse until they could access transport to take the body to where it was found.

Perhaps what is most important is not the murderer/s and his motive, but the effects it had on much of the populace. It was what they thought was the case that was crucial. This was that it helped bolster credibility in Oates' lies. The victims of the killing were all those Catholics who were to be hanged because one of their principal witnesses had been given that credibility. Therefore, perhaps those who found the body had an interest in promoting Oates' allegations by using the suicide to give ballast to his tales.

Bibliography

Archives

Bodleian Library
Carte MSS 130, 216, 219, 263, 432
Rawlinson Mss A 136

The British Library
Additional Manuscripts
32509
38105
41804
61903

East Sussex Record Office
DUN10/5/80, Busbridge letter, 1679
FRE 5206 Feake letter, 1685
XA30/53, Parish Registers
XA78/3 Quarter Sessions records
XA78/17 Hastings Court records: Oates

Essex Record Office
Q/SR/439/35
T/R 896

Lambeth Palace Library
VB1/3
VM1/18

The National Archives
Admiralty
ADM33/115; 51/11
Chancery

C8/358/14
Privy Council
PC2/64
State Papers Domestic
SP29/417, 419
SP44/335
Copies of material held elsewhere
PRO31/3/141

Surrey History Centre
LM/1331/65
LM/COR/9/10

Primary Sources

Osmund Airly, ed., *Gilbert Burnet's A History of my own Time* II, (Oxford: Clarendon Press, 1900).

John Akerman, ed., *Moneys received and paid to the Secret Service in the reigns of Charles II and James II* (London, 1851).

Anon, *The Tryal and Conviction of Thomas Knox and John Lane* (London: Robert Pawlett, 1680).

Anon, *Trial of Viscount Stafford* (1681).

Anon, *A Dialogue between two porters* (London, 1681).

Anon, *A Letter from Amsterdam to a Friend in Paris* (1679).

Anon, *The Life of Titus Oates*, (London: E. Mallett, 1685).

Anon, *The Little Infant, Titus, or Oates exulted above his brethren* (London, 1685).

Anon, *The Birth and Education, Life and Conversation of Dr Titus Oates* (London, 1705).

Anon, *A New Discovery of Titus Oates*, (London, 1701).

Anon, *Dr Oats's answer to Count Teckley's Letter intercepted at Dover* (1683).

Anon, *Trial of Titus Oates* (1685).

Anon, *The Tryal of Edward Coleman*, (c.1678).

Anon, *Elegy upon the much unlamented death of Dr Titus Oates* (London, 1705).

Anon, *The Life and History of Titus Oates* (London, 1705).

Anon, *The Doctor degraded* (1685).

Anon, *The Memoires of Titus Oates* (London: T. Graves, 1685).

Anon, *An essay tending to prove that perjury deserves not only the pillory but a much severer punishment* (London: J. Hindmarsh, 1685).

Anon, *An Exact and faithful Narrative of the Horrid Conspiracy of Thomas Knox, William Osborne and John Lane* (London: Thomas Pankhurst, 1680).

Anon, *Vindication of the English Catholics*, (1680).

Anon, *The Life and Death of Captain William Bedloe* (London: George Larkin, 1681).

Anon, *Miracles upon Miracles or Great News from the King's Bench Prison in Southwark, of a monster called by the name of Titus upon Oates* (1687).

Anon, *Annals of Queen Anne* (London, 1706).

Anon, *A Second Collection of Tracts on all subjects* (1750).

Anon, *Admissions to the College of St. John's Cambridge* (Cambridge University Press, 1895)

Richard Baxter, *The Autobiography of Richard Baxter* (London: J. Dent and Sons, 1925).

Guy de la Bedoyere, *The Letters of Samuel Pepys* (Woodbridge: Boydell, 2006).

E.S. de Beer, ed., *The Diary of John Evelyn*, V (Oxford University Press, 1955).

T.A. Bireli, ed., 'The History of English persecution of Catholics and the Presbyterian Plot', *Catholic Record Society*, Vol. 48 (1953).

Thomas Bramston, *Autobiography of Sir Thomas Bramston, K.B.*, (London: Camden Society, 1845).

Thomas Brown, *The Salamanca Wedding: A True Account of a Swearing Doctor's Marriage with a Muggletonian Widow in Bread Street* (London, 1693).

Thomas Brown, *The Works of Thomas Brown* (London: Sam. Briscoe, 1720).

John Buchanan-Brown, ed., The *Remains of Thomas Hearne*, (London, 1966).

W.E.Buckley, ed., *Memoirs of Thomas, Earl of Ailesbury* (Westminster, 1890).

Richard Bulstrode, *Memoirs and Reflections upon the reigns of King Charles I and King Charles II* (London, 1721).

Edmund Calamy, *Historical Account of my own Life*, I, (London: Colburn and Bentley, 1829).

Roger Castlemaine, *Compendium* (London: Thomas Dawks, 1680).

Andrew Clarke, ed., 'The Life and Times of Anthony Wood', I-III, *Oxford History Society*, 19, 21, 26 (1891-1894).

J.S. Clarke, *Life of James II*, I (1816).

John Dalrymple, *Memoirs of Great Britain and Ireland*, II (Dublin, 1773).

F.H. Blackburne Daniell, ed., *Calendar of State Papers Domestic: Charles II, 1675-1676*, (London: HMSO, 1907)

Ibid, 1678 (1913)

Ibid, 1679-1680 (1915)

Ibid, 1680-1681 (1921)

Ibid and Francis Bickley, eds., 1683 (1934)

Thomas Crosby, *History of the English Baptists* (London, 1738-1740).

John Dryden, *Selected Poems*, (Harmondsworth: Penguin, 2021).

Adam Elliott, *A Modest Vindication of Titus Oates* (London, 1682).

Philip Ellis, *The Ellis Correspondence*, II (London, 1829).

Edward Ellys, *A Complaint of Edward Ellys* (c.1696).

Keith Feiling and F.R. Needham, eds., 'The Journals of Edmund Warcup, 1676-1684', *English Historical Review*, 40 (1925).

C.H. Firth, ed., 'Scotland under the Protectorate, 1653-1659', *Scottish History Society*, 31 (1899).

Fountainhall, Lord ed., *Historical Observes of memorable occasions* (1840).

William Fuller, *The Whole Life of William Fuller* (London, 1703).

Anchitell Grey, *ed., Grey's Debates of the House of Commons*, VI, (London, 1769).
Lord Grey, *The Secret History of the Rye House Plot* (London, 1754).
Thomas Edwards, *Grangraema I-III* (1646).
Tim Harris, ed., *The Entring Books of Roger Morrice: The Reign of James II, 1685-1687* (Suffolk: Boydell, 2007).
Edward Hasted, *History and Topographical Survey of Kent* Volume 6, (Canterbury, 1797).
HMC 2nd Report.
HMC 5th report, (1876).
HMC 6th report, appendix 5, (1877).
HMC Fitzherbert MSS.
HMC Ormonde, New Series V.
E. Hockliffe, ed., 'The Diary of Ralph Josselin', *Camden Society*, 3rd series, X (1908).
T.B. Howell, *Complete Collection of State Trials*, V-X (1828).
Charles Jackson, ed., 'The Diary of Abraham de la Pryme', *Surtees Society*, LIV (1870).
John Cordy Jeafferson, ed., *Middlesex County Records, 1667-1688* (London, 1892).
Journal of the House of Commons, IX-XII
Journal of the House of Lord Journals, IX-X, XIV
C.S. Knighton, ed., *Pepys' Later Diaries* (Stroud: Sutton, 2004).
Christopher Kirkby, *A Complete and true Narrative* (1679).
Mark Knights, ed., *The Entring Books of Roger Morrice: The Reign of William III, 1689-1691* (Suffolk: Boydell, 2007).
Roger L'Estrange, *Brief History of the Times*, III, (London: C. Brome, 1687).
Narcissus Luttrell, *A Brief Historical Relation*, vols 1-5, (Oxford University Press, 1857).
Andrew Marvell, *An Account of The Growth of Popery and Arbitrary Power* (London, 1677).
Christopher Morris, ed., *The Journeys of Celia Fiennes* (Cambridge University Press, 1949).
John Nickolls, ed., *The Journal of George Fox*, (Cambridge University Press, 1952).
Roger North, *Examen, or an Enquiry* (London: D. Gyles, 1740).
Titus Oates, *Sound advice to Roman Catholics*, (London, 1689).
Ibid, *Tragedy of the Popish Plot Reviv'd* (London, 1696).
Ibid, *The Witch of Endor, or The Witchcraft of the Roman Jesebel* (London, 1679).
Ibid, *A Sermon preached at St. Michael's, Wood Street* (London, 1679).
Ibid, *A sermon preach'd in an Anabaptist Meeting House in Wapping on Sunday the 1st of February*, (London, 1699).
Ibid, *Oates' Letter to the Right Honourable Sir Leoline Jenkins* (1684).
Ibid, *A Display of Tyranny* (London, 1689).
Ibid, *Proposals humbly offered to the high and mighty Prince William* (London, 1689).
Ibid, *To the Knights, Citizens and Burgesses in Parliament: The Deplorable Case and Humble Petition of Dr Titus Oates* (London, 1689).
Ibid, *Picture of King James* (London: R. Baldwin, 1696).

John Phillips, *The Secret History of the reigns of K. Charles II and K. James II* (London, 1690).

Pat Rogers, ed., *Daniel Defoe: A Tour through the Whole Island of Great Britain* (Harmondsworth: Penguin, 1971).

William A. Shaw, ed., *Calendar of Treasury Books XIII, 1678-1679* (London: HMSO, 1912).

Ibid, *VI, 1679-1680* (1913).

Ibid, *IX, 1689-1692* (1931).

Ibid, *X, 1693-1696* (1935).

William Smith, *Intrigues of the Popish Plot* (London, 1685).

John Spurr, ed., *The Entring Books of Roger Morrice: The Reign of Charles II, 1677-1685* (Suffolk: Boydell, 2007).

Helen Stocks, ed., *Records of the Borough of Leicester, 1603-1688* (Cambridge 1923).

Adam Taylor, *The History of the English General Baptists,* (London, 1818).

Stephen Taylor, ed., *The Entring Books of Roger Morrice: The Reign of James II, 1687-1689* (Suffolk: Boydell, 2007).

Edward M. Thompson, ed., *The Correspondence of the Hatton Family* (London: Camden Society, 1878).

E.K. Timings, ed., *Calendar of State Papers Domestic: James II, 1685* (1960).

Ibid, 1686-1687 (1964).

Ibid, 1687-1689 (1972).

Frances and Margaret Verney, eds., *Memoirs of the Verney Family, II* (London: Longman, 1907).

James Welwood, *Memoirs of the most Memorable Transactions* (London, 1704).

John Harold Wilson, ed., *Rochester-Saville Letters, 1671-1680* (Columbus: Ohio State University Press, 1941).

Joseph Wilson, *Memorabilia Cantabrigiana* (London, 1803).

Newspapers

Post Boy, 1699

Cambridge General Advertiser, 1840

Domestic Intelligencer, 1679

Dublin Evening Herald, 2002

English Gazette, 1680

English Intelligencer, 1679

Hastings and St. Leonard's Observer, 1873, 1927, 1949, 1957

Hastings Independent Press, 2020

Kent Times, 1889, 1893

Kent and Sussex Courier, 1971

Leeds Mercury, 1911.

London Gazette, 1684, 1688

Mercurius Anglicus, 1679

Protestant Domestic Intelligencer, 1680
Protestant Intelligencer, 1681
Rutland Times, 1994, 1996

Secondary Sources

Anon, Western Martyrology (London: Blackwood & Co, 1873).

J.A. Alsop, 'Titus Oates' deathbed', *Historical Research*, 64, issue 155 (October 1991).

J. Manwaring-Baines, Historic *Hastings* (St. Leonard's on Sea: Cinque Port Press Ltd, 1986).

Anthony Belt, *Hastings: A Survey* (1937).

Alan Betteridge, 'Early Baptists in Leicester and Rutland', *Baptist Quarterly*, 25.5 (January 1973) and 25/8 (October 1973).

Lord Birkenhead, *Famous Trials of History* (London: Hutchinson & Co, 1926).

Alan Bray, *Homosexuality in Renaissance England* (Columbia University Press, 1984).

John Dickson Carr, *The Murder of Sir Edmund Godfrey* (London: Hamish Hamilton, 1936).

Sir George Clark, *The Later Stuarts, 1660-1714* (Oxford University Press, 1950).

C.H. Firth, *Cromwell's Army* (London, 1902).

Paul Hammond, 'Titus Oates and Sodomy' in Jeremey Black, ed., *Culture and Society in England, 1660-1800* (Manchester University Press, 1997).

Ibid, *Figuring Sex between Men from Shakespeare to Rochester* (Oxford: Clarendon, 2002).

Tim Harris, *Restoration, Charles II and his kingdoms, 1660-1685* (London: Penguin, 2005).

Ibid, *Revolution, 1685-1720* (London: Penguin, 2005).

Tim Hitchcock and Michele Cohen, *English Masculinities, 1660-1800* (Longman, 1999)

Geoffrey Holmes, *The making of a Great Power: Later Stuart and early Georgian Britain, 1660-1722*, (Pearson, 1993).

Robert Hutchinson, *The Audacious Crimes of Colonel Thomas Blood* (Weidenfeld and Nicolson, 2015).

Ronald Hutton, *Charles II* (Oxford: Clarendon, 1989).

James William Johnson, *A Profane Wit: The Life of John Wilmot, Earl of Rochester* (Rochester: New York, 2004).

Don Jordan, *The King's City*, (London: Little Brown Book Group, 2017).

Kealy, A.G., *Chaplains of the Royal Navy, 1622-1902* (Portsmouth: Wilkins and Sons, 1903).

Anna Keay, *The Restless Republic: Britain without a Crown* (London: Collins, 2022).

John Kenyon, *The Popish Plot* (Harmondsworth: Penguin, 1972)

Stephen Knight, *The Murder of Justice Godfrey* (London: Granada, 1978)

Jane Lane, *Titus Oates* (London: Andrew Dakers, 1949).

Byrant Lillywhite, *London Coffee Houses* (London: Allen and Unwin, 1963).

Sue Limb and Patrick Cordingley, *Captain Oates: Soldier and Explorer* (London: Batsford, 1982).

Andrea MacKenzie, *Conspiracy, Culture in Stuart England: The Mysterious Murder of Sir Edmundbury Godfrey* (Woodridge: Boydell Press, 2022).

Ian McCormick, ed., *Secret Sexualities* (London: Routledge, 1997).
Jason MacElligott, ed., *Fear, Exclusion and revolution* (Ashgate, 2006).
Alan Marshall, *The Strange death of Edmund Godfrey* (London: Sutton, 1999).
John Miller, *Popery and Politics, 1660-1688* (Cambridge University Press, 1973).
Ian Mortimer, *The Time Traveller's Guide to Restoration Britain* (London: Bodley Head, 2017).
J.G. Muddiman, ed., *The Bloody Assizes*, (Edinburgh: William Hodge, 1929).
Charles Petrie, *The Jacobite Movement* (London: Eyre and Spottiswoode, 1959).
John Pollock, *The Popish Plot* (London: Duckworth, 1944).
N.A.M. Rogers, *Mastery of the Seas, 1649-1815* (London: Penguin, 2004).
L.F. Salzman, *The Story of the English Towns; Hastings* (1921).
Thomas Seccombe, *Twelve Bad Men* (London: Unwin, 1894).
Victor Stater, *Hoax: The Popish Plot that never was* (Yale University Press, 2022).
James Stephens, *A History of the Criminal Law of England* I (London: MacMillan, 1883).
Simon Thurley, *Palaces of Revolution: Life, death and art at the Stuart Court* (London: William Collins, 2021).
H.D. Traill, *The First Earl of Shaftesbury* (London: Longman, 1886).
Various authors, 'Ten Worst Britons', *BBC History Magazine*, 7, (2006).
Victoria County History of Oxford, Vol, IV.
Ibid, *Essex*, IV (1956).
Bryam Waites, ed., 'Who was who in Rutland', *Rutland Record* 8, (1988).
Melinda Zook, *Radical Whigs and conspiratorial politics in late Stuart England* (Pennsylvania State Press, 1999).

Online sources

www.theclergydatabase.org.uk
www.oldbaileyonline

Fiction

Kate Braithwaite, *The Plot* (Luitie Books, 2024)

Notes

Introduction

1. Sir George Clark, *The Later Stuarts, 1660-1714* (Oxford University Press, 1950), pp.92-93.
2. Charles Petrie, *The Jacobite Movement* (London: Eyre and Spottiswoode, 1959), p.57.
3. Geoffrey Holmes, *The making of a Great Power: Later Stuart and early Georgian Britain, 1660-1722*, (London: Pearson, 1993), pp.122-123.
4. Alan Marshall, *The Strange death of Edmund Godfrey* (Stroud: Sutton, 1999), p.34.
5. Tim Harris, *Restoration, Charles II and his kingdoms, 1660-1685* (London: Penguin, 2006), p.136.
6. Don Jordan, *The King's City: London under Charles II*, (London: Little Brown Book Group, 2017), p.378.
7. Various authors, 'Ten Worst Britons', *BBC History Magazine*, 7, (2006).
8. Victor Stater, *Hoax: The Popish Plot that never was* (Yale University Press, 2022), pp.x, xii, 282.
9. Jane Lane, *Titus Oates* (London: Daker, 1949).
10. Ibid; Petrie, *Jacobite Movement*, p.56.
11. St. Margaret's church, London, parish registers, Ancestry.co.uk

Chapter 1

1. *Dictionary of National Biography* XII, (London, 1895), p.741
2. Anon, *The Life of Titus Oates*, (London, printed by E. Mallett, 1685), p.1.
3. Andrew Clarke, ed., 'The life and Times of Anthony Wood, antiquary of Oxford, as described by himself, 1664-1681', II, *Oxford History Society*, 21, (1892), p.417.
4. Anon, *The Birth and Education, Life and Conversation of Dr Titus Oates* (London, 1705), p.2.
5. *Journals of the House of Commons*, III, 1643-1644, (London, 1802), p.706.
6. Thomas Edwards, *Gangrgema*, I, (London, 1646), p.120.
7. Ibid, II, p.3.
8. Alan Betteridge, 'Early Baptists in Leicestershire and Rutland', *Baptist Quarterly*, 25/5 (January 1973), p.208-209.
9. Edwards, *Gangraena*, III, p.189.
10. Anna Keay, *The Restless Republic: Britain without a Crown* (Collins: London, 2022), p.152.

11. Anon, *The Life*, p.1.
12. Adam Taylor, *The History of the English General Baptists,* (London, the author, 1818), pp.116, 239.
13. Clarke, 'Life and Times', II, p.417.
14. Taylor, *History*, pp.116-118.
15. Roger North, *Examen or an Enquiry*, (London: F. Gyles, 1740), p.221.
16. Essex Record Office, Q/SR 328/75.
17. Margaret Emmison, ed., *Essex Sessions Records, 1641-1645* (1946), p.176.
18. Keay, *Restless Republic*, p.154.
19. HMC 5th report, (1876), p.390.
20. E. Hockliffe, ed., 'The Diary of Ralph Josselin', *Camden Society*, 3rd series, X (1908), p.33.
21. British Library Additional Manuscripts, 32509, f.59v.
22. Betteridge, 'Early Baptists in Leicestershire and Rutland', *Baptist Quarterly*, 25/5 (January 1973), p.207, 209 and 25/8 (October 1973), p.357.
23. HMC 5th Report (1876), pp.397, 403.
24. Ibid, 6th Report, Appendix, (1877), p.215.
25. HMC 7th Report, (1879), p.26.
26. C.H. Firth, *Cromwell's Army* (London: Methuen and Co., 1902), p.342.
27. *Journal of the House of Lords, 1646,* IX, (London, HMSO, 1767-1830), pp.570, 619, 673, X, *1648-1649,* (London, HMSO, 1767-1830), p.258.
28. John Nickalls, ed., *The Journal of George Fox* (Cambridge University Press, 1952), p.45.
29. Keay, *Restless Republic*, p.40.
30. Anon, *Cradle*, p.2.
31. Bryan Waites, ed., 'Who was who in Rutland', *Rutland Record*, 8 (1980), p.283.
32. North, *Examen*, pp. 221, 223.
33. T.A. Bireli, ed., 'The History of English persecution of Catholics and the Presbyterian Plot', *Catholic Record Society*, Vol. 48 (1953), p.192.
34. E.S. De Beer, ed., *Diary of John Evelyn*, III, (1955), pp.123-124.
35. Anon, *Life*, p.1.
36. Ibid, p.2.
37. Anon, *The Birth and Education*, p.2.
38. Bireli, 'The History', p.191.
39. Helen Stocks, ed., *Records of the Borough of Leicester, 1603-1688* (Cambridge, 1923). pp.385-386.
40. C.H. Firth, ed., 'Scotland under the Protectorate, 1653-1659', *Scottish History Society*, 31 (1899), p.252.
41. Ibid, pp.238, 240-241.
42. Ibid, p.252.
43. C.H. Firth, ed., *Selections from the Papers of* William *Clarke*, III, (London: Camden Society, 1892), p.31.

44. Thomas Crosby, *The History of the English Baptists* III, (London: Thomas Crosby, 1740), p.169.
45. Anon, *Vindication of the English Catholics*, (1680), p.6.
46. Anon, *The Life and History of Titus Oates* (London, 1705), pp.4-5.
47. Anon, p.5.
48. Pat Rogers, ed., *Daniel Defoe: A Tour through the Whole Island of Great Britain* (Harmondsworth: Penguin, 1971), p. 140; John Macky, *A Journey through England*, I (London: J. Hooke, 1722), p.149.
49. East Sussex Record Office, Parish Register of All Saints' church, Hastings, XA30/53; Clarke, 'Life, II', p.417.
50. Anon, *Life*, p.2.
51. T.B. Howell, *Complete State Trials*, VII, (London, 1828), p.128.
52. The National Archives, PC2/66, p.404.
53. Anon, *The Life and History*, pp.6-7.
54. Ibid, pp.7-8.
55. Charles Robinson, ed., *Register of the Merchant Taylors' School, 1562-1699* (Farncombe and Co., Lewes, 1862), p.272.
56. Info. St. John' college, Cambridge; William Smith, *Intrigues of the Popish Plot*, (London, 1685), p.25.
57. North, *Examen*, p.221.
58. Smith, *Intrigues of the Popish Plot*, pp.25, 5.
59. HMC 2nd Report (1874), Appendix, p.117 (translated from the Latin).
60. Anon, *Life*, p.2.
61. Anon, *The Life and History*, p.8.
62. Clarke, 'Life', II, p.417.
63. De Beer, *Diary*, III, p.138.
64. Adam Elliott, *A Modest Vindication of Titus Oates* (London, 1682), p.1.
65. Elliott, *Modest Vindication*, p.2.
66. Anon, *Life*, p.2.
67. Birelli, 'The history of English persecution', p.192.
68. Joseph Wilson, *Memorabilia Cantabrigiana* (London, 1803), p.69.
69. Anon, *The Life and History*, p.9.
70. BL. Add. Mss, 32509, f.59v.
71. De Beer, *Diary*, III, p.136.
72. Christopher Morris, ed., *The Journeys of Celia Fiennes* (Cambridge University Press, 1949), pp.65-66.
73. Anon, *Life and History*, p.2.
74. Clarke, 'Life', II, p.417.
75. Roger Castlemaine, *Compendium* (London: Thomas Dawks, 1680), p.80.
76. Anon, *The Birth and Education*, p.2.
77. *The Observator*, 25 October 1682.
78. Ibid.
79. Anon, *Life and History*, p.9.

80. Ibid, pp.9-11.
81. Ibid, p.11.

Chapter 2

1. CCEd | Clergy of the Church of England Database (theclergydatabase.org.uk) Accessed 16 September 2023.
2. *Victoria County History of Essex IV* (Oxford University Press, 1956), p.255; ERO, T/R 86, pp.32, 27, 50, 72.
3. Titus Oates, *A Tragedy of the Popish Plot Reviv'd*, (London, 1696), pp.34-35.
4. Edward Hasted, *History and Topographical Survey of Kent*, Volume 6, (Canterbury: Simmons and Kirkby, 1797), pp.192-203; *Melville's Directory and Gazetteer of Kent* (1857), p.218; Lambeth Palace Archives, VB1/3/189.
5. *Kent Times*, 9 February 1893.
6. LPA, VB1/3/233.
7. Howell, *Complete State Trials*, VII, p.435.
8. North, *Examen*, p.222.
9. Smith, *Intrigues of the Popish Plot*, p.2.
10. Elliott, *Modest Vindication*, p.33.
11. Anon, *The Life and History*, p.12.
12. History Of The Church (bobbingchurch.org).
13. Howell, *Complete State Trials*, VII, p.435.
14. Edward Dunkin, ed., 'Calendar of Sussex Marriage Licences', *Sussex Record Society* (1900), p.93.
15. Clarke, 'Life', II, p.417.
16. Ibid, pp.417-418.
17. Anon, *Life*, p.2.
18. *A Letter from Amsterdam to a friend in Paris* (1679).
19. ESRO, XA30/53.
20. ESRO, PAR361/12/1.
21. John Manwaring Baines, *Historic Hastings* (Cinque Press: St. Leonard's, 1986), pp.117-118.
22. Anon, *The History and Life*, p.12
23. ESRO, XA78/3.
24. Clarke, 'Life', II, p.417.
25. TNA, Privy Council, 2/64, p.405.
26. F.H. Blackburne-Daniell, ed., *Calendar of State Papers Domestic, 1675-1676*, (London, 1907), pp.68-69.
27. TNA, PC2/64, p.408.
28. Clarke, 'Life', II, p.417.
29. ESRO, XA78/3.
30. Anon, *Life*, p.2; Oates, *A New Discovery of Titus Oates*, (London, 1701), preface; Clarke, 'Life', II, p.417.
31. Castlemaine, *Compendium*, pp.66-67.

32. Ibid, p.67.
33. Clarke, 'Life', II, p.418.
34. *London Gazette* 22-25 July 1675.
35. Gilbert Burnet, *History of His own Time*, II, (Oxford, 1833) p.148.
36. Anon, *Letter from Amsterdam*, p.1?
37. Kealy, A.G., *Chaplains of the Royal Navy, 1622-1902* (Portsmouth: Wilkins and Sons, 1903).
38. TNA, PC2/66, p.394.
39. Ibid, ADM33/115; 51/11.
40. Oates, *Tragedy of the Popish Plot Reviv'd*, p.36.
41. *Letter from Amsterdam*, p.2.
42. Elliott, *Modest Vindication*, p.34.
43. N.A.M. Rogers, *Mastery of the Seas, 1649-1815* (London: Penguin, 2004), p.407.
44. Blackburne-Daniell, *CSPD 1680-1681*, (London: HMSO, 1920-1921), pp.350-351.
45. ESRO, XA78/17.
46. Smith, *Intrigues*, pp.2, 5.
47. Anon, *Life*, pp.2-3
48. Anon, *The Life and History*, pp.13-15.
49. Smith, *Intrigues of the Popish Plot*, pp.2, 5.
50. Ibid, pp.5-6.
51. Roger L'Estrange, *Brief History of the times*, III, (London: C. Brome, 1687), p.11.
52. CSPD 1679-1680, p.628.
53. *Diaries of the Popish Plot*, pp.1-2.
54. *Oxford Dictionary of National Biography*, (2004), 54, pp.966-969
55. Burnet, *History*, II, p.147.
56. *Diaries of the Popish Plot*, pp.2-3.
57. TNA, PC2/66, p.396.
58. Burnet, *History*, II, p.148.
59. Anon, *Vindication of the English Catholics*, p.1.
60. Howell, *Complete State Trials*, VII, pp.103-104.
61. Ibid, p.357.
62. Ibid, p.358.
63. Anon, *Life*, p.3.
64. *Letter from Amsterdam*, p.3.
65. TNA, SP29/417/299.
66. *Trial of Oates*, pp.34, 21.
67. Ibid, pp.3-5.
68. Anon, *Life*, p.3.
69. Ibid, p.3.
70. Warner, 'History', p.193.
71. Ibid, p.194.
72. *Trial of Titus Oates* (1685), pp.13, 29.

73. Ibid, p.15.
74. Anon, *Life*, p.3.
75. Anon, *The Life and History*, p.15.
76. Anon, *Trials*, pp.18, 20.
77. Elliott, *Modest Vindication*, p.21.
78. *Trial of Titus Oates*, p.17.
79. Ibid.
80. Ibid, pp.25, 23.
81. Ibid, p.19.
82. Ibid, pp.25, 15, 28.
83. Ibid, p.33.
84. lbid, p.22.
85. lbid, p.33.
86. lbid, p.19.
87. Ibid p.24.
88. Howell, *Complete State Trials*, VII, p.370.
89. *Trial of Oates*, pp.34, 21.
90. *HMC House of Lords*, XIII, 1675-1681, p.99.
91. Blackburne-Daniell, CSPD 1678, pp.544-545.
92. L'Estrange, *Brief History*, I, pp.88, 90.
93. *Trial of Titus Oates*, p.35.
94. Ibid, p.31.
95. Ibid, p.18.
96. Ibid, p.27.
97. Anon, *Life*, p.3.
98. Ibid, pp.3-4.
99. Howell, *Complete State Trials*, X, p.1447.
100. Anon, *The Life and History*, p.16.
101. L'Estrange, *Brief History*, I, p.103.
102. Smith, *Intrigues*, p.6.
103. *Observator*, (1684), p.75.
104. Smith, *Intrigues*, pp.6-7.
105. Crosby, *Baptists*, III, p.168.
106. Lane, *Oates*, pp.45-47.
107. John Miller, *Popery and Politics, 1660-1688* (Cambridge University Press, 1973), p.155.
108. Andrea Mackenzie, *Conspiracy Culture in Stuart England: The Mystery of Sir Edmund Bury Godfrey* (Suffolk: Boydell Press, 2022), p.135.2/992.
109. L'Estrange, *Brief History*, pp.126, 125, 122, 131.
110. *Diaries*, pp.5-6.
111. BL. Add.Mss. 28047, f.5v.
112. North, *Examen*, pp.195, 95.

113. Burnet, *History*, II, pp.171-172.
114. *Diaries of the Popish Plot*, pp.6-7.

Chapter 3

1. Christopher Kirkby, *A Complete and True Narrative*, (London, 1679), p.1.
2. Clarke, 'Life', I, p.516.
3. Kirkby, *A Complete and True Narrative*, p.1.
4. Ibid, p.2; TNA, PC2/66, p.392
5. North, *Examen*, p.172.
6. Kirkby, *Narrative*, p.2.
7. *House of Lords Journal*, XIII, p.324.
8. Kirkby, *Narrative*, p.3.
9. TNA, PC2/66, p.392.
10. Burnet, *History*, II, p.154.
11. *Diaries of the Popish Plot*, p.36.
12. Howell, *State Trials*, VII, p.167.
13. TNA, PC2/66, p.393.
14. North, *Examen*, p.170.
15. Kirkby, *Narrative*, p.3.
16. Ibid.
17. Smith, *Intrigues*, p.8.
18. TNA, PC2/66, p.393.
19. Ibid, p.393.
20. Blackburne Daniell, ed., *Calendar of State Papers Domestic: Charles II, 1678*, (London: HMSO, 1913), pp.425-428.
21. TNA, PC2/66, p.393.
22. Ibid, p.394.
23. Ibid.
24. Ibid, pp.394-395.
25. CSPD, 1678, pp.431-432.
26. Howell, *State Trials*, VII, p.396.
27. Mackenzie, *Conspiracy Culture*, p.645.1/992.
28. TNA, PC2/66, p.398.
29. Ibid, p.399.
30. Ibid, p.400.
31. British Library, Add.Mss. 38015, f.283.
32. Thomas Bramston, *Autobiography of Sir Thomas Bramston* (London: Camden Society, 1846), p.179-180.
33. TNA, PC2/66, pp.402-403.
34. Ibid, p.403.
35. Ibid.
36. Ibid, p.404.

37. Ibid.
38. Ibid.
39. Ibid.
40. Ibid.
41. Ibid, p.406.
42. Ibid.
43. De Beer, *Evelyn's Diary*, IV, p.154.
44. Ibid, p.626.
45. Burnet, *History*, II, p.154.
46. Clarke, *Life of James II*, I, p.514.
47. Burnet, *History*, II, p.157n.
48. Bireli, 'The History', p.415.
49. Howell, *State Trials*, VII, pp.167-8
50. Clarke, *Life*, I, pp.526-527.
51. Ibid, p.168.
52. Smith, *Intrigues*, p.9.
53. Baxter, *Autobiography*, p.242.
54. Andrew Browning, ed., *The Memoirs of Sir John Reresby*, (London, 1936), p.152.
55. Burnet, *History*, II, p.152.
56. L'Estrange, *Brief History*, II, p.28.
57. Thomas Ailesbury, *Memoirs of Thomas, Earl of Ailesbury*, I, (London: Roxburgh Club, 1890), p.29.
58. TNA, SP29/407/6.
59. BL, Add.Mss. 61905, f.77r.
60. Ibid.
61. L'Estrange, *Brief History, III,* p.40.
62. *HMC, Calendar of the Manuscripts of the Marquess of Ormonde New Series, V*, (London, 1908), pp.207, 221.
63. Ibid, p.206.
64. *HMC, Calendar of the Manuscripts of Sir William Fitzherbert*, (London, 1893), p.115.
65. L'Estrange, *Brief History*, II, p.38.
66. E.N. Williams, *Dictionary of English and European History, 1485-1789* (Penguin, 1984), p.367.
67. De Beer, *Evelyn's Diary*, IV, p.26.
68. Richard Baxter, *Autobiography of Richard Baxter*, (J.M. Dent and Sons, 1925), pp.224-225.
69. Ibid, pp.226-227.
70. De Beer, *Evelyn's Diary,* III, pp.607-608.
71. Baxter, *Autobiography*, p.224.
72. De Beer, *Evelyn's Diary*, IV, p.136.
73. Andrew Marvell, *An Account of The Growth of Popery and Arbitrary Power* (London, 1677), p.1.

74. Clark, *The Later Stuarts*, p.93.
75. MacKenzie, *Conspiracy Culture*, p.63.5, 66.0, 86.0/992.
76. Robert Hutchinson, *The Audacious Crimes of Colonel Thomas Blood* (Weidenfeld and Nicolson, 2015), pp.49-53.
77. Baxter, *Autobiography*, p.232.
78. Burnet, *History*, II, p.154.
79. Narcissus Luttrell, *A Brief Historical Relation of State Affairs*, I, (Oxford University Press, 1857), pp.1-2.
80. Burnet, *History*, II, p.154.
81. Burnet, *History*, II, p.157.
82. De Beer, *Evelyn's Diary*, IV, p.155.
83. Clarke, *Life*, I, p.526.
84. Smith, *Intrigues*, p.8.
85. John Dalrymple, *Memoirs of Great Britain and Ireland*, II (Dublin, 1773), p.247.
86. Burnet, *History*, II, pp.151.
87. Ibid, p.152.
88. *HMC Fitzherbert*, p.114.
89. De Beer, *Evelyn's Diary*, IV, p.155.
90. Ailesbury, *Memoirs*, p.27.
91. *HMC Ormonde* NS V, p.380.
92. CSPD, 1678, p.471.
93. L'Estrange, *Brief History*, p.34.
94. Bireli, 'The History', p.199.
95. TNA, PRO31/3/141, f.55r.
96. *Journal of the House of Commons*, 9, 1667-1687, (London, 1802), p.519.
97. Surrey History Centre, LM/1331/65.
98. *Journal of the House of Commons*, 9, p.520.
99. CSPD, 1678, p.480.
100. Anchitell Grey, *ed., Grey's Debates of the House of Commons*, VI, (London, 1769), pp.112-128.
101. Luttrell, *Brief Historical Relation*, I, pp.2-4.
102. Ibid, p.316.
103. Ibid, p.317.
104. Ibid, p.324.
105. Ibid, pp.613-630.
106. Howell, *State Trials*, VI, pp.1469-70.
107. BL. Add. Mss. 32509, f.19r.
108. Ibid, f.50v.
109. *Journal of the House of Lords*, XIII, p.313-330.
110. L'Estrange, *Brief History*, p.31.
111. Ailesbury, *Memoirs*, p.28.
112. Burnet, *History*, II, p. 153.

113. Simon Thurley, *Palaces of Revolution: Life, Death and Art at the Stuart Court* (2021), p.331.
114. *Journal of the House of Lords*, XIII, pp.331-332.
115. Ibid, p.332.
116. Ibid.
117. Ibid, p.341.
118. *HMC Ormonde* NS V, pp.232-233.
119. CSPD, 1678, pp.511, 533.
120. L'Estrange, *Brief History*, p.37.
121. Burnet, *History* II, pp.160.
122. Anon, *The Life and Death of Captain William Bedloe* (London: George Larkin, 1681), p.102.
123. Burnet, *History,* II, p.161.

Chapter 4

1. Howell, *State Trials*, VI, pp.1502-1512.
2. Luttrell, *Brief Relation*, I, p.4.
3. Burnet, *History*, II, p.169.
4. *The Tryal of Edward Coleman*, (c.1678), pp.5-9.
5. Ibid, p.17-18.
6. Ibid, pp19-21.
7. Ibid, pp.22-23.
8. Ibid, pp.24-26.
9. Ibid, pp.29-30.
10. Ibid, pp.63-64, 70.
11. CSPD, 1678, pp.519, 539.
12. Grey, *Grey's Debates*, VI, pp.285-304.
13. *Journal of the House of Lords*, XIII, p.388.
14. Ibid, p.389.
15. Ibid.
16. Ibid.
17. Clarke, *Life*, I, p.529.
18. *HMC Ormonde* NS V, p.255.
19. Bodleian Library, Carte Mss 432, 216.
20. *HMC Ormonde*, NS, V, p.245.
21. Ailesbury, *Memoirs*, I, p.29-30.
22. Burnet, *History*, II, p.173.
23. Burnet, *History*, II, p.166.
24. *HMC Ormonde* V, p.487.
25. De Beer, *Diary*, IV, p.158.
26. *Journal of the House of Lords*, XIII, pp.361-364.
27. Grey, *Debates*, VI, pp.285-304.

28. Ibid.
29. Ibid.
30. Ibid.
31. TNA, SP44/54, 3.
32. CSPD 1678, pp.514, 548.
33. Grey, *Debates*, VI, pp.304-325.
34. Ibid, pp.326-337.
35. De Beer, Evelyn's *Diary*, IV, pp.156, 157.
36. Titus Oates, *A sermon preach'd in an Anabaptist Meeting House in Wapping on Sunday the 1st of February*, (London, 1699), pp.2-3.
37. Howell, *State Trials*, VII, pp.79-90.
38. Ibid, p.91.
39. Ibid, p.92.
40. Ibid, pp.93-94.
41. Ibid, p.94.
42. Ibid, pp.95-96.
43. Ibid, p.96.
44. Ibid, p.97.
45. Ibid, p.98.
46. Ibid, pp.99-100.
47. Ibid, pp.101-102.
48. Ibid, pp.102-103.
49. Ibid, pp.104-106.
50. Ibid, p.106.
51. Ibid, pp.107-108.
52. Ibid, pp.113-114.
53. Ibid, pp.123-124
54. Ibid, pp.128-130.
55. *Burnet's History*, II, p.183.
56. Ibid, pp.185.
57. *HMC House of Lords MSS*, p.70.
58. CSPD 1678, p.554.
59. Bod. Lib., Rawlinson A, 136, 221.
60. TNA, SP29/417/299.
61. CSPD 1678, p.595.

Chapter 5

1. ESRO, DUN10/5/80.
2. TNA, PC2/67, pp.33, 57.
3. Bod. Lib, Rawlinson A, pp.136, 236.
4. *HMC Lords MSS*, p.121.
5. *Journal of the House of Lords*, XIII, pp.586-587. 546-548.

6. John Spurr, ed., *The Entring Books of Roger Morrice: The Reign of Charles II, 1677-1685* (Suffolk: Boydell, 2007), p.103.
7. Bod. Lib Rawlinson A 136, 232-240.
8. *Journal of the House of Lords*, XIII, pp.543-545.
9. Bod. Lib., Rawlinson 136, 16, 18, 23.
10. *Journal of the House of Lords*, XIII, pp.498-502.
11. Bod. Lib. Rawlinson A, 136, 22, 166, 16, 153-154.
12. Ibid, 143.
13. Ibid, 228.
14. Ibid, 33
15. Ibid, 133.
16. Oates, *A Sermon preached at St. Michael's, Wood Street* (London, 1679), dedication.
17. Ibid, *The Witch of Endor, or The Witchcraft of the Roman Jesebel* (London, 1679), dedication.
18. Ibid, *An Exact Discovery of the Mystery of Iniquity as it is now practiced among the Jesuits* (17689).
19. Ibid, *A Sermon*, preface.
20. Ibid, *The Witch*, preface.
21. Ibid.
22. Ibid.
23. Ibid, *Sermon*, preface.
24. Ibid, *The Witch*, pp.1-41.
25. Ibid, *Sermon*, pp.1-31.
26. Jessop, ed., *Lives of the Nor*ths, 1, (London, 1890), p.202.
27. Oates, *An Exact Discovery.*
28. Bod. Lib., Rawlinson A 136, 5.
29. CSPD 1679, p.22.
30. Bod. Lib. Rawlinson A 136, 14, 143.
31. John Akerman, ed., *Moneys received and paid to secret services of Charles II and James II* (London, 1851), pp.3-11.
32. William A. Shaw, ed., *Calendar of Treasury Books VI, 1678-1679* (London: HMSO, 1913), p.13.
33. Akerman, *Moneys received and paid*, pp.9-10.
34. Howell, *Complete State Trials*, VII, p.1447.
35. *Observator* (1683), p.20.
36. Holmes, *The making of a great power*, p.456.
37. CSPD 1679-1680, p.40.
38. Ibid, p.69.
39. Ibid, p.72.
40. Ibid, p.87.
41. CSPD, 1679-1680, pp.77, 106.
42. Anon, *An Exact and Faithful Narrative*, (1680), p.12.

43. Spurr, *The Entring Book*, p.112.
44. *Journal of the House of Commons*, IX, p.576-578, 585-586.
45. *Grey's Debates*, VII, pp.49-50
46. Howell, *State Trials*, VII, pp.159-167.
47. Ibid, pp.168- 230.
48. *HMC Ormonde, NS*, V, p.68.
49. Howell, *State Trials*, VII, pp.322-323.
50. Ibid, pp.323-324.
51. Ibid, pp.324-325.
52. Ibid, p.325-326.
53. Ibid, pp.326-328.
54. Ibid, pp.328-329.
55. Ibid, pp.328-329.
56. Ibid, pp.329-330.
57. Ibid, pp.331-332.
58. Ibid, pp.333-334.
59. Ibid, p.357.
60. Ibid, pp.358-359.
61. Ibid, pp.360-362.
62. Ibid, pp.361-386.
63. Ibid, pp.394-400.
64. Burnet, *History*, II, p.221.
65. Howell, *State Trials*, pp.401-402.
66. Ibid, pp.401-411.
67. Ibid, pp.411-412.
68. Ibid, pp.413-418.
69. *Domestic Intelligencer*, 22 July 1679.
70. Ibid, 11 November 1679.
71. Howell, *State Trials*, VII, pp.417-426.
72. Ibid, pp.426-427.
73. Ibid, pp.427-428.
74. Ibid, pp. 428-431.
75. Ibid, pp.431-432.
76. Ibid, pp.432-435.
77. Ibid, pp.435-436.
78. Ibid, pp.437-453.
79. Ibid, pp.453-462.
80. Ibid, pp.463-465.
81. Ibid, pp.466-478.
82. Ibid, pp.478-479.
83. Ibid, pp.479-499
84. Burnet, *History*, II, p.223.

85. Bod Lib., Rawlinson A 136, 237-240.
86. De Beer, *Evelyn's Diary*, IV, p.174.
87. Ibid.
88. OBOL, Trial of Wakeman and others
89. Howell, *State Trials*, VII, pp.619-621.
90. Ibid, pp.622-624.
91. Ibid, p.625.
92. Ibid, pp.626-627.
93. Ibid, p.627.
94. Ibid, p.628.
95. Ibid, pp.628-629.
96. Ibid, p.629.
97. Ibid, pp.630-631.
98. Ibid, pp.649-650.
99. Ibid, pp.650-653.
100. Ibid, pp.654-679.
101. Ibid, pp.680-686.
102. De Beer, *Evelyn's Diary*, IV, p.174.
103. OBOL
104. De Beer, *Evelyn's Diary*, IV, p.174.
105. Richard Bulstrode, *Memoirs and Reflections upon the reigns of Charles I and Charles II* (London, 1721), p.298; Thomas Bramston, *Autobiography of Sir Thomas Bramston, KB*, (London: Camden Society, 1846), p.181.
106. De Beer, *Evelyn's Diary*, IV, p.174.
107. *Burnet's History*, II, p.227.
108. Browning, *Memoirs*, pp.2-6.
109. *Domestic Intelligencer*, 22 July 1679.
110. Ibid, 7 November 1679.
111. TNA, SP29/417/246.
112. *HMC Ormonde* NS V, p.487.
113. Anon, *The Life and History*, p.40.
114. *English Intelligencer*, 9 August 1679.
115. Ibid, 30 August 1679.
116. *Domestic Intelligencer*, 15 August 1679.
117. Ibid, 2 September 1679.
118. Ibid, 30 September 1679.
119. Keith Feiling and F.R. Needham, eds., 'The Journals of Edmund Warcup, 1676-1684', *English Historical Review* 40 (1925), pp.243-244.
120. Clark, 'Life', II p.465.
121. Ibid, II, p.467.
122. Ibid, I, p.463.
123. CSPD 1681, p.556.

124. TNA, PC2/68, pp.422, 449, 485, 453.
125. *Journal of the House of Lords*, XIII, p.529-531.
126. Ibid, pp.567-569.
127. Margaret M. Verney, ed., *Memoirs of the Verney Family*, IV (Longman: London, 1899), p.259.
128. J.H. Wilson, ed., *Rochester-Saville Letters, 1671-1680* (Columbus: Ohio State University, 1941), p.73.
129. Anon, *An Exact and Faithful narrative of the horrid Conspiracy of Thomas Knox, William Osbourne and John Lane* (London: Thomas Parkhurst, 1680), p.15.
130. Howell, *State Trials*, VII, pp.763-767.
131. Ibid, pp.10, 19.
132. Anon, *The Tryal and Conviction of Thomas Knox and John Lane* (London, 1680), pp.7, 11-13, 67.
133. Howell, *State Trials*, VII, pp.799-804.
134. CSPD 1679-1680, p.308.
135. *Mercurius Anglicus*, 16-19 November 1679.
136. Bod. Lib., Carte, 228, 163.
137. *HMC Ormonde*, NS V, p.579.
138. Feiling and Needham, 'Journals', p.243.
139. Edward M. Thompson, ed., *Correspondence of the Family of Hatton*, I, (London: Camden Society, 1878), p.198.
140. Smith, *Intrigues*, p.22.
141. Ibid, p.15.
142. North, *Examen*, pp.223-224, 205.
143. Ibid, p.176.
144. Bod. Lib. Rawlinson 136, 253-255.
145. *Domestic Intelligencer*, 10 July 1679.
146. Ibid, 14 November 1679.
147. Feiling and Needham, 'Journals', p.244.

Chapter 6

1. *HMC Ormonde*, NS, V, pp. 572, 575-576; Hatton, *Correspondence*, I, p.220.
2. Howell, *State Trials*, VII, p.811-837.
3. Ibid, pp.837-844.
4. Ibid, p.845.
5. Ibid, pp.845-846.
6. Ibid, pp.847-848
7. Ibid, pp.851-852.
8. Ibid, pp.853-854.
9. Ibid, pp.855-858.
10. Ibid, pp.858-860.
11. Ibid, pp.860-861.

12. Ibid, pp.862-866.
13. Ibid, pp.866-867.
14. Ibid, pp.866-868.
15. Ibid, pp.871-872.
16. Bod. Lib. Carte Mss, 216, 116.
17. Smith, *Intrigues of the Popish* Plot, p.22; *Protestant Intelligencer*, 27 January 1680.
18. *Protestant Intelligencer*, 27 January and 24 February 1680.
19. Elliott, *A Modest Vindication*, pp.22-23.
20. Ibid, p.24.
21. Ibid, introduction.
22. Ibid, p.27.
23. Ibid.
24. *Protestant Domestic Intelligencer*, 6 April 1680.
25. J.C. Jeafferson, ed., *Middlesex County Records*, V, *1678-1688* (London), p.126.
26. Ibid, pp.131-133.
27. C.S Knighton, ed., *Pepys' later diaries* (Stroud: Sutton, 2004), p.80; CSPD 1681, p.669.
28. *HMC Lords Mss*, p.145.
29. Howell, *State Trials*, VII, pp.1070- 1071.
30. Ibid, pp.1072-1074.
31. Ibid, pp.1074-1075
32. Ibid, pp.1075-1078.
33. Ibid, pp.1079-1083.
34. Ibid, pp.1093-1095.
35. Ibid, pp.1107-1113.
36. Akerman, *Moneys received and paid*, pp.12-21.
37. CSPD, 1679-1680, pp.597, 609.
38. Burnet, *History*, II, p.300.
39. CSPD, 1679-1680, p.35.
40. Ibid, p.608.
41. CSPD, 1680-1681, p.24.
42. Ibid, p.43.
43. Ibid, p.40.
44. Ibid, p.617-619, 682-685.
45. Jeafferson, *Middlesex County Records*, V, p.138.
46. *HMC Lords MSS*, p.98.
47. *Journal of the House of Lords*, XIII, pp.687-689, 714-716.
48. Ibid, p.141.
49. *Trial of Viscount Stafford*, pp.6-8.
50. Ibid, pp.8-13.
51. Ibid, p.13.
52. Ibid, pp.17, 22.
53. Ibid, pp.36-41.

54. Ibid, p.62.
55. Ibid, pp.62-63.
56. Ibid, pp.63-64.
57. Ibid, pp.64-65.
58. Ibid.
59. Ibid, pp.125-126.
60. Ibid, pp.126-129
61. Ibid, p.133.
62. Ibid, pp.159-160
63. Ibid, pp.161-166.
64. Ibid, pp.166-167.
65. Ibid, pp.211-21.
66. Ibid, pp.229-230
67. Howell, *Complete State Trials*, VII, pp.1504-1505.
68. Ibid, pp.1505-1507.
69. Ibid, p.1518.
70. De Beer, Evelyn's *Diary*, IV, p.230.
71. Ibid, pp.230-231.
72. Ailesbury, *Memoir*, I, p.57.
73. *HMC Ormonde* NS V, p.513.
74. *English Gazette*, 29 December 1680 – 1 January 1681.
75. Browning, *Memoirs*, pp.208-209.
76. Smith, *Intrigues of the Popish Plot*, p.29.
77. North, *Examen*, p.272.
78. Smith, *Intrigues of the Popish Plot*, pp.30-31.
79. Feiling and Needham, 'Journals', p.252.
80. CSPD, 1682, pp.237, 236.
81. TNA, SP29/419, 110.
82. Melinda Zook, *Radical Whigs and conspiratorial politics in late Stuart England* (Pennsylvania State Press, 1999), p.38.
83. Ibid, 110, 112.
84. TNA, SP, 29/417/289
85. CSPD, 1680, p.296.
86. Ibid, pp.307, 333.
87. *Protestant Intelligencer*, 15 March 1681.
88. TNA, PC2/69, p.270.
89. Akerman, *Moneys paid and received*, pp.34-35.
90. CSPD, 1680-1681, p.660.
91. Ibid, pp.217, 228, 236-237, 351, 426.
92. Ibid, pp.163-173.
93. Howell, *Complete State Trials*, VIII, p. 362.

94. Ibid, pp.372-373.
95. Feiling and Needham, 'Journals', p.252.
96. Howell, *Complete State Trials*, VIII, pp.638-639.
97. Ibid, pp.639-641.
98. Ibid, pp.650-651.
99. CSPD 1680-1681, p.411.
100. Smith, *Intrigues of the Popish Plot*, p.29.
101. *HMC Le Fleming*, p.183.
102. CSPD 1681, p.439.
103. Bulstrode, *Memoirs*, p.329.
104. Anon, *A Dialogue between two porters* (1681).
105. Luttrell, *Brief Relation*, II, p.126.
106. *Protestant Intelligencer*, 10 September 1681.
107. CSPD, 1680-1681, p.657.
108. Feiling and Needham, 'Journals', p.256.
109. CSPD 1681, p.380.
110. CSPD, 1680-1681, pp.623-625, 628.
111. *Currant Intelligencer*, 2-5 July 1681.
112. Howell, *State Trials*, VIII, p.811
113. Ibid, p.583.
114. Luttrell, *Brief Relation*, I, pp.159, 196, *Protestant Intelligencer*, 18 February 1682 and 1 July 1682.
115. TNA, PC2/69, pp.127, 133.
116. Ibid, pp.608, 695-697.
117. John Dryden, *Selected Poems*, (2001), pp.131-2.
118. CSPD, 1683, p.18.
119. CSPD, 1683-1684, p.136.
120. Anon, *The Life*, p.4.
121. Smith, *Intrigues of the Popish plot*, pp.30-31.
122. North, *Examen*, p.223.
123. Lord Grey, *The Secret History of the Rye House Plot* (London, 1754); CSPD 1683, pp.340, 351.
124. *Observator*, 365, (1683).
125. CSPD, 1683, p.340.
126. Feiling and Needham, 'Journals', p.258.
127. Guy de Bedoyere, ed., *The letters of Samuel Pepys* (Suffolk: Boydell, 2006), p.166.
128. Anon, *The Life of Titus Oates*, p.1; Wood, 'Life' III, p.36.
129. CSPD, 1680-1681, p.604.
130. Luttrell, *Brief Relation*, I, p.248.
131. Anon, *Dr Oats's answer to Count Teckley's Letter intercepted at Dover* (1683).
132. *Observator*, (1683), p.20.

Chapter 7

1. Oates, *Oates' Letter to the Right Honourable Sir Leoline Jenkins* (1684).
2. Bod. Lib., Rawlinson A 136, 283.
3. Ibid, 289-291.
4. L'Estrange, *Brief History*, III, p.37.
5. Feiling and Needham, 'Journals', p.260.
6. *London Gazette* 16 June 1684.
7. Bulstrode, *Memoirs*, p.379.
8. Howell, *State Trials*, X, pp.125-135.
9. Ibid, pp.135-136
10. Ibid, pp.137-138.
11. Ibid, pp.138-140.
12. Ibid, p.140.
13. *London Gazette* 16 June 1684.
14. Luttrell, *Brief Relation*, II, pp.308, 313.
15. TNA, SP44/335, p.245.
16. Old Bailey online.
17. *HMC Fitzherbert*, p.25.
18. CSPD 1685, pp.113, 141-142.
19. Browning, *Memoirs*, p.341.
20. De Beer, *Evelyn's Diary*, IV, p.438.
21. Anon, *Trials of Titus Oates*, (1685), p.4
22. Ibid, p.5.
23. Ibid, p.7.
24. Ibid.
25. Ibid, p.8
26. Ibid.
27. Ibid, p.9.
28. Ibid.
29. Ibid, p.10.
30. Ibid.
31. Ibid
32. Ibid, p.11.
33. Ibid.
34. Ibid, pp.11-12.
35. Ibid, p.12.
36. Ibid, p.12
37. Ibid, p.13
38. Ibid, pp.13-14
39. Ibid, p.15.
40. Ibid, p.15

41. Ibid, p.16
42. Ibid, p.17
43. Ibid, p.18
44. lbid, p.43.
45. Ibid, p.43.
46. Ibid, p.44.
47. Ibid, p.45-6.
48. Ibid, p.46.
49. Ibid, p.47
50. Ibid p.48
51. Ibid, p.49.
52. Ibid, p.50.
53. Ibid, p.51.
54. Ibid, pp. 51-2.
55. lbid, pp.52-53.
56. Ibid, p.53.
57. Ibid, p.54.
58. Ibid, p.55.
59. Ibid, pp.56-7.
60. Ibid, p.58.
61. Ibid, pp.59-60.
62. Ibid, pp.61-2.
63. Ibid, p.63
64. Ibid, p.66.
65. Ibid, pp.69-70
66. Ibid, pp.71-73.
67. Ibid, pp.73-4.
68. Ibid, pp.75-76.
69. Howell, *Complete State Trials*, X, p.1193.
70. *Trials*, pp.77-83
71. Ibid, p.85.
72. Howell, *Complete State Trials*, X, p.1198.
73. Ibid, pp.1226-1227.
74. Ibid, pp.1241-1242.
75. Ibid, p.1244.
76. Ibid, pp.1248-1254.
77. Ibid, pp.1250-1259.
78. Ibid, pp.1261-1281.
79. Ibid, p.1282.
80. Ibid, p.1283-1289.
81. Ibid, p.1290.

82. Ibid, pp.1291-1311.
83. De Beer, *Evelyn's Diary*, IV, pp.438-439.
84. Ailesbury, *Memoirs* I, pp.138, 140, 137.
85. De Beer, *Evelyn's Diary*, IV, p.440.
86. Howell, *Complete State Trials*, X, p.1316.
87. Anon, *Trials*, p.60
88. Fountainhall, *Historical Observes*, p.164.
89. Bod. Lib., Carte Mss 130, 293.
90. Browning, *Memoirs*, p.365.
91. Edward Chamberlayne, *Anglia Notitia* (London, 1671), p.50.
92. De Beer, *Evelyn's Diary*, IV, p.445.
93. Burnet, *History, III*, p.38.
94. ESRO, FRE5206.
95. Luttrell, *Brief Relation*, II, p.343.
96. Fountainhall, *Historical Observes*, p.164.
97. CSPD, James II, 1, 1685, pp. 156-157; Anon, *The Doctor degraded* (1685).
98. SHS, LM/COR/9/10.
99. Edmund Calamy, *Historical Account of my own Life*, I, (London, 1829), p.120.
100. Stocks, *Records*, p.581.
101. Stephen Taylor, ed., *The Entring Book of Roger Morrice, The Reign of James II, 1687-1689* (Suffolk: Boydell, 2007), p.462.
102. Anon, *An essay tending to prove that perjury deserves not only the pillory but a much severer punishment* (London, 1685), p.11
103. Ibid, p.19.
104. Anon, *The Memoires of Titus Oates* (1685).
105. *The Little Infant Titus, or Oates elevated above his Brethren* (London, 1685).
106. L'Estrange, *Brief History*, I, p.130.
107. HMC 9th Report, p.56.
108. Harris, *The Entring Book of Roger Morrice: The Reign of James II, 1685-1687* (Suffolk: Boydell, 2007), pp.41, 263.
109. Clarke, 'Life', III, p.274; Petrie, *Jacobite Movement*, p.57.
110. CSPD, 1688, p.8.
111. Oates, T*o the Knights, Citizens, and Burgesses in parliament: The Deplorable Case and humble Petition of Dr Titus Oates* (1696).
112. BL. Add.Mss. 41804, f.26r.
113. CSPD, James II, 1686-1687, p.265.
114. Harris, *Entring Book*, pp.290-291, 307.
115. CSPD, 1686-7, pp.234-235.
116. Philip Ellis, *The Ellis Correspondence*, II, (London, 1829), p.340.
117. Anon, *Miracles upon Miracles or Great News from the King's Bench Prison in Southwark, of a monster called by the name of Titus upon Oates* (1687).
118. L'Estrange, *Brief History*, pp.30-31.

119. Ibid. p.33.
120. Ibid, II, p.45.
121. Luttrell, *Brief Historical Relation*, l, p.454.
122. Oates, *Tragedy of the Popish Plot Reviv'd*, p.58.
123. Luttrell, *Brief Historical Relation*, I, p.459.
124. Charles Jackson, ed., 'The Diary of Abraham de la Pryme', *Surtees Society*, LIV (1870), p.9.
125. *London Gazette* 4 October 1688; Bramston, *Autobiography*, p.318.
126. Taylor, *Entring Book*, p.364.
127. Ibid, p.426.

Chapter 8

1. Hatton, *Correspondence,* II, p.125.
2. J.G. Muddiman, ed., *The Bloody Assizes*, (Edinburgh: William Hodge, 1929), p.5.
3. Taylor, *The Reign of James II*, p.482.
4. Ibid p.461.
5. Oates, *Proposals humbly offered to the high and mighty Prince William* (1689).
6. Mark Knights, ed., *The Entring Book of Roger Morrice: The Reign of William III, 1689-1691* (Suffolk: Boydell, 2007), p.3.
7. TNA, SP116/450.
8. Ibid.
9. Ailesbury, *Memoir*, I, p.144.
10. *Journal of the House of Lords*, XIV, pp.167, 209, 213.
11. *Journal of the House of Commons*, X, pp.144-145.
12. *Journals of the House of Lords*, XIV, pp.218-225.
13. Ibid, pp.226, 228.
14. Ibid, pp.230, 234, 236.
15. *Journal of the House of Commons*, X, pp.176-177.
16. Hatton, *Correspondence*, II, p.135/
17. CSPD 1689-1690, pp.31, 197.
18. Knights, *Entring Book*, V, pp.119-129.
19. *Journals of the House of Lords*, XIV, pp.276-277, 318.
20. *Journals of the House of Commons*, X, p.237.
21. Shaw, *Calendar of Treasury Books XIII, 1689-1692* 1931), p.53
22. Ailesbury, *Memoir*, I, p.144.
23. Oates, *Sound advice to Roman Catholics*, (London, 1689), p.1.
24. Ibid, pp.1-19.
25. Muddiman, *Bloody Assizes*, p.9.
26. Oates, *Display of Tyranny* (1689), pp. dedication, 26, 36, 38, 64.
27. Anon, *The Life and History*, pp.61-62.
28. John Phillips, *The Secret History of the reigns of K. Charles II and K. James II* (London, 1690), pp.83-84.

29. Ibid, pp.93, 187-188.
30. Luttrell, *Brief Historical Relation*, II, p.443.
31. Ancestry.co.uk, Luttrell, *Brief Historical Relation III*, p.165.
32. Anon, *The Birth and Education*, p.8.
33. Anon, *The Life and History*, p.45.
34. Thomas Browne, *The Salamanca Wedding: A True account of a swearing Doctor's Marriage with a Muggletonian Widow in Bread Street*, (London, 1693), p.1.
35. Ibid, p.2.
36. Ibid.
37. Ibid, p.3.
38. Ibid, pp.3-4.
39. Ibid, p.4.
40. Ailesbury, *Memoirs*, I, p.154.
41. Luttrell, *Brief Historical Relation, III*, pp.173, 179.
42. Ibid, p.187.
43. Ancestry.co.uk
44. Shaw, *Calendar of Treasury Books*, X, 1693-1696, (London, 1935), p.716.
45. Luttrell, *Brief Historical Relation, III*, p.563.
46. Oates, *To the Knights, Citizens and Burgesses in Parliament: The Deplorable Case and Humble Petition of Dr Titus Oates* (1696).
47. Oates, *Picture of King James* (London: R. Baldwin, 1696), prologue.
48. De Beer, *The Diary of John Evelyn*, V (Oxford University Press, 1955), p.238.
49. *A Complaint of Edward Ellys* (c.1696).
50. TNA, C8/358/14.
51. *Journals of the House of Commons*, XII, p.600; CTB, XIII, 1697-1698, pp.18, 44, 103, 392.
52. William Fuller, *The Whole Life of William Fuller* (London, 1703), p.62.
53. Ibid, p.63.
54. Ibid p.64.
55. CSPD William III, 1697, p.484.
56. Luttrell, *Brief Historical Relation, IV*, p.558.
57. Crosby, *History of the Baptists*, III, pp.169, 172-173.
58. https://www.joh.cam.ac.library/special_collections/early_books/oates.htm. Accessed 11 October 2023.
59. Anon, *The Life and History*, p.68.
60. *Post Boy*, 21-23 February 1699.
61. Crosby, *History*, pp.173-175.
62. Ibid, pp.175-176.
63. Ibid, pp.177-179.
64. Ibid, pp.181-182.
65. Luttrell, *Brief Historical Relation*, IV, p.190.
66. Anon, *A Second Collection of Tracts on all subjects* (), p.421.

67. Ibid, pp.421-422.
68. Ibid, p.420.
69. North, *Examen*, p.235.
70. *The Works of Mr Thomas Brown* (London, 1720), pp.241-242.
71. Anon, *The Life and History*, p.76.
72. *The Postman*, 12-14 July 1705, cited in J.D. Alsop, 'Titus Oates' Deathbed', *Historical Research*, 64, issue 155 (October 1991), p.432.
73. James Welwood, *Memoirs of the most remarkable transactions* (London, 1704), p.102.
74. Anon, *The Birth and Education*, p.8.
75. John Buchanan-Brown, ed., The *Remains of Thomas Hearne*, (London, 1966), p.4.
76. Luttrell, *Brief Historical Relation*, V, p.572.
77. *Annals of Queen Anne* (London, 1706), p.285.
78. Anon, *Elegy upon the much unlamented death of Dr Titus Oates* (1705).
79. Anon, *The Life and History*, pp.3-4, 77.
80. Ibid, p.78.
81. Information from John Gauss.

Chapter 9

1. North, *Examen*, p.225.
2. Cited in Bonamy Dobree, *English Literature in the early Eighteenth Century* (Oxford, 1959), p.387.
3. Thomas Smollett, *A Complete History of England from the descent of Julius Caesar to the Treaty of Aix La Chappelle, 1748*, Vol. VIII, (London, 1758-1760), pp.125-127.
4. David Hume, *History of England*, II (1754-1761), p.512.
5. James Macpherson, *The History of Great Britain*, I, (London: Cenggae Gale, 1775), pp.246-248.
6. T. F. Henderson, ed., *Macaulay's History of England*, (London: Routledge, 1907), p.61.
7. *The Western Martyrology*, (London: J. Blackwell and Co., 1873), pp.98-102.
8. Thomas Seccombe, ed., *The Lives of Twelve bad men* (London: T. Fisher Unwin, 1894), pp.98, 254.
9. Pollock, *Popish Plot*, p.3.
10. Ibid, p.7.
11. Lane, *Titus Oates*, p.9.
12. Ibid, pp.363-364.
13. *Punch*, 14 September 1949.
14. Kenyon, *Popish Plot*, cover blurb.
15. Knight, *Killing*, pp.47, 50, 143.
16. Ibid, p.121.
17. Marshall, *The strange death*, p.61.
18. In Our Time: Titus Oates and his Popish Plot, https://www.bbc.co.uk/programmes/b079rbcj

19. Fake news: Titus Oates and the Popish Plot, https://www.youtube.com/watch?v:wQe
20. Louis F. Saltzman, *The Story of the English Towns: Hastings* (London, 1921), pp.62-63.
21. Anthony Belt, *Hastings: A Survey*, (Hastings: Kenneth Saville, 1937), p.47.
22. *Kent Times*, 23 March 1889.
23. *Dublin Evening Herald*, 5 November 2002.
24. *Hastings and St. Leonard's Observer*, 6 September 1873; 5 February 1927, 27 August 1949.
25. Ibid, 7 September 1957.
26. *Rutland Times*, 31 May 1996.
27. Alan Palmer, *Dictionary of Twentieth Century History, 1900-1989* (1989), pp.263-264.
28. *Hastings and St. Leonard's Observer*, 29 January 1927.
29. *Hastings Independent Press*, 7 April 2020.
30. *Leeds Mercury*, 5 August 1911; *Kent and Sussex Courier*, 29 January 1971.
31. *Rutland Times*, 9 December 1994.
32. *Cambridge General Advertiser*, 8 April 1840.
33. Sue Limb and Paul Cordingley, *Captain Oates: Soldier and Explorer* (London: Batsford, 1982), p.12.

Appendix One

1. L'Estrange, *Brief History*, p.36.

Appendix Two

1. Chamberlayne, *Anglia Notitia*, p.44.
2. Alan Bray, *Homosexuality in Renaissance England* (Columbian University Press, 1982), pp.13-16.
3. Ian MaCormick, ed., *Secret Sexualities* (1997), p.7; Timothy Hitchcock and Michele Cohen, *English Masculinities, 1660-1800* (Longman, 1999), p.3; Paul Hammond, *Figuring Sex between men from Shakespeare to Rochester* (Oxford, 2002), p.10.
4. Harris, *Restoration*, pp.243-244.
5. Old Bailey online.
6. *Dictionary of National Biography*, Vol. XII, pp.741-748.
7. Pollock, *Popish Plot*, pp.4-5.
8. Ibid, p.338.
9. Lane, *Titus Oates*, p.27.
10. Ibid, pp.30-31.
11. Ibid, p.340.
12. Kenyon, *Popish Plot*, pp.54-55, pp.180-185.
13. Ibid, p.301.
14. Knight, *The Killing*, pp.47-50.
15. Marshall, *The strange death*, pp.60-61.
16. *ODNB*, Volume 41, pp.335-340.
17. Stater, *Hoax*, pp.38-39.

18. Jenni Uglow, *A Gambling Man: Charles II's Restoration Game,* (New York: Farrar, Struass and Giroux, 2009), p.519.
19. Paul Hammond, 'Titus Oates and Sodomy' in Jeremy Black, ed., *Culture and Society in England, 1660-1800* (Manchester University Press, 1997), p.88, 89, 91.
20. Ibid, pp.85, 91, 93.
21. Ibid, pp.86, 95, 98-99.
22. MacKenzie, *Conspiracy Culture*, p.631/2/992.

Appendix Three

1. Ailesbury, *Memoirs*, p.29; Slater, *Hoax*, p.62; Knight, *Killing*, pp.191-220.
2. Marshall, *Strange Death*, p.146.
3. Mackenzie, *Conspiracy Culture*, p.51.0/992.
4. Burnet, *History*, (1724), p.429.
5. James Stephens, *A History of the Criminal Law in England*, I (London: MacMillan, 1883), p.393.
6. H.D. Traill, *The First Earl of Shaftesbury* (London: Longman, 1886), p.128n.
7. Lord Birkenhead, *Famous Trials of History* (1926), p.75.
8. John Dickson Carr, *The Murder of Sir Edmund Godfrey* (London: Hamilton Hamish, 1936), p.321.
9. Alan Marshall, *Strange Death,* pp.155-156.
10. Mackenzie, *Conspiracy Culture*, p.941.3/992.
11. Knight, *The Killing*, pp.177-178.
12. Marshall, *Strange Death.*
13. Mackenzie, *Conspiracy Culture*, p.631.2/992.
14. Kenyon, *Popish Plot*, pp.308-309.

Index